THE LEGAL ATLAS
OF THE
UNITED STATES

Julius Fast & Timothy Fast

Facts On File, Inc.

To Cathy,

Without whose generous help
in re-writes and overall support,
we could never have completed this work.

THE LEGAL ATLAS OF THE UNITED STATES

Copyright © 1997 by Julius Fast & Timothy Fast

Facts On File, Inc.
11 Penn Plaza
New York NY 10001

Library of Congress Cataloging-in-Publication Data
Fast, Julius, 1918–
The legal atlas of the United States/by Julius Fast and
Timothy Fast.
p. cm.
Includes bibliographical references and index.
ISBN 0-8160-3128-2
1. Law—United States—Atlases. I. Fast, Timothy.
II. Title
KF387.F35 1997
349.73'022'3—dc21 97-5621

Facts On File books are available at special discounts when
purchased in bulk quantities for businesses, associations,
institutions or sales promotions. Please call our
Special Sales Department in New York at 212/967-8800 or
800/322-8755.

LAYOUT: DALE WILLIAMS
COVER DESIGN: SEMADAR MEGGED

Printed in China

MAN FOF 10 9 8 7 6 5 4 3 2 1

This book is printed on acid-free paper.

CONTENTS

THE
LEGAL ATLAS
OF THE
UNITED STATES

MAJOR CITIES

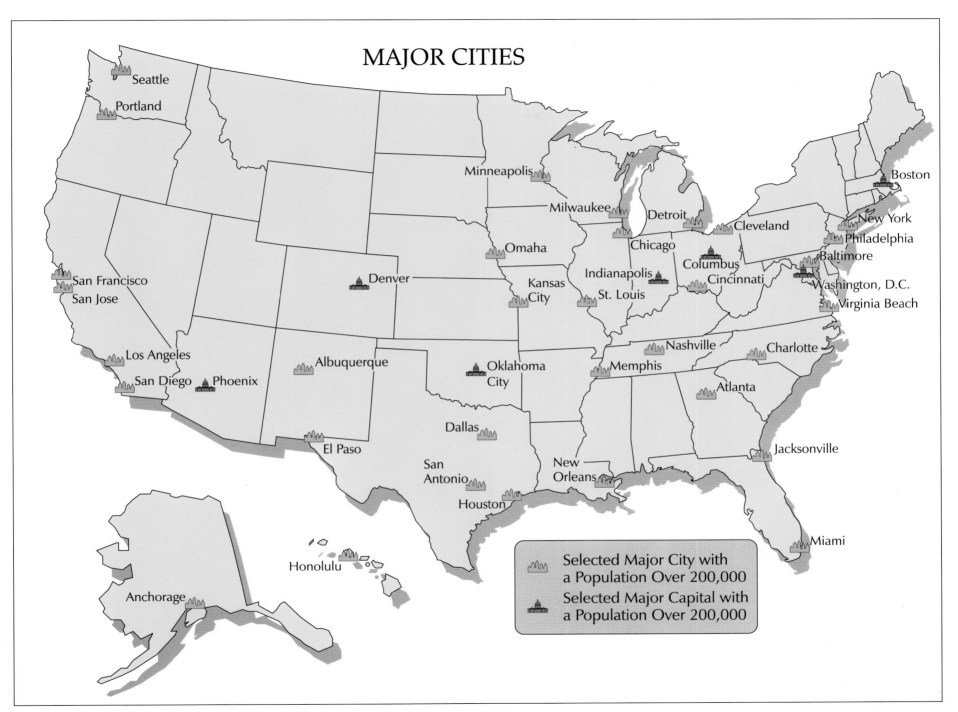

Seattle
Portland
Minneapolis
Milwaukee
Detroit
Cleveland
Boston
Chicago
New York
Omaha
Philadelphia
Columbus
Baltimore
San Francisco
Denver
Kansas City
Indianapolis
Cincinnati
Washington, D.C.
San Jose
St. Louis
Virginia Beach
Los Angeles
Nashville
Charlotte
San Diego
Phoenix
Albuquerque
Oklahoma City
Memphis
Atlanta
Dallas
El Paso
Jacksonville
San Antonio
New Orleans
Houston
Miami
Honolulu
Anchorage

Selected Major City with a Population Over 200,000

Selected Major Capital with a Population Over 200,000

GEOGRAPHIC REGIONS*

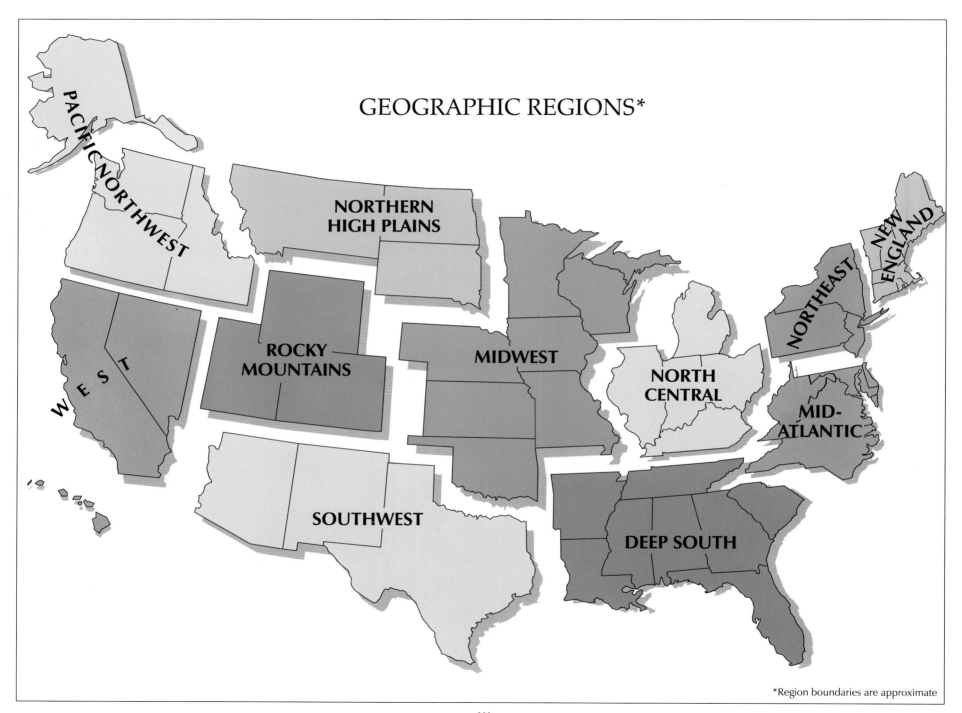

PACIFIC NORTHWEST

NORTHERN HIGH PLAINS

NEW ENGLAND

NORTHEAST

WEST

ROCKY MOUNTAINS

MIDWEST

NORTH CENTRAL

MID-ATLANTIC

SOUTHWEST

DEEP SOUTH

*Region boundaries are approximate

INTRODUCTION

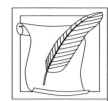

"The law," according to Brooks Adams, "is the envelope with which any society surrounds itself for its protection." The law provides the rules of conduct within that society, and the punishments for those not abiding by those rules. The law as the foundation of every civlized society shapes the lives of citizens. The United States, as well as every other civilized society, depends on the law for its very survival.

Although this atlas examines the current legal issues in this country, one must recognize that the law as we know it today has evolved over the nation's history. Recognizing this, Judge Oliver Wendell Holmes wrote in 1881, "The law embodies the story of a nation's development through many centuries. In order to know what it is, we must know what it has been, and what it tends to become."

Our current system of law is to a large extent based on earlier systems of law such the ancient Babylonian Code of Hammurabi, the laws of Manu from India, the Mosaic code from Palestine, the codes of law of Solon of Athens, Roman law and the Germanic codes.

In more recent centuries, the French Napoleonic code became the source of civil law, while in England the Royal Courts developed common law. Common law is a judicial system based on precedent and founded on the theory that the law administered by the king's courts represents the common customs of the land.

This English common law provided the greatest influence on colonists of the new nation, who adopted the portions that they deemed appropriate and rejected the rest. Over the past two centuries, the law in America has changed to address the needs of each period in the nation's development. It remains dynamic, influencing and being influenced by new circumstances it encounters.

In America, the critical roles of the legal profession and legal institutions are to make and apply the laws of the nation. This atlas examines, on a state to state basis, some of the types of laws that we believe most affect Americans, family law and personal law.

And since crime is a constant concern for most Americans, we will illustrate the major classifications of crime in America. The first is violent crime, which includes murder, rape, robbery and aggravated assault. In addition, we will examine the property crimes of burglary, larceny, theft, arson and motor vehicle theft.

By presenting the data in map form, regional patterns can be observed. Good examples of these can be found in several maps. The map "Divorce Rate" (Family Law section), shows low divorce rates in the northern Midwest and the Northeast. Another regional pattern can be found on the map "Weapons Possession 1991" (Personal Law section). The map reveals that the southern half of the United States has a greater arrest rate than the northern half. Regional patterns can also extend through a series of maps. In general, the rates for crimes against property are greater in the South than in the North.

Patterns do not have to be limited to geographic areas. The rate of abortions in the United States follows the distribution of the population (see "Abortion Rate 1988" in the Personal Law section). States with a large population tend to have a greater rate of abortion.

Although the atlas presents maps giving state and regional views of the United States, the maps can offer some insight into relations between laws and their overall effect. Two maps in the Corrections section, "Executions" and "Change in the Murder Rate 1973-1993," show the influence of capital punishment on the murder rate. Half of all states that have had ten or more executions, have shown a drop in the murder rate. Of the states that do not have a death penalty, half have shown an increase in the murder rate.

It is often said that a picture is worth a thousand words. By compiling this atlas, we hope that we have created both the pictures and the words that make it easier to investigate the occurrence of certain laws and crimes in each of our nation's fifty states.

UNDERSTANDING MAPS

Maps, like charts and diagrams, are information in a visual format. But unlike those other graphic forms, maps have the unique ability to associate information with a place.

Through the use of symbols and color, maps can show where something is located, regional geographic patterns and qualitative or quantitative information about the region depicted.

Thematic mapping, the kind used in this atlas, involves designing a map that depicts the spatial distribution of a particular set of data. If you glance through the sections of this atlas, you will discover two basic types of thematic maps that depict different kinds of geographic information.

Choropleth Maps

Choropleth maps are the most common thematic map type used in this atlas and one of the easiest to read. In a choropleth map, information is ranked from the highest to the lowest values and then divided into several groups or classes. Each data class is represented on the map by a different color. The colors are arranged from light to dark or through a logical progression of hues (for example: yellow to orange to red) to parallel the progression of low to high values.

In a few cases, particularly when we are examining a group of related laws, a state may fit into more than one category. To represent this, the colors that represent each category are striped within the state. An example of this can be found in the map "Criteria for Release via Parole" (Corrections section).

Typically data are divided into no more than six classes, since it is hard to distinguish more than seven shades of a color distributed throughout a map. Because choropleth maps divide data into discrete classes, the choice of how data are divided influences the appearance of the map. For the majority of the choropleth maps, the data have been classed, or grouped, into round numbers (for example: 10, 20, 100, 250 etc.).

Graduated Circle/Symbol Maps

Instead of using color to classify state data, we can use symbols of different sizes placed within each state to represent its data values. An example of a graduated symbol map is "Population of Major Cities " in this section. "Motor Vehicle Theft in Major Cities" (Property Crime section) is an example of a graduated symbol map. For data pertaining to the major cities, the graduated circle or symbol is centered on the actual location of the city.

Where data can be divided into subclasses, as with the map "Racial Distribution of Judges" (the Justice System section), a pie chart is used as a special kind of symbol map. Most of us are familiar with pie charts from their use in diagrams or charts. A circle is divided into wedges, each representing a percentage of the total "pie."

In addition to understanding different mapping techniques, it is important to have the ability to tell one geographic region, state or city from another. For those who are unfamiliar with some states' locations, we have included a map labeling all of the states as a guide.

It is also helpful to know the locations of large urban areas. To familiarize yourself with the location of the major metropolitan areas referenced in this atlas, we have included a map showing the location of 40 major cities, all with populations greater than 200,000 as of 1990. Finally you will discover that we refer to various portions of the country by regional geographic names. Regions such as the Midwest, Deep South and Southwest are not well defined. In fact, geographers often disagree as to what areas are included in a given region. To give you our definition of these different regions, a map has been included that identifies 11 geographic regions of the United States. Be aware that the boundaries between any two areas are not exact and that this regional map serves only as a guide to the text.

A WORD ABOUT DATA

One of the most important data-handling techniques is that of standardization. In many cases, mapping data in raw form is not very useful. If raw data were mapped, most of the maps in this atlas would simply reflect the population distribution of the United States. That is, states with larger populations would consistently show greater values than the more sparsely populated ones. To prevent this, data have been standardized to eliminate differences based on population size.

One way to standardize data is to express data as rates, or as the number of occurrences for a specified number of units. As an example, City A with a population of 50,000 might have 150 practicing lawyers, whereas City B, population 80,000, might have 200 lawyers. Even though City B has a higher actual number of practicing lawyers, data standardization using a rate will show that City A actually has a greater number of lawyers relative to its population. If we establish our unit as 1,000 persons, we can see that City A has 3.0 attorneys for every 1,000 persons, whereas City B has only 2.5.

Percentages are a special kind of rate. The base population of each state, whatever its actual size, is considered to be 100 percent. Data are then expressed as a proportion of that amount. For example, 50 percent of robberies in one state are committed by juveniles, as compared to 20 percent in another. It no longer matters that the total number of juveniles differs from state to state. We are interested in relative proportions.

The map "Population" can be used as a guide to the overall population distribution as of 1990. With it, the map "Population of Major Cities" can also be used as a guide when looking at those maps that deal with crime and arrest rates in major urban areas.

In addition to standardizing data, we have tried to collect data from the same time period. Data for the majority of the maps are from 1990. For those maps whose information is for years other than 1990, the date is noted on the map. As much as possible, data were standardized against the base populations from the same time period.

Familiarize yourself with the mapping techniques, carefully examine the legend and find examples of each category on the map. Look at individual states and see where they fit in the legend. Finally, look at the country as a whole and try to get a feeling for any regional patterns that emerge.

POPULATION

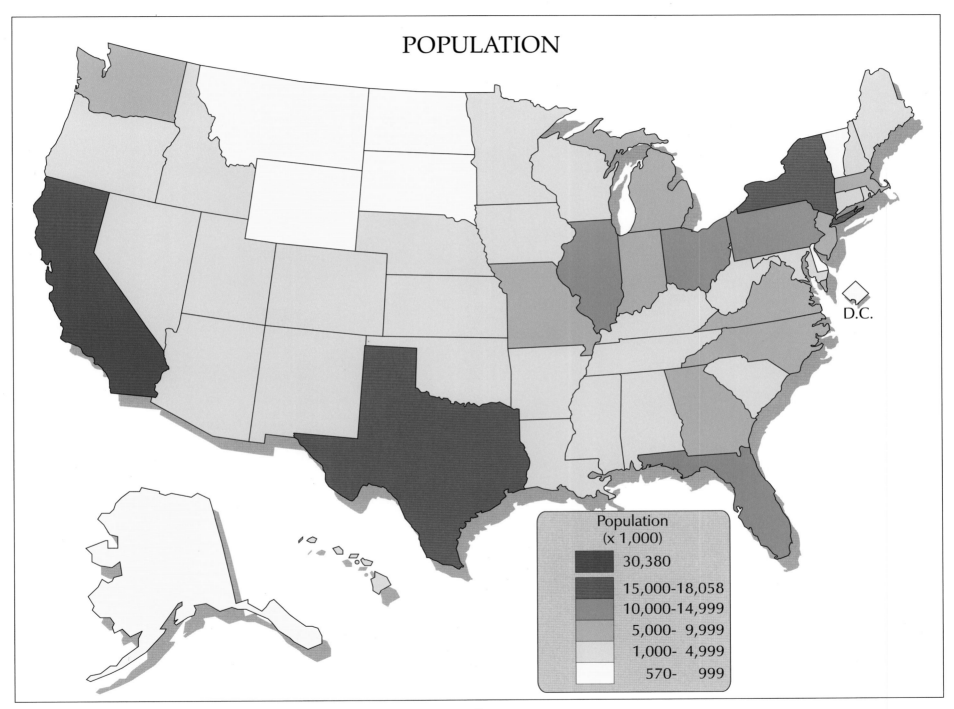

D.C.

Population
(x 1,000)

30,380

15,000-18,058

10,000-14,999

5,000- 9,999

1,000- 4,999

570- 999

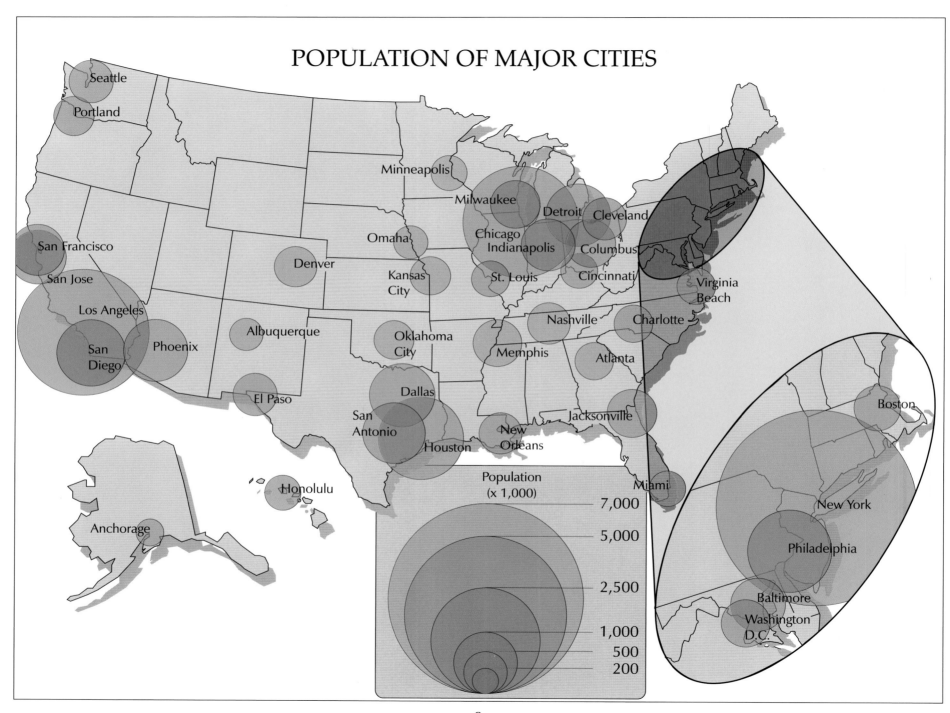

POPULATION OF MAJOR CITIES

Seattle
Portland
San Francisco
San Jose
Los Angeles
San Diego
Phoenix
El Paso
Anchorage
Honolulu
Albuquerque
Denver
Minneapolis
Milwaukee
Omaha
Chicago
Indianapolis
Kansas City
St. Louis
Oklahoma City
Dallas
San Antonio
Houston
Memphis
New Orleans
Nashville
Atlanta
Jacksonville
Miami
Detroit
Cleveland
Columbus
Cincinnati
Charlotte
Virginia Beach
Boston
New York
Philadelphia
Baltimore
Washington D.C.

Population
(x 1,000)
7,000
5,000
2,500
1,000
500
200

FAMILY LAW

The term "family law" covers a wide range of legal issues involving the family. Our concept of family law has developed slowly over many centuries. In Roman law, the father was the head of the family, possessing both religious and economic authority, and literally having the power of life and death over all family members.

This Roman system later became the model for the law of Western Europe, and, to an extent, of the United States. However, as 19th-century women began to acquire the legal right to own property and control their children, a code of family law developed that modified the authority of the father and addressed the new rights of women, more specifically mothers, in the family.

While the legal definition of "family" may be somewhat vague, many states have acknowledged the necessity for the special legal treatment of families and have established "family courts." These courts recognize the importance of family relationships. Marital problems such as divorce, annulment, legal separations, alimony, child support and child custody are typically handled in family court, family court judges having much the same power as judges in courts of general jurisdiction.

Crimes of a more serious nature, such as assault, robbery and murder, are usually tried in criminal court regardless of the child's age.

Family law, as presented in this atlas, covers laws of marriage, divorce and adoption. Various related laws, such as those covering the age of consent, grounds for divorce, division of property in divorce, support for spouses and children, requirements for adoption and parental rights, are also covered.

CONSENTING ADULTS

The map "Laws Regulating Consenting Adults" gives an idea of the criminal and legal aspects of sex in and out of marriage for 25 states and the District of Columbia. Because data are unavailable for the remaining 25 states, determining spatial patterns is difficult. In 13 states it is a crime for an unmarried man and woman to live together, although this law is rarely enforced. Also rarely enforced are laws obtaining in five states—Idaho, Minnesota, Georgia, Virginia and West Virginia, and also in the District of Columbia—making it a crime for a man and woman to engage in sex without benefit of marriage.

In 11 states and the District of Columbia, there is no law

against a man and woman living together without benefit of marriage, and in 18 states an unmarried couple may have sexual intercourse without breaking the law.

Consensual sodomy, usually defined as anal or oral sex between an unmarried couple, is a crime in 13 states, but legal in 12 states and the District of Columbia. It is a crime between a married couple in eight states, but legal in marriage in 18 states and the District of Columbia. Six states—Montana, Kansas, Oklahoma, Missouri, Arkansas and Tennessee—have no criminal laws regarding cohabitation or sodomy.

LOVE AND MARRIAGE

The map, "Marriage Rate" shows that Nevada has the highest number of marriages (105 per 1,000 people). Because its laws incorporate neither a residency requirement nor a waiting period, many "spur-of-the-moment" marriages take place in the state.

Hawaii, Arkansas, Idaho and South Carolina follow in the number of marriages with rates of 15 to 16 per 1,000.

The lowest marriage rates, seven marriages per 1,000 people, are found in North Dakota, West Virginia and Pennsylvania. Altogether, 13 states, located mostly in the north, and the District of Columbia fall within the lowest range.

OLD ENOUGH TO MARRY

In the United States, a person 18 years of age is considered to be of legal age, mature enough to make his or her own decisions, and can be married without parental consent. Many states, however, allow marriage at ages below 18 with parental consent.

The map "Marriage Laws: Age of Consent" tells us that in 26 states and the District of Columbia, the legal age of consent with parental approval is 16 for both men and women. With the exception of Utah and California, the age of consent is lowest in the Northeast and the South. Texas, Alabama, New York, Massachusetts and New Hampshire have ages of consent with parental approval ranging from 12 to 14. In Mississippi and Georgia, there is no age limit set for marriage for either men or women with parental consent.

LICENSES AND BLOOD TESTS

Individuals need not be residents of a state to be married there, but they must fulfill the licensing and testing requirements in the state in which they marry. The map "Marriage Laws: Blood Tests and Licenses" shows that in most states a waiting period from one to five days is required before you can obtain a license to marry The license, once obtained, is valid for a minimum of 20 days in Iowa and South Dakota to a maximum of 180 days (six months) in Montana and Maryland. Of the six states with the highest marriage rate, only South Carolina and Tennessee require a waiting period of one and three days respectively. From one to five days is the waiting period in just over half of all states. Of the 26 states that require a waiting period, 19 set the period at three days.

While a blood test for marriage is required in 29 states, it is not essential in 20. In New York State, blood tests may be required in certain locations. Geographically, blood tests are required in the Deep South, except for South Carolina, along with the Rocky Mountain, North Central and Northeastern states. In general, there is little correlation between age of consent and those states that demand blood tests.

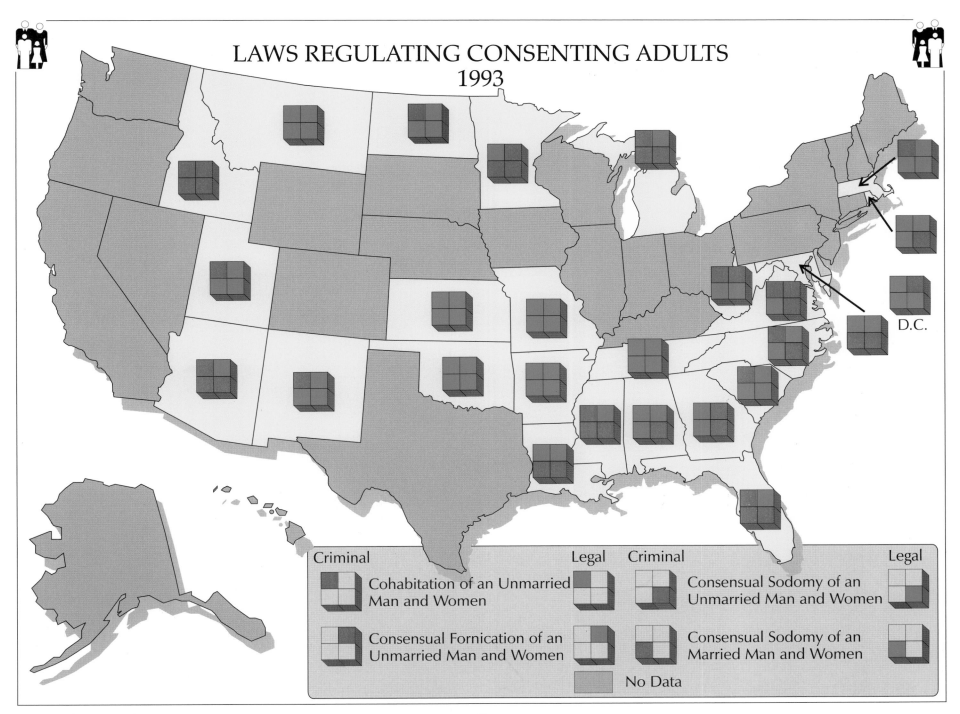

LAWS REGULATING CONSENTING ADULTS
1993

D.C.

Criminal		Legal	Criminal		Legal
	Cohabitation of an Unmarried Man and Women			Consensual Sodomy of an Unmarried Man and Women	
	Consensual Fornication of an Unmarried Man and Women			Consensual Sodomy of an Married Man and Women	
	No Data				

MARRIAGE RATE

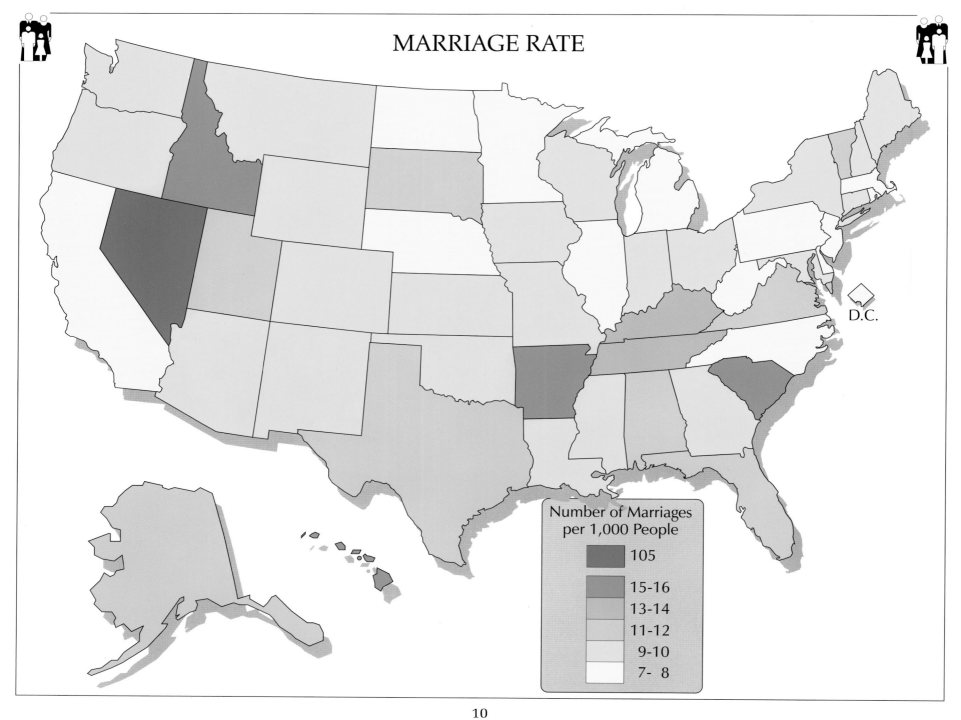

D.C.

Number of Marriages
per 1,000 People

105

15-16

13-14

11-12

9-10

7- 8

MARRIAGE LAWS: AGE OF CONSENT
1991

D.C.

Women

<15 15 16 17 18

Men

18

17

16

15

<15

No Age Limit

Legal Age of Consent with Parental Approval

* Not represented on map

11

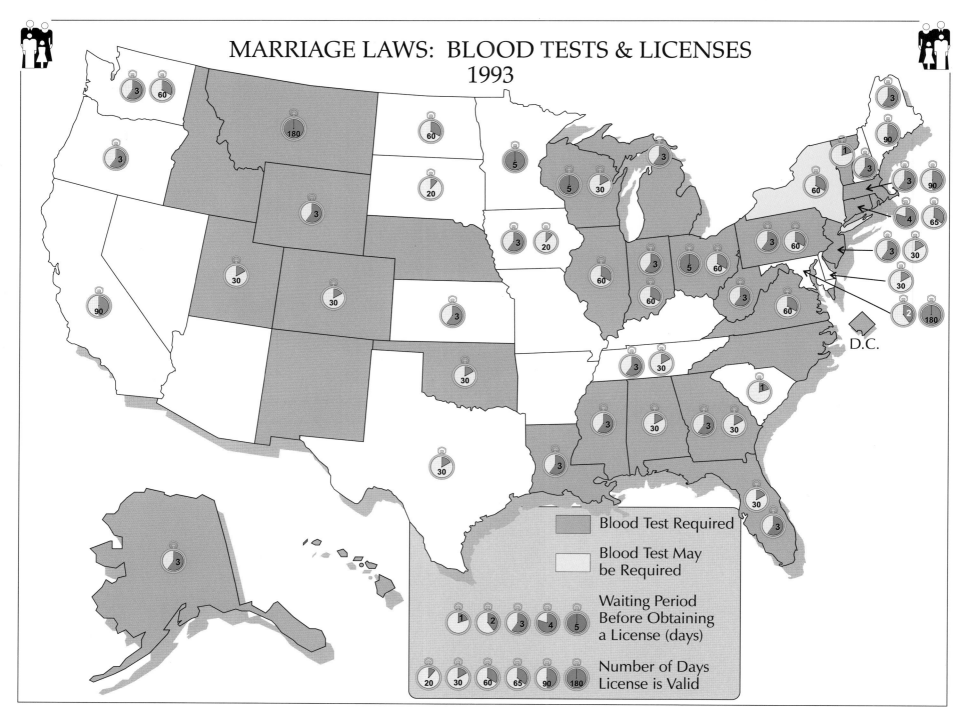

MARRIAGE LAWS: BLOOD TESTS & LICENSES
1993

Blood Test Required

Blood Test May be Required

Waiting Period Before Obtaining a License (days)

Number of Days License is Valid

D.C.

COMMON-LAW MARRIAGE

Common-law marriage is defined legally as a situation where two people of the same or opposite sex live together, have a sexual relationship, share their money and have the same set of friends and acquaintances.

In recent years, there has been a dramatic increase in the number of unmarried couples living together. The 1990 census reported that about two million Americans said that they lived with a member of the opposite sex without the benefit of marriage. Several factors, including the stigma that may be associated with living together, may boost the true figure much higher, by some estimates as high as eight million.

Common-law marriages grew from necessity early in the nation's history. In pioneer times, communities were frequently isolated and people, such as judges and clergy, who could legally perform marriages, were scarce. When two people agreed to live together without the benefit of legal documents, common law acknowledged that a marriage had taken place. As the country grew and communities became less isolated, the courts in some regions decided that only the traditional form of marriage, performed by those legally authorized to do so, should be recognized. Common-law marriages were thought to undermine the stability of family life.

Today, as the map "Common Law Marriage and Cohabitation" shows, 14 states and the District of Columbia still recognize the existence of common-law marriage in which residents can legally live together as spouses.

Most other states will recognize a common-law marriage that was contracted in one of these 14 states. Though rarely enforced, laws against nonmarital cohabitation are on the books in ten states. The remainder of the states do not recognize common-law marriage, but have no criminal statutes against it. Paradoxically, in Idaho, common-law marriage is recognized legally, but nonmarital cohabitation is a crime.

Contrary to a generally held belief, the length of cohabitation does not confer common-law status in a marriage. It is the existence of some form of legal documentation, such as cosigning a lease or filing a joint tax return, that confers common-law marriage status.

In common-law marriages, the courts do not offer a spouse much, if any, protection if one partner dies or the relationship is dissolved. Only a written cohabitation agreement provides the legal protection both sides need.

WHEN THE MARRIAGE FAILS

The map "Divorce Rate" shows the heaviest divorce rates do not occur in the most populous states. California, with over 30 million people, has one of the country's lowest divorce rates, but a contributing factor may be that nearby Nevada has the most liberal divorce laws and may attract a large number of Californians who are seeking a quick and simple divorce.   Other factors may be that southern California has a large Hispanic and thus Catholic population for whom divorce is prohibited by religion. California's community property laws may also be a factor, although other states with similar laws have higher divorce rates. Across the board, there seems to be no relationship between community property laws and divorce rates.

What emerges is a low divorce rate in the North Central and Northeastern coastal states. The West and the South have relatively high divorce rates, with the exception of largely Catholic Louisiana.

GROUNDS FOR DIVORCE

There are 13 different grounds for divorce in the United

States. The 12 "traditional" grounds for divorce are illustrated in the three maps covering "Selected Grounds For Divorce." The thirteenth, No Fault Divorce, is a newer addition to divorce law and is depicted later. Alabama recognizes the largest number of grounds for divorce, allowing all of the 12 traditional grounds. Georgia, Massachusetts, Mississippi, North Dakota, Rhode Island, Washington and West Virginia each recognize 10 of these selected grounds. Six states—Colorado, Hawaii, Michigan, Minnesota, Nebraska and Nevada—permit only one ground for divorce.

Adultery has long been the first and most accepted ground for divorce. While most of the Southern states and the North Atlantic states accept it, the Pacific Coast states, along with Florida, do not. Adultery is also an accepted ground for divorce in Utah, Idaho, the Dakotas, Illinois and Alaska.

Although adultery as sufficient reason to end a marriage is accepted in 30 states and the District of Columbia, there are differences from state to state in what legally constitutes an act of adultery. For example, in Alabama, an act of adultery may be proved by circumstantial evidence. Proving adultery is more complicated in South Carolina, where a person must be found to spend the night undressed in bed with another person. The same states (with the exception of Louisiana) that recognize adultery as a ground for divorce also recognize cruelty.

Half of all states allow a divorce on the grounds that a couple have been living separate and apart. The time required to be spent apart varies from a low of only six months in Montana, Louisiana and Vermont to a high of five years for Idaho. The majority (17) of the states fall within a time period of less than two years.

Unlike living separate and apart, which is usually a result of an agreement by both partners, desertion covers those instances where one spouse has abandoned the other, usually without mutual consent. Only four New England states set the number of years of desertion at greater than one. It is interesting to note that Vermont, which allows a divorce after living separate and apart for only six months, requires a seven year time period for desertion.

Eight of the 24 states that allow alcoholism as a ground for divorce are located in the South. However, the majority of the states that recognize alcoholism as a reason for divorce are in the North. All but two states allowing drug addiction as a ground for divorce—Alaska and North Dakota—are located east of the Mississippi. Insanity may be a reason for divorce in 25 states, with 22 of them setting specific time periods. States that allow divorce on the grounds of a felony conviction or imprisonment follow a similar pattern to alcoholism, with the greatest concentration in the South and Northeast.

Impotence is a ground for divorce in 30 states, half of these states seeing impotence as grounds for annulment as well. Being pregnant at the time of marriage, presumably by someone other than the groom, is cause for divorce in Idaho, Kansas, Oklahoma, Mississippi, Alabama, Georgia, Tennessee, Virginia and West Virginia. Bigamy is grounds for divorce in most states, and in 30 states it is also grounds for annulment. Non support is a recognized reason in 15 states.

RESIDENCY REQUIREMENTS

The map "Durational Residency Requirements" lists the residency requirements, that is, the time you must live in each state before getting a divorce. It ranges from a month and a half in Idaho and Nevada to a year in 10 other states. In general, there is an East-West distribution of residency requirements with the West allowing a shorter residency period than the East.

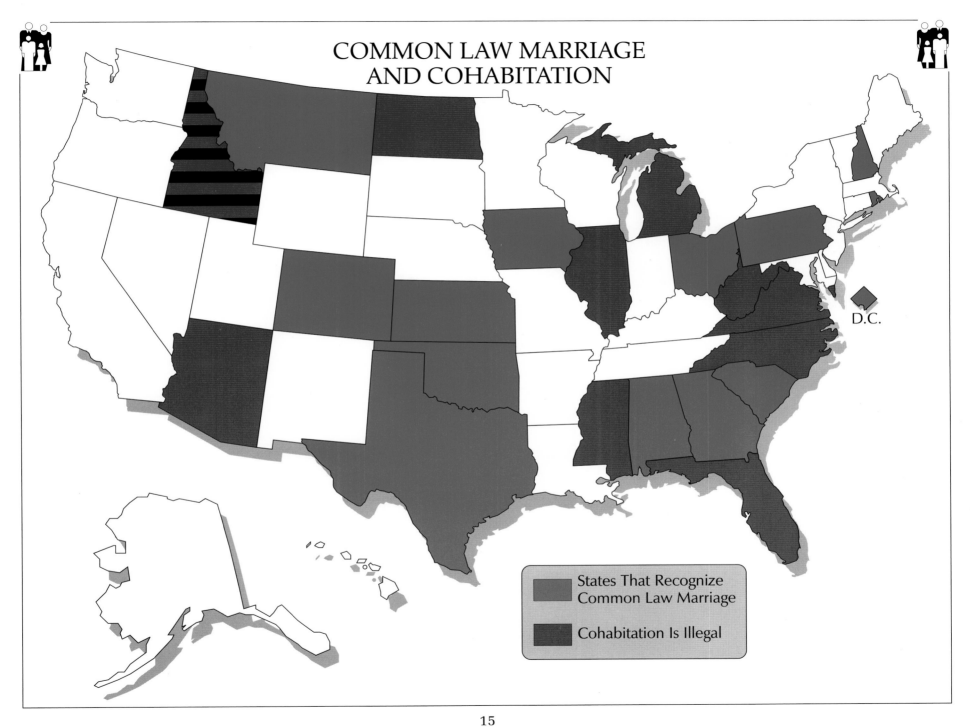

COMMON LAW MARRIAGE AND COHABITATION

D.C.

States That Recognize Common Law Marriage

Cohabitation Is Illegal

15

DIVORCE RATE*

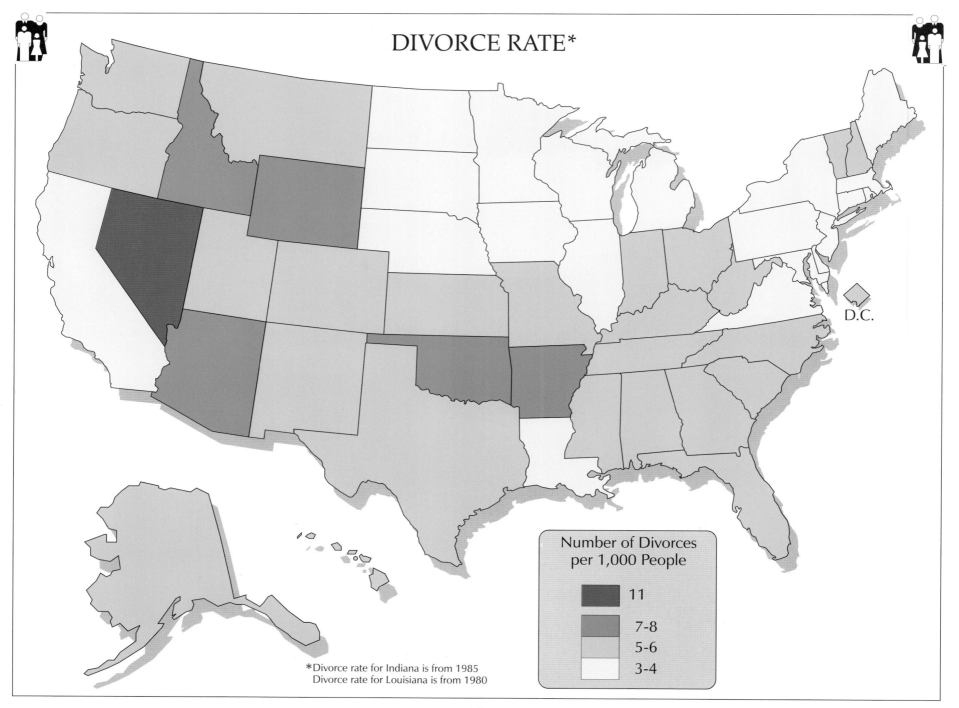

D.C.

Number of Divorces
per 1,000 People

11

7-8

5-6

3-4

*Divorce rate for Indiana is from 1985
Divorce rate for Louisiana is from 1980

16

SELECTED GROUNDS FOR DIVORCE
1993

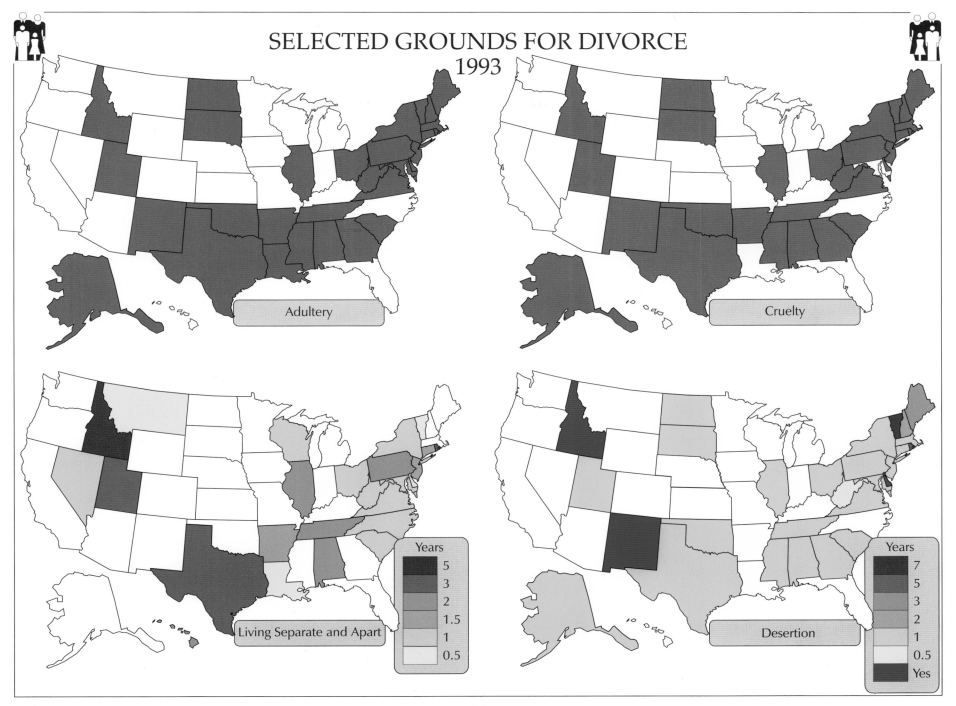

Adultery

Cruelty

Living Separate and Apart

Years
5
3
2
1.5
1
0.5

Desertion

Years
7
5
3
2
1
0.5
Yes

SELECTED GROUNDS FOR DIVORCE
1993

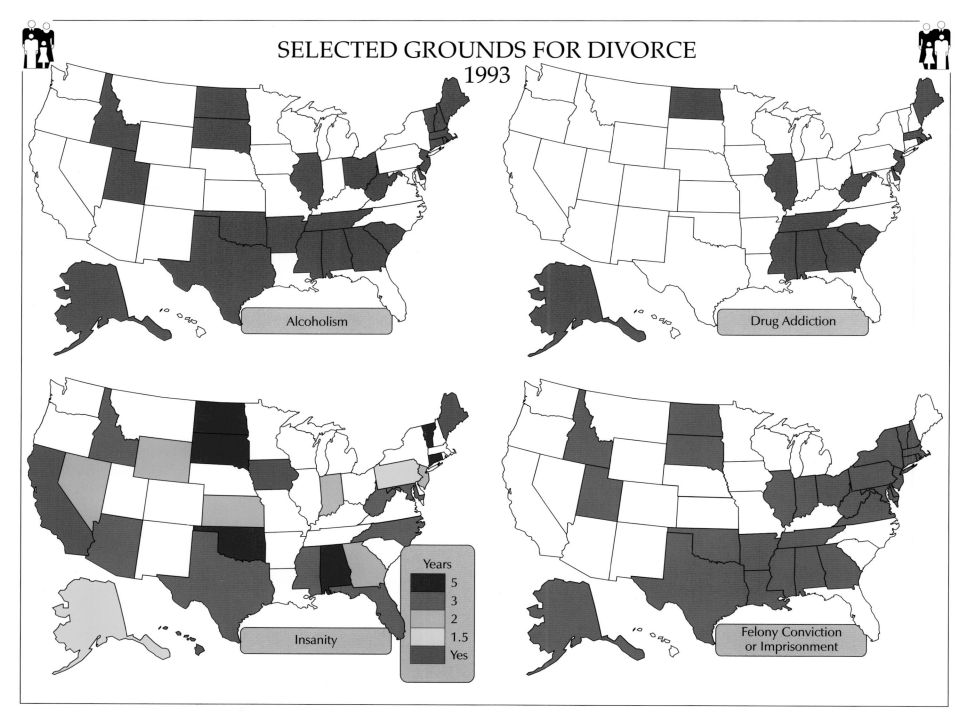

Alcoholism

Drug Addiction

Insanity

Felony Conviction or Imprisonment

Years
5
3
2
1.5
Yes

SELECTED GROUNDS FOR DIVORCE
1993

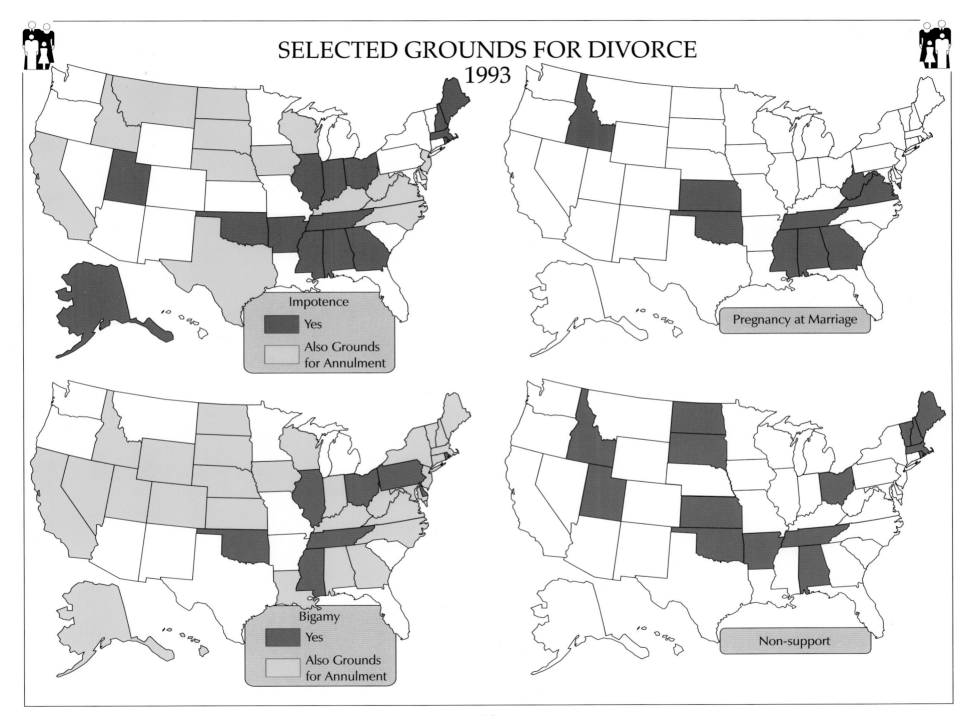

Impotence
- Yes
- Also Grounds for Annulment

Pregnancy at Marriage

Bigamy
- Yes
- Also Grounds for Annulment

Non-support

Nebraska, Iowa and Louisiana are the only states west of the Mississippi River requiring a full year of residence before granting a divorce. Illinois is the only state east of the Mississippi requiring less than six months.

NO-FAULT DIVORCE

A no-fault divorce needs no other grounds than that both partners cannot continue to live together. The usual phrases are *irreconcilable differences* or *irretrievable breakdown*.

Such a divorce does not mean that there is no fault involved in the breakup. A couple may have irreconcilable differences because one partner has persistently slept around or abused the other. In these cases, the "fault" can determine what payments are made and what shape custody of any children will take.

The grounds listed on the previous maps apply to divorces where one partner is at fault. In these cases, the innocent partner usually applies for the divorce. There is, however, increasing popularity for the kind of divorce where neither partner is at fault, a no-fault divorce. The map "No-Fault Divorce" shows that 34 states have no-fault divorce laws in which *irreconcilable differences* or *irretrievable breakdown* constitute one of the reasons for the divorce, or the only reason. In 11 states, *irreconcilable differences* or *irretrievable breakdown* can be the sole reason for divorce. In 20 states it must be added to traditional grounds. In Alabama, *no-fault* can either be the sole ground for divorce or added to other traditional grounds.

WHO GETS WHAT

The map "Division of Property in Divorce" shows the country divided into community property states and equitable distribution states. A community property state recognizes a form of joint ownership between husband and wife. Each owns one half of whatever they have earned or acquired during the marriage. The wages earned by either spouse during the marriage are community property, and anything bought with those wages, a house, a car, a summer cabin, is also community property. Both partners have equal ownership even if only one worked during the marriage. Property bought before the marriage, or with money earned before the marriage, is not considered community property.

In equitable distribution states, the judge looks at the assets of both husband and wife, the length of the marriage and the contributions each made to the marriage, and then he attempts to divide the property fairly.

Ten states, predominately in the South and West, are community property states. In seven states all the property the couple owns is divided equally, but in Nevada, Arizona and Mississippi, the division tends towards the equitable. Thirty-nine states have equitable distribution. In 18 states, clustered in the northern plains and the North Central region, all the property a couple owns is divided equitably. In 21 states only the property acquired during the marriage is divided.

Gifts and inheritances are excluded from the settlement in 21 states, mostly in the Midwest and South Central region, and in 12 states the contribution one spouse (usually the wife) made to the other to obtain a professional degree is considered when the assets are split.

The map "Factors Affecting Property Distribution in Divorce" shows some of the factors a judge may take into consideration when dividing property in a divorce. The states that recognize monetary contributions, the money one partner contributes during the marriage, are often the same states that favor equitable distribution.

When one partner is found guilty of economic misconduct, using family money in an illegal manner, that too becomes a factor in the division. Twenty-three states recognize economic misconduct and take it into consideration when awarding property. All but 13 states have specific statutory guidelines for the judges in settling property disputes in a divorce.

Although many states have no-fault divorce rules in practice, fault may still be considered in the division of property. Twenty-four states consider fault a factor and may favor the partner not at fault with a larger settlement. Eighteen states exclude fault from their decisions.

SPOUSAL SUPPORT

Spousal support, the more modern term for alimony, is the payment made by one spouse, after a divorce, to support the other. Depending on the divorce agreement, it can be temporary until the divorced partner gets into an earning situation, or it can be permanent until the partner remarries or dies.

After a divorce, it is usually the husband who supports the ex-wife, but with changing economic times, women are frequently earning more than their husbands and are in more stable job situations. In these cases, the wife may be the partner paying spousal support. Unfortunately, statistics have not been available on the state by state percentages of women who are providing spousal support.

Many factors go into the determination of which spouse pays support, if indeed any is to be paid. Among the factors considered by the court are:

1) the length of the marriage
2) the age of each partner
3) the education of each partner
4) the job skills and earning potential of each partner
5) the standard of living to which each is accustomed
6) each partner's independent financial resources.

Finally, some courts may apply moral standards and find against the partner whose conduct caused the divorce. A court may also refuse to grant support to a spouse who has committed adultery.

Some states limit the number of years that spousal support must be paid, usually from three to seven years, or require payment until the divorced spouse gets back on his or her economic feet.

Spousal support payments stop not only if the ex-partner remarries, but also if he or she begins to live with someone else. If the spouse paying support dies, the payments may still continue if the divorced partner is named as a beneficiary in the other's will or insurance policy, or if he or she can make a claim against the deceased's estate.

A basic question that has troubled the experts involved in divorce is what guidelines should be used for spousal support. Most states favor an equitable distribution of property. In this situation, the assets of the couple, the length of marriage and the contribution each made during the marriage are all considered, and the property is then divided in a fair manner.

Another aspect of spousal support depends on marital misconduct. The map "Spousal Support" shows that marital fault is not considered in only four Southern states, Louisiana, Georgia, North Carolina and Virginia. In 30 states, spousal support can be barred by marital misconduct. Usually it is the wife who is found guilty of some sort of misconduct in the situation that led to the divorce. In most cases, the misconduct is sexual in nature. In fewer cases, it could be abuse of a child or the other spouse.

DURATIONAL RESIDENCY REQUIREMENTS

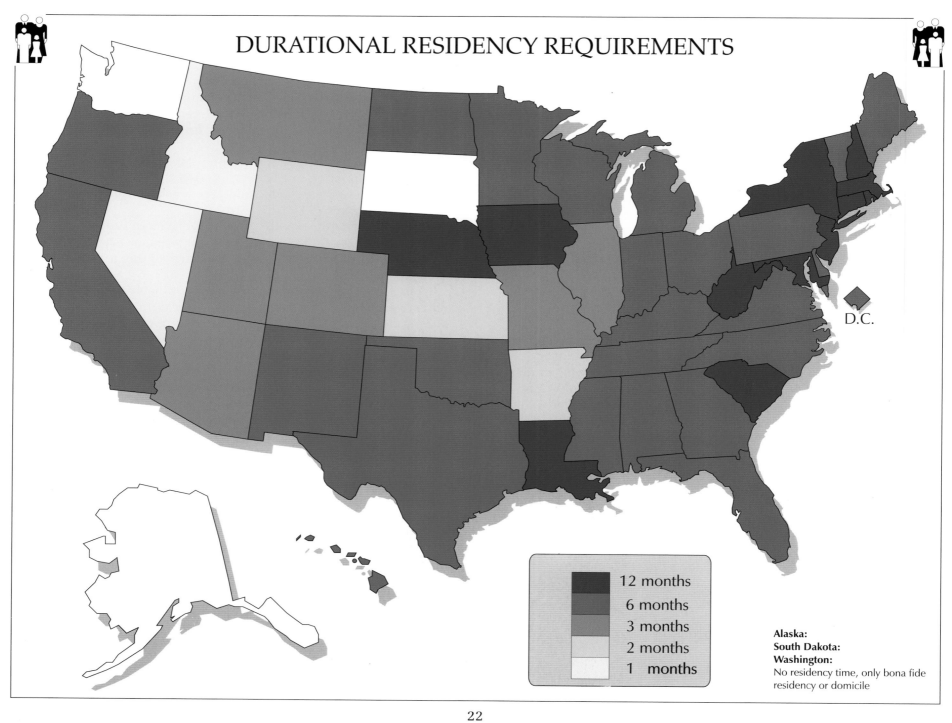

D.C.

12 months
6 months
3 months
2 months
1 months

Alaska:
South Dakota:
Washington:
No residency time, only bona fide
residency or domicile

NO-FAULT DIVORCE

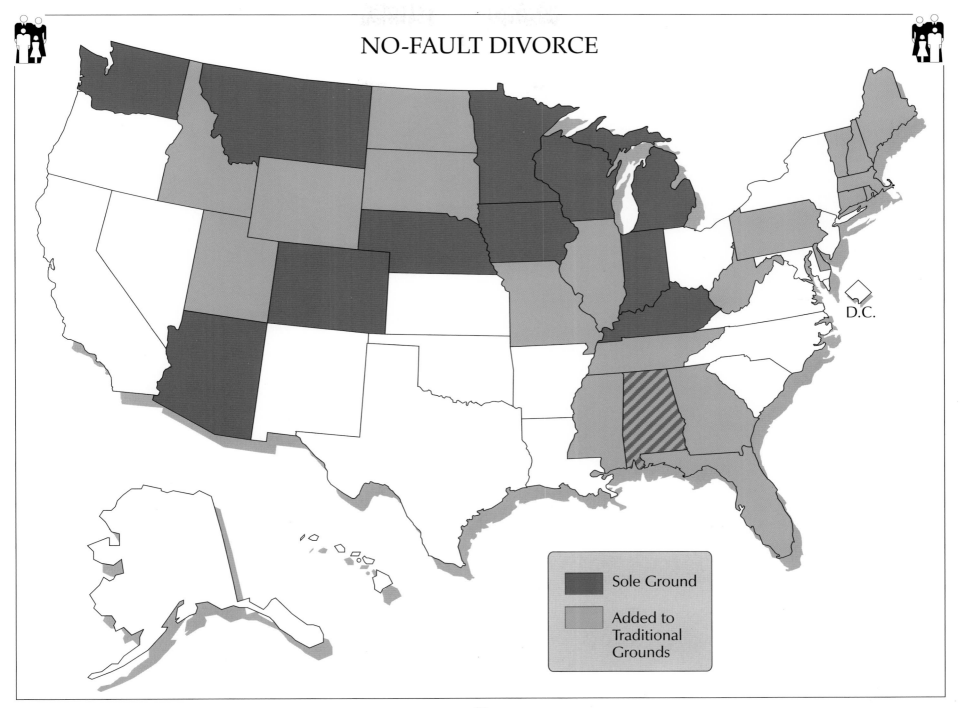

Sole Ground

Added to Traditional Grounds

D.C.

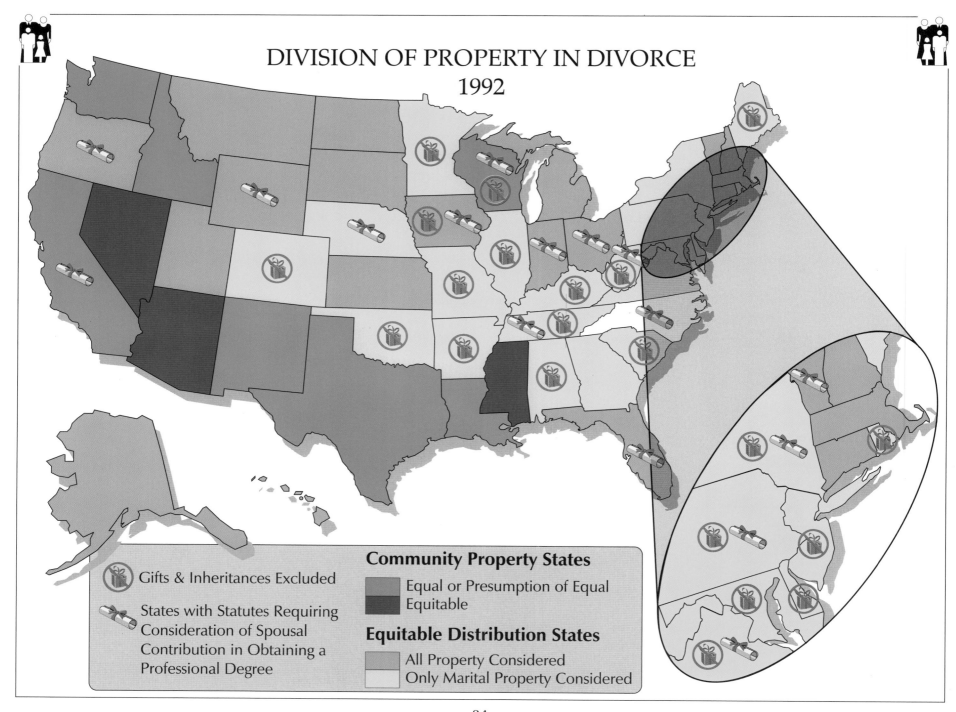

DIVISION OF PROPERTY IN DIVORCE
1992

Gifts & Inheritances Excluded

States with Statutes Requiring Consideration of Spousal Contribution in Obtaining a Professional Degree

Community Property States
Equal or Presumption of Equal
Equitable

Equitable Distribution States
All Property Considered
Only Marital Property Considered

FACTORS AFFECTING PROPERTY DISTRIBUTION IN DIVORCE
1992

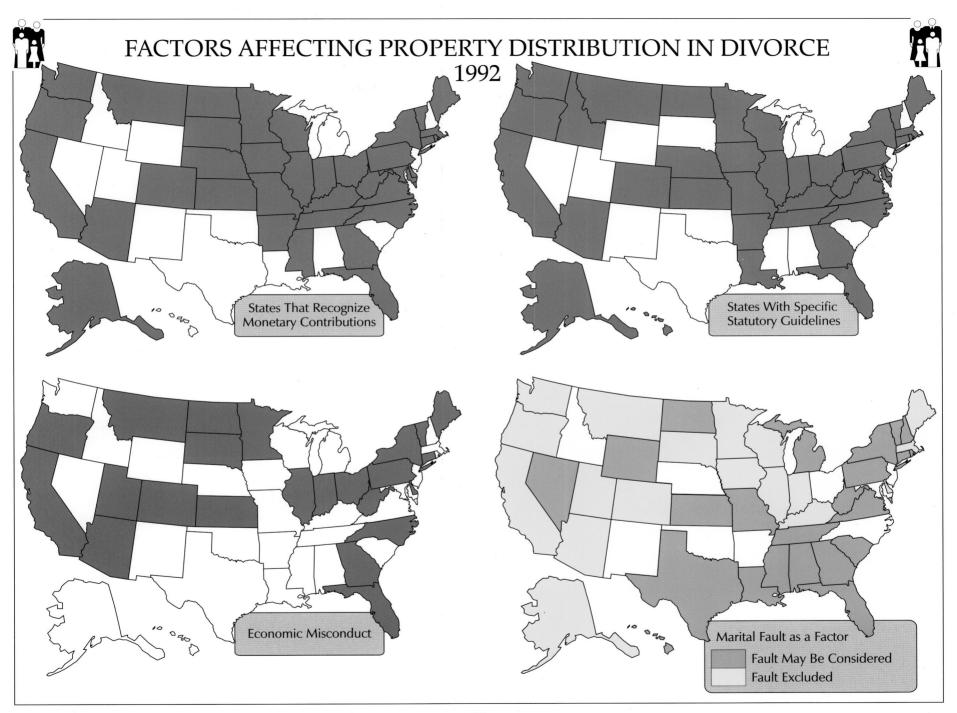

States That Recognize Monetary Contributions

States With Specific Statutory Guidelines

Economic Misconduct

Marital Fault as a Factor

Fault May Be Considered

Fault Excluded

SPOUSAL SUPPORT

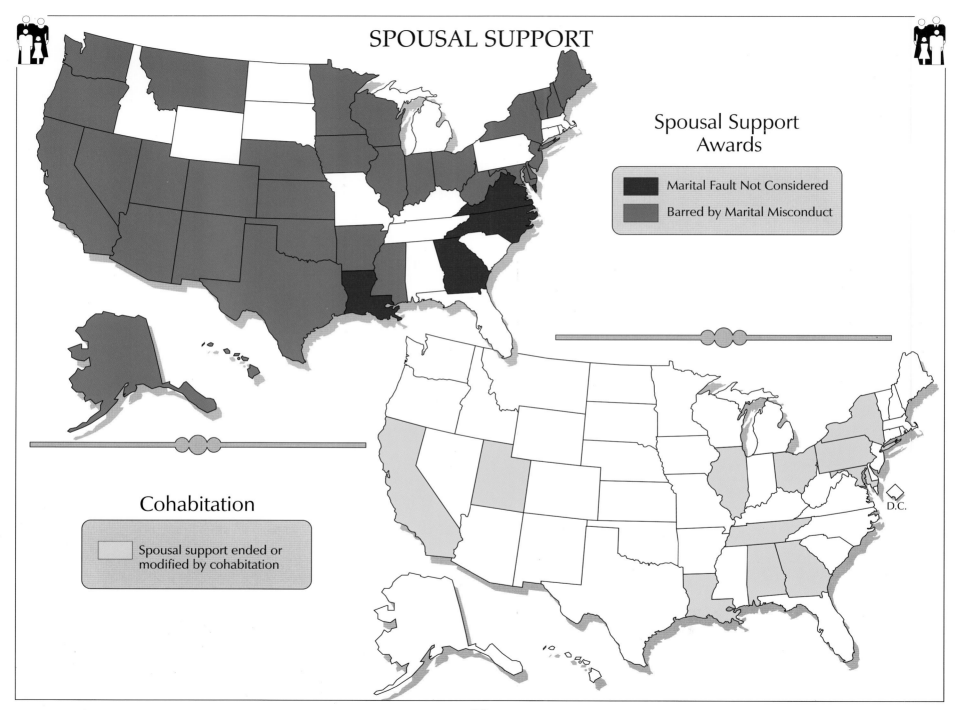

Spousal Support Awards

- Marital Fault Not Considered
- Barred by Marital Misconduct

Cohabitation

- Spousal support ended or modified by cohabitation

D.C.

Eleven states find that a woman entering into a living arrangement with another man after a divorce is no longer entitled to spousal support. Spousal support is either terminated, or in more lenient courts, modified to adjust to the circumstances of cohabitation.

SHARING THE CHILDREN

In awarding custody of children after a divorce, family court judges must decide what custody arrangement is in the best interest of the child. Often this decision takes the form of a joint custody arrangement. Before entering joint custody, where both parents have the child with them for stated times, the court will want proof that the parents are mature and willing to work with each other after the divorce. They must be cooperative, stable and available. If both parents can agree to a sensible custody plan, it is almost always accepted. If there is evidence of hostility or incompetence, the court will usually refuse joint custody, finding that it "lacks stability" for the child.

In the map "Joint Custody" we see that joint custody is encouraged in 17 states. In Mississippi, Vermont, Massachusetts and Rhode Island, it is encouraged, and the child's wishes are considered. In Alabama, New Jersey and New York, each case depends on the court decision.

In 22 states, joint custody is permitted, but is neither encouraged nor discouraged. In Pennsylvania, Maryland North Carolina and Oregon, while it is neither encouraged or discouraged, the child's wishes are taken into consideration.

Joint custody is not permitted, or is discouraged in Wyoming, North and South Dakota, Nebraska, Arkansas, Georgia, South Carolina and West Virginia. However, in South Carolina and Arkansas the wishes of the child influence the decision.

The logistics of joint custody are handled in a number of ways. Usually children live with one parent and visit the other on a regular basis. Parents share responsibility for important decisions such as education and medical care. Joint custody rarely means that children spend half the time with mom and half with dad.

PATERNITY

Most states grant illegitimate children, those born to parents not married to each other, the same rights as those born within a marriage. Regardless of the circumstances of birth, every child is entitled to financial support from the biological father. An illegitimate child can share in a father's estate, provided the child can prove paternity. A child becomes "legitimate" when the parents marry, or if the father, in a written document, acknowledges the child as his.

Proving paternity is a very important consideration. The courts will usually presume that a child is legitimate if the parents are married and lived together for at least ten months before the child's birth. However, as the first of the eight maps entitled "Paternity Legislation" shows, in all but 18 states, a husband can use scientific tests, usually blood tests, to prove he is not the father. However, as blood tests can prove only that a man is not a child's father, proving that he is the father has, until recently, been difficult. With the development of human leukocyte antigen (HLA) testing, claimed to be at least 98 percent accurate, in which tissue type and genetic factors can be matched, paternity identification is much easier. Now a child in these 32 states can use these tests to prove he or she is the son or daughter.

In nine states, the alleged father must pay temporary support during the legal paternity trial. Nine states will accept testimony that proves paternity, while 24

JOINT CUSTODY

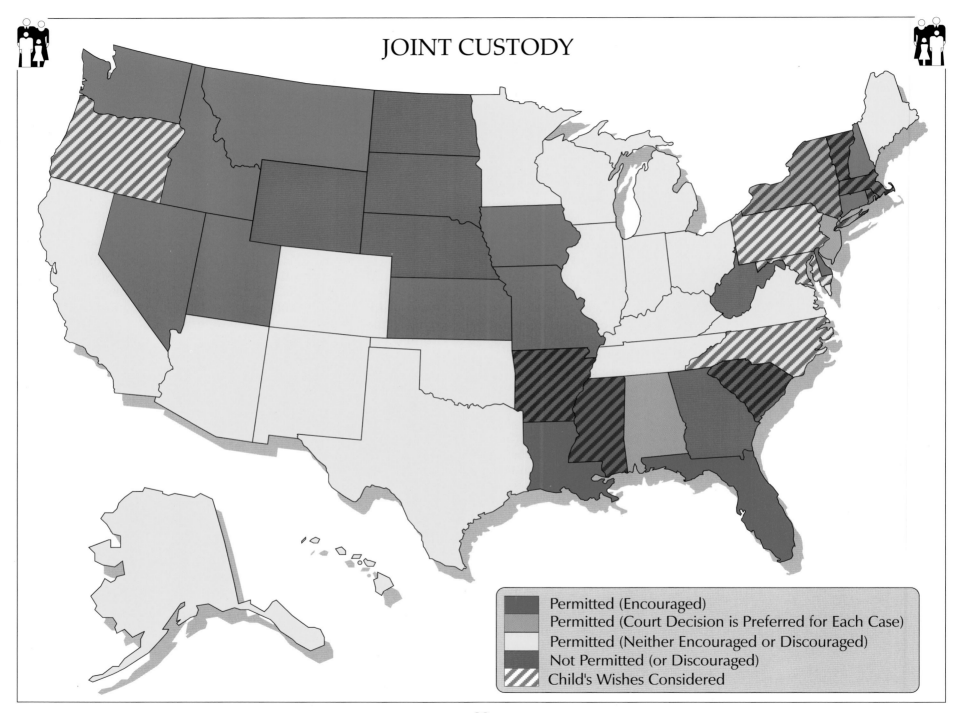

Legend:
- Permitted (Encouraged)
- Permitted (Court Decision is Preferred for Each Case)
- Permitted (Neither Encouraged or Discouraged)
- Not Permitted (or Discouraged)
- Child's Wishes Considered

PATERNITY LEGISLATION
1982

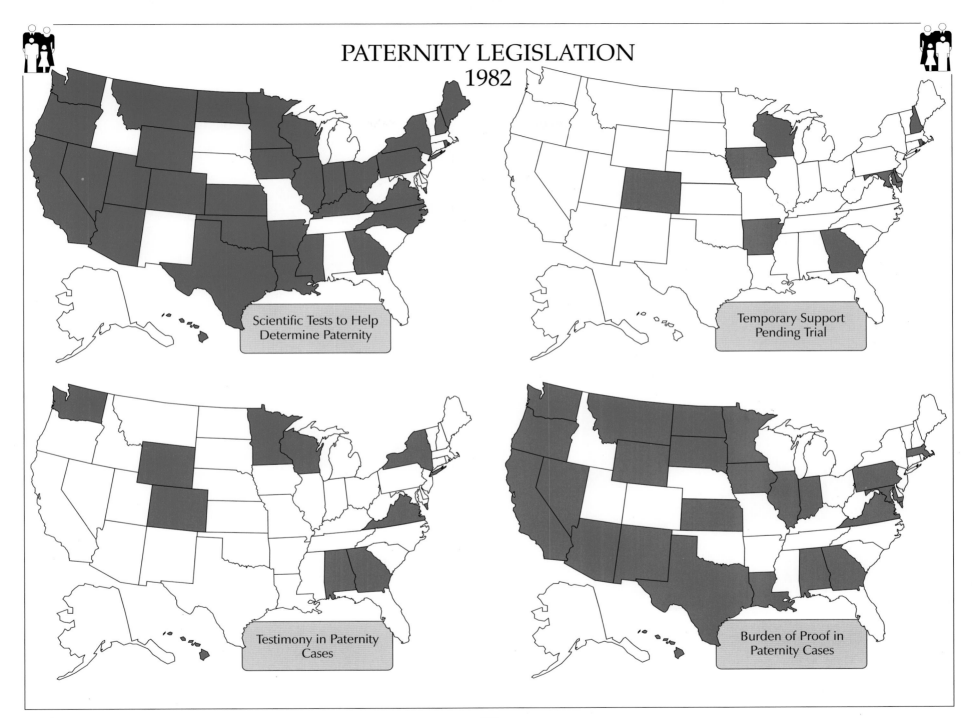

Scientific Tests to Help Determine Paternity

Temporary Support Pending Trial

Testimony in Paternity Cases

Burden of Proof in Paternity Cases

PATERNITY LEGISLATION
1982

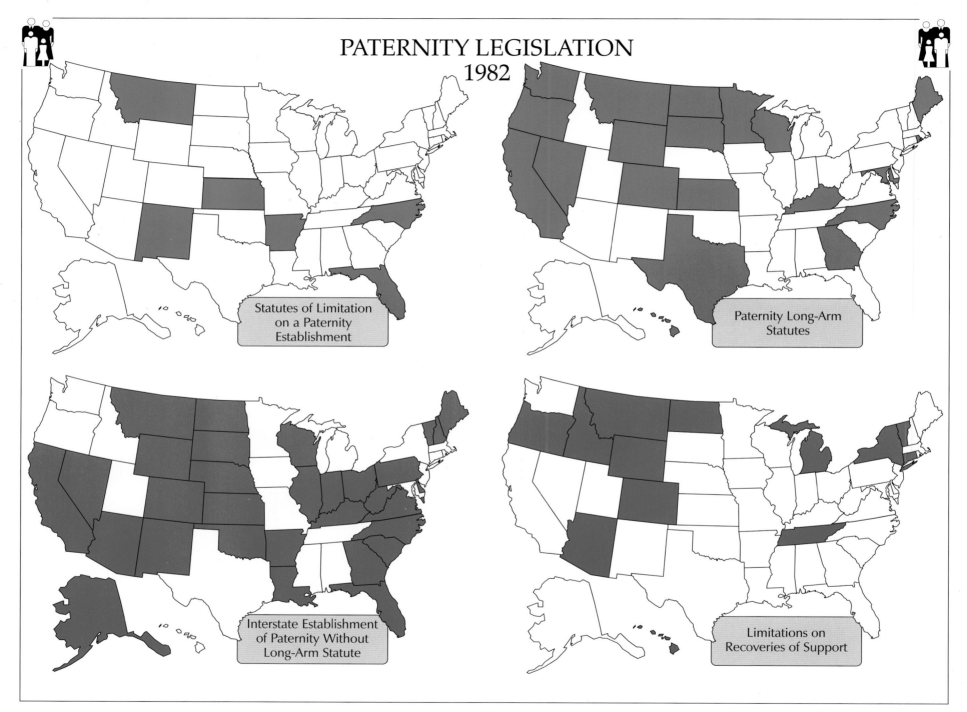

Statutes of Limitation on a Paternity Establishment

Paternity Long-Arm Statutes

Interstate Establishment of Paternity Without Long-Arm Statute

Limitations on Recoveries of Support

states place the burden of proof on the child seeking paternal recognition.

Six states, North Carolina, Florida, Arkansas, Kansas, New Mexico and Montana, put a statute of limitation on establishing paternity. Twenty states have "long arm" statutes which will locate the father in other states, and 31 states will allow the establishment of the putative father in other states without the long arm statute. Finally, nine Northern states along with Colorado, Arizona, Tennessee and Hawaii impose time limitations on the recovery of support.

ADOPTION

When we think of adoption, we usually envision a happy couple holding a newborn baby, but in fact anyone can be adopted by anyone else. Stepparents can adopt stepchildren. An adult, married or single, can adopt another adult. A couple can adopt an unrelated child of any age.

Adoption is a legal procedure that cuts the adoptee's legal ties to his or her biological parents and forges new ones to someone else—the adoptive parent. The adoptive parent must then assume the same responsibilities for an adopted child as he or she would for a biological child. A legal relationship of parent-child is created.

The biological parent who gives up a child for adoption relinquishes all rights in relation to the child, including visitation rights. The child, in turn, usually loses all rights to support and inheritance from the biological parent.

There are various age and residency requirements for adoptive parents. In 12 states, as indicated in the map "Age & Residency Requirements for Adoption" anybody can adopt. Twenty-seven states are more restrictive, but still allow any adult to adopt, while six states restrict adoption to married couples. In eight states, Wyoming, New Mexico,

Minnesota, Wisconsin, Indiana, Kentucky, Georgia and Delaware, you must be a state resident to adopt, while in Tennessee and New Jersey United States citizenship is required.

The lower map shows the difference in age allowed between adoptive parent and adoptee. While an adult can be adopted, in New Mexico the adoptive parent must be 20 years older than the adoptee. In Idaho, West Virginia and New Jersey, there must be a 15 year difference. In eight predominately Western states, a ten year difference is required. Rhode Island mandates only a one year difference. The remaining 37 states have no requirement as to age differences between adoptive parents and adoptee.

Adopted children do have certain rights, and usually these rights concern a desire to learn the identity of their biological parents. The map "Adoptees' Rights" shows that, in 38 states, access to information about birth parents is prohibited, but in three states, Idaho, Kansas and Alabama, access is relatively easy, with no consent needed. In Florida, New Mexico, Kentucky, Hawaii and West Virginia, access to information is only allowed if the biological parent agrees. In Alaska, Louisiana, Delaware and Virginia, access to information can be obtained only with a court order when it is needed because of medical necessity or other extraordinary reasons.

Looking at the map "Adoption Rate & Type," there seems to be no geographic pattern to the distribution of adoptees per state. California, Ohio and New Jersey have the lowest rates of adoption, with Maryland, Delaware, Connecticut, Louisiana, Arizona, Nevada, Idaho and Hawaii running a close second. The greatest number of adoptions have occurred in Alaska, Arkansas, Oklahoma, Montana, North Dakota, Indiana, West Virginia, Maine and Florida.

The adoption of foreign-born infants was greatest in Hawaii, with predominately Asian-born infants. Texas,

Nevada and the states in the Deep South adopt the smallest number of foreign-born children.

The availability of foreign children varies. In some years Korean children are easy to adopt, and in other years, children from South America. With the collapse of the Communist regimes in Eastern Europe, a great number of Russian and Eastern European born orphans became available for adoption.

TAKING THE CHILDREN AWAY

When a child is at risk and the parents are found inadequate or harmful, the state may choose to "terminate" the parents' right to that child. There are seven maps labeled "Statutes Concerning Involuntary Termination of Parental Rights." The four with a subhead of "Legal Procedures and Issues" detail the legal rights of parents in these situations. Taken as a whole, the seven maps show that 27 states have varying degrees of termination ranging from outright adoption to permanent foster care. In 23 states, there are no statutes concerning the right of the state to terminate parental rights.

In the first group of four maps, the map "Right to Counsel" shows that most states allow both parent and child the right to counsel, but Tennessee, Mississippi and Montana allow only the child the right to counsel. Oregon, Colorado, New Mexico, Kansas and Ohio reserve the right to counsel only for the parents.

The map "Right of Appeal" notes that most states, 36, allow both parents and child the right to appeal an involuntary termination of parental rights.

In cases involving termination, 23 states allow legal procedures to the putative father, the man who is commonly accepted as the child's father even though he is not married to the mother.

The fourth map in this group shows that 13 states set time limits for completing termination litigation.

The two maps "Issues Concerning Return to Home" cover the relationships that the courts consider significant and the child's preference in deciding whether or not to terminate parental rights.

The map "Significant Relationships" takes into account the relationships between parents and child and between foster parents and child before terminating parental rights. Six states, Kansas, Oklahoma, Iowa, Missouri, Connecticut and Rhode Island give primacy to the parent or parents before making a decision. Five states, Georgia, Tennessee, West Virginia, Delaware and New Hampshire, consider the foster parents, and 17 states consider both parents and foster parents.

The map titled "Child's Preference" shows that eight states take the age of the child into consideration in determining termination of parental rights. Two states, Florida and New Mexico, consider the nature and depth of the child's wishes. Only five states consider both the child's age and the child's desires in the termination of parental rights.

The seventh map in the series, "Statutes Concerning Involuntary Termination of Parental Rights, Alternative Placement," explains that, when it comes to alternative placement of the child after termination of parental rights, the largest number of states, 21, put the child in the custody or guardianship of another party, but do not allow adoption.

Seventeen states favor other forms of long-term care, such as orphanages or group homes. In 18 states there is court-ordered permanent foster care and only nine states allow the child to be put up for open adoption.

AGE & RESIDENCY REQUIREMENTS
FOR ADOPTION

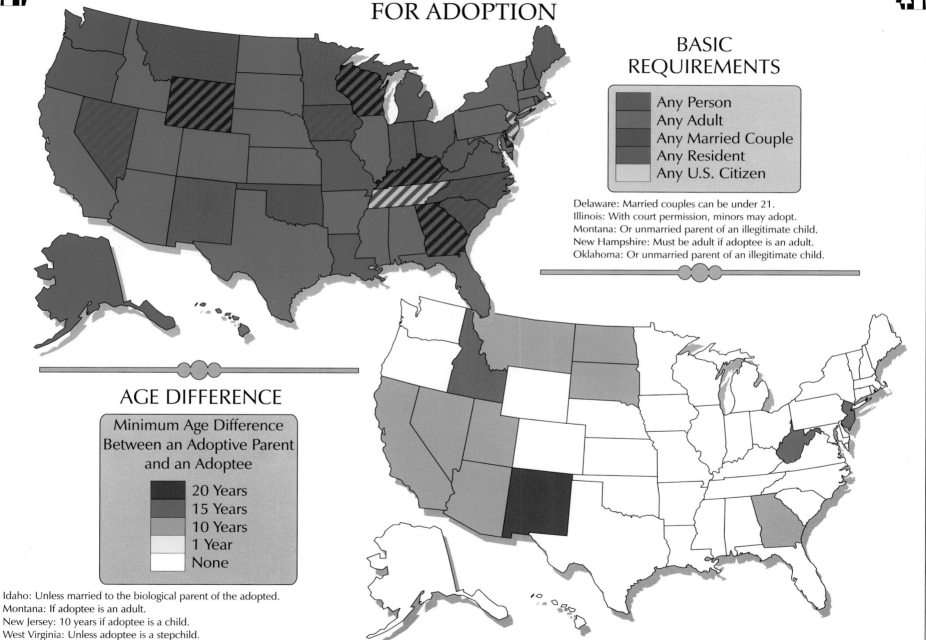

BASIC REQUIREMENTS

- Any Person
- Any Adult
- Any Married Couple
- Any Resident
- Any U.S. Citizen

Delaware: Married couples can be under 21.
Illinois: With court permission, minors may adopt.
Montana: Or unmarried parent of an illegitimate child.
New Hampshire: Must be adult if adoptee is an adult.
Oklahoma: Or unmarried parent of an illegitimate child.

AGE DIFFERENCE

Minimum Age Difference Between an Adoptive Parent and an Adoptee

- 20 Years
- 15 Years
- 10 Years
- 1 Year
- None

Idaho: Unless married to the biological parent of the adopted.
Montana: If adoptee is an adult.
New Jersey: 10 years if adoptee is a child.
West Virginia: Unless adoptee is a stepchild.

ADOPTEES' RIGHTS

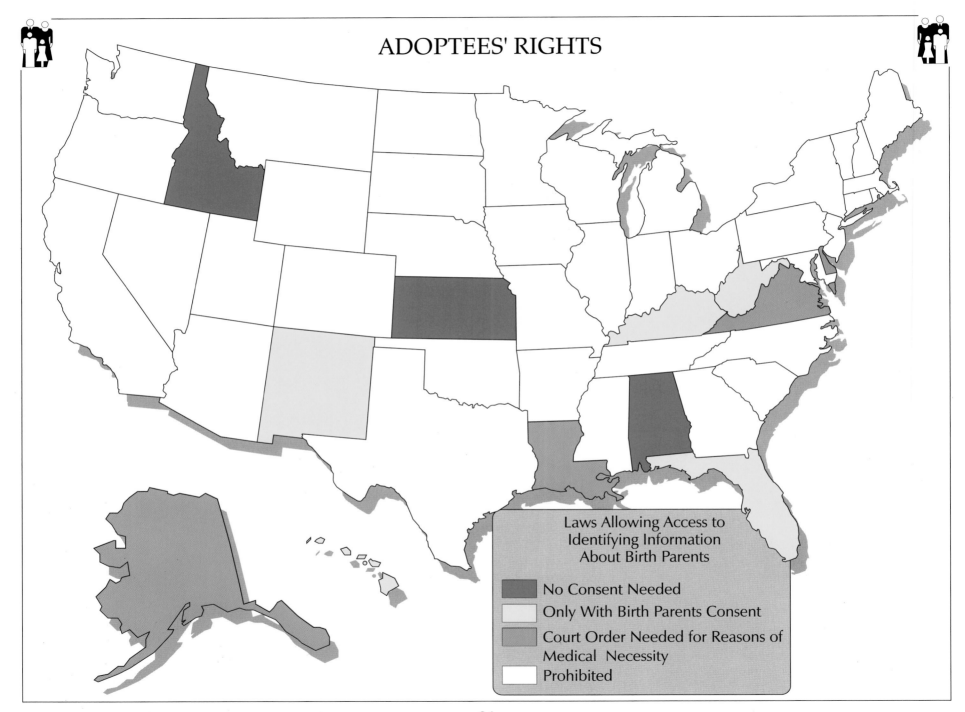

Laws Allowing Access to Identifying Information About Birth Parents

- No Consent Needed
- Only With Birth Parents Consent
- Court Order Needed for Reasons of Medical Necessity
- Prohibited

ADOPTION RATE & TYPE
1986

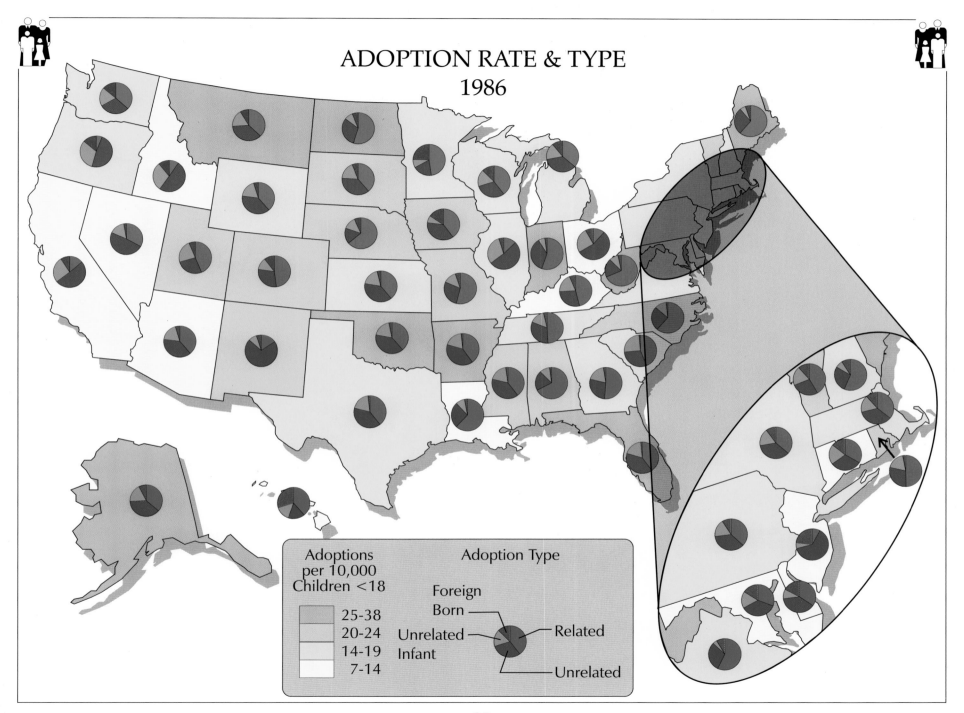

Adoptions per 10,000 Children <18

	25-38
	20-24
	14-19
	7-14

Adoption Type

Foreign Born
Unrelated
Infant
Related
Unrelated

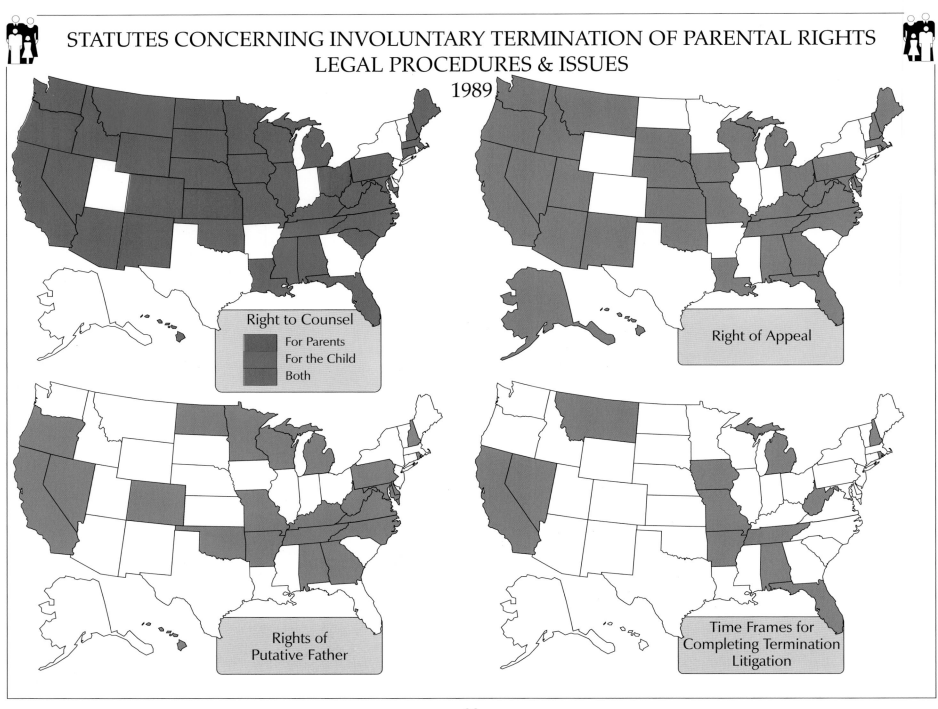

Right to Counsel

For Parents
For the Child
Both

Right of Appeal

Rights of
Putative Father

Time Frames for
Completing Termination
Litigation

STATUTES CONCERNING INVOLUNTARY TERMINATION OF PARENTAL RIGHTS
ISSUES CONCERNING RETURN TO HOME
1989

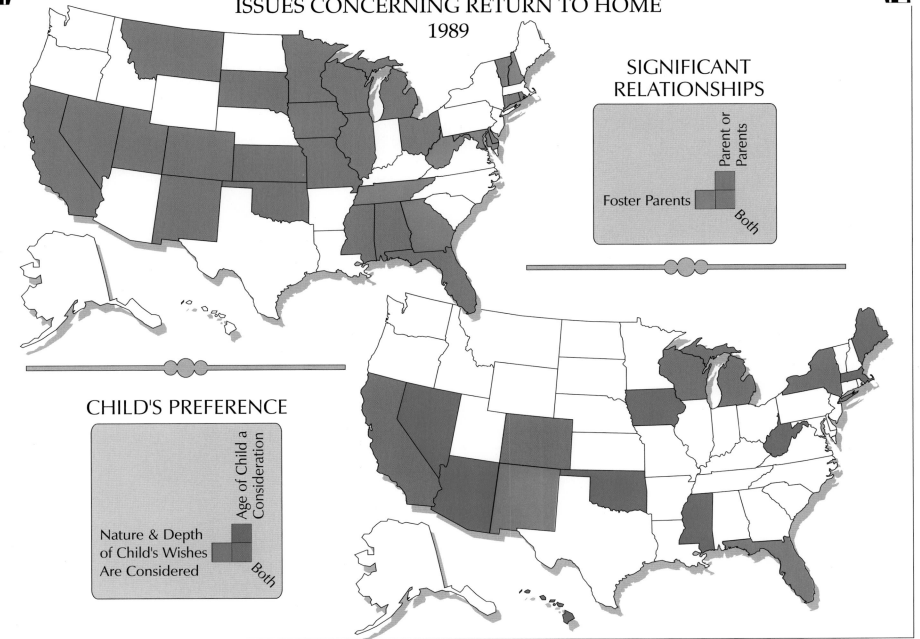

SIGNIFICANT
RELATIONSHIPS

Parent or Parents

Foster Parents

Both

CHILD'S PREFERENCE

Age of Child a Consideration

Nature & Depth
of Child's Wishes
Are Considered

Both

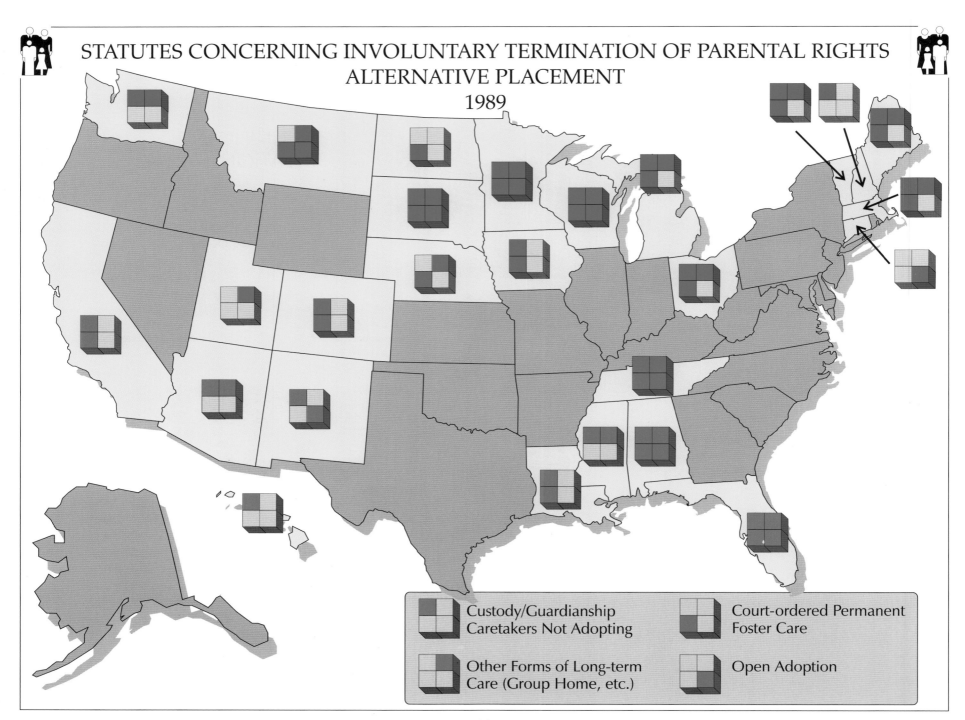

STATUTES CONCERNING INVOLUNTARY TERMINATION OF PARENTAL RIGHTS
ALTERNATIVE PLACEMENT
1989

Legend:
- Custody/Guardianship Caretakers Not Adopting
- Court-ordered Permanent Foster Care
- Other Forms of Long-term Care (Group Home, etc.)
- Open Adoption

PERSONAL LAW

In the strict context of the law, a person can be a corporation, company, an association, a firm or a partnership, as well as an individual. Laws dealing solely with the individual, or personal law, are the focus of this section.

The basis for laws that primarily affect the individual is the Constitution of the United States. Drafted in 1787, the Constitution laid the foundation for the individual rights of freedom of speech, religion and due process. In addition to the Constitution, individual states have passed various laws that govern its individuals. Though usually staying within the framework of the United States Constitution, state laws may vary widely across the country. Here we examine several broad groups of personal law issues in which laws vary from state to state.

ABORTIONS

Prior to 1973, only four states, Alaska, Hawaii, Washington and New York, permitted abortions. In the 1973 decision of Roe v. Wade, the United States Supreme Court, in an extremely controversial ruling, decided that a woman has the right to an abortion. In *Roe* v. *Wade*, the nine

months of pregnancy were broken into three separate trimesters with different laws regulating each trimester. During the first trimester, neither the federal nor state government has any say in whether a woman can have an abortion. Most of the nation's 201 abortions per 1,000 live births occur in the first trimester. However, a state can pass laws regulating the performance of an abortion during the second trimester. Abortions during this period can be prohibited by the state, but the circumstances are somewhat ambiguous. In the final trimester, the state can prohibit abortion in almost every situation, except when the mother's life is threatened.

Eight maps, labeled "Laws Regulating Abortions," deal with state laws. Since *Roe* v. *Wade*, the right to an abortion has been under attack. In 1989, the Supreme Court, in *Webster* v. *Reproductive Health Services*, ruled that states could restrict access to abortion, and a number of states have done that. In 1983 four states—Colorado, Florida, Rhode Island and South Carolina—required the husband to be notified or to grant consent for a married woman seeking an abortion. By 1992 the number of states requiring husband notification had more than doubled.

Laws that limit a minor's access to an abortion are far more widespread. Nearly three-quarters of all states require parental or state-mandated counseling for minors seeking an abortion. A decade ago only 16 states imposed such a requirement. Alabama, Michigan and Pennsylvania have enacted 24-hour waiting periods. North Dakota, Missouri and Louisiana have imposed a "gag" rule which prevents certain healthcare providers from giving counseling or referrals regarding abortions. These three states, along with 22 others, require that women be given state-prepared material intended to dissuade them from having an abortion.

Sixty percent of all states prohibit abortions after the fetus is considered viable, usually after 20 weeks. Of these states, only Missouri and Louisiana require a physician test for viability. Alabama also requires a physician's testing; however, a post-viable abortion is not prohibited. Six states, Arizona, North Dakota, Missouri, Louisiana, Kentucky and Pennsylvania, prohibit the use of public facilities for abortion. In addition, Missouri prohibits a public employee from participating in the performance of an abortion.

The Hyde Amendment, passed in 1976, prohibits the use of federal Medicaid funds for abortions of indigent women. While this amendment did not affect state laws, 38 states have their own policies that severely restrict the use of state money for abortions. In these 38 states, public funds cannot be used for abortion unless the mother's life is in danger. Eight of these states will allow abortions in cases of incest, rape or life endangerment. Only 12 states have no restrictions on the use of public funds for abortions.

To summarize the "Laws Regulating Abortions" maps, five states—Washington, Oregon, Hawaii, New Jersey and Vermont—offer no restrictions on the availability of abortions. At the other end of the spectrum, South Dakota, Louisiana, Pennsylvania and Missouri are among the most restrictive in abortion laws.

The map "Abortion Rate, 1988" shows that the states having the highest abortion rates are generally concentrated on the East and West coasts. With the exception of Nevada, they are also the states that provide non-restricted, public-funded abortions. Nevada's high rate, in spite of its lack of public funding, may be due to the fact that prostitution is legal there.

Only a few states (Wisconsin, Illinois, Florida, South Carolina, Delaware and Rhode Island) have both restrictive abortion laws and a high abortion rate. For the majority of states, there is a correlation between the abortion rate and the restrictivness of abortion laws.

SMOKING

If you want to light up a pipe, a cigarette or a cigar in any part of a restaurant or any public area these days, there are only four states where you may legally do so: Kentucky, Mississippi, Alabama and Georgia. Laws that restrict smoking are on the increase. Behind the current smoking bans is the fact that clinical studies have indicated more and more health risks, not only from smoking, but also from inhaling the smoke of others.

The map, "Restrictions on Smoking in Public Places, 1993" shows there are extensive restrictions in Hawaii, Minnesota, New York, New Hampshire and Vermont These are states with traditional emphasis on liberal environmental issues. In these states, there is no smoking in any public places.

Twenty-four states have moderate restrictions, laws which prohibit smoking in government office buildings, hospitals, elevators, public libraries and theaters. Seventeen states have minimal restrictions, such as bans on smoking in set-aside areas in public places. The lightest restrictions are found in the Southern states. Many of the states with minimal or no restrictions have strong economic ties to the tobacco industry.

LAWS REGULATING ABORTIONS
1992

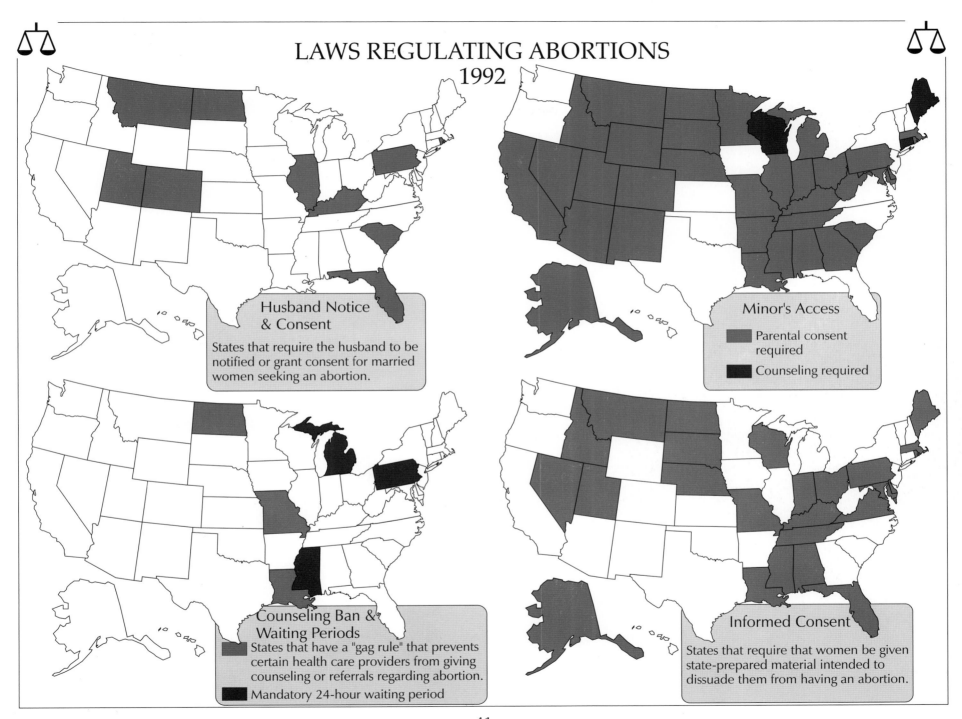

Husband Notice & Consent

States that require the husband to be notified or grant consent for married women seeking an abortion.

Minor's Access

- Parental consent required
- Counseling required

Counseling Ban & Waiting Periods

States that have a "gag rule" that prevents certain health care providers from giving counseling or referrals regarding abortion.

- Mandatory 24-hour waiting period

Informed Consent

States that require that women be given state-prepared material intended to dissuade them from having an abortion.

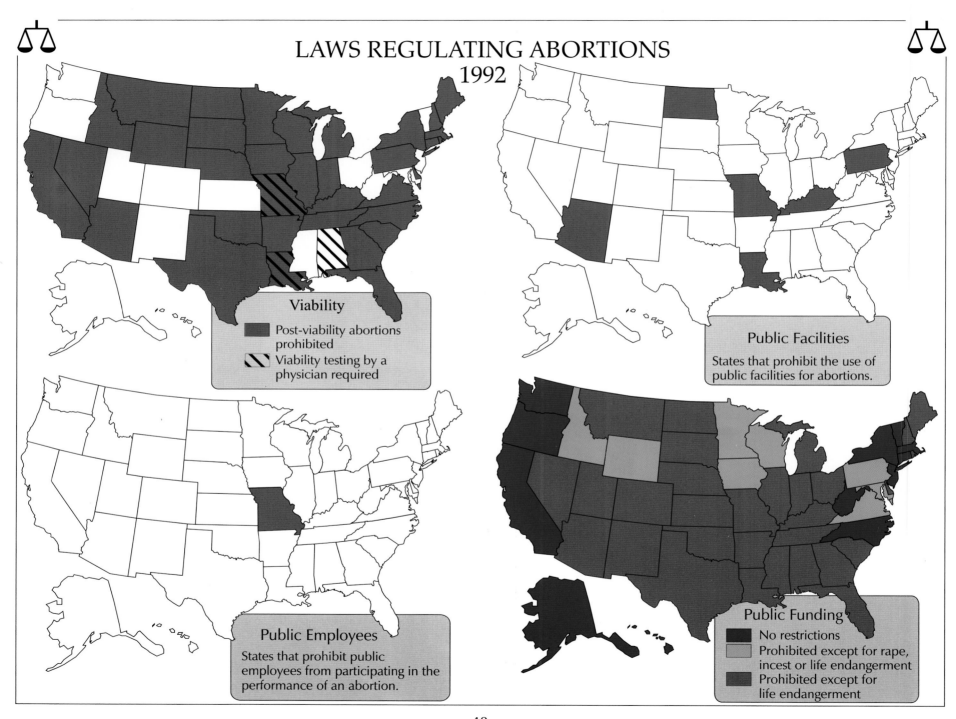

LAWS REGULATING ABORTIONS
1992

Viability
Post-viability abortions prohibited

Viability testing by a physician required

Public Facilities
States that prohibit the use of public facilities for abortions.

Public Employees
States that prohibit public employees from participating in the performance of an abortion.

Public Funding
No restrictions

Prohibited except for rape, incest or life endangerment

Prohibited except for life endangerment

ABORTION RATE
1988

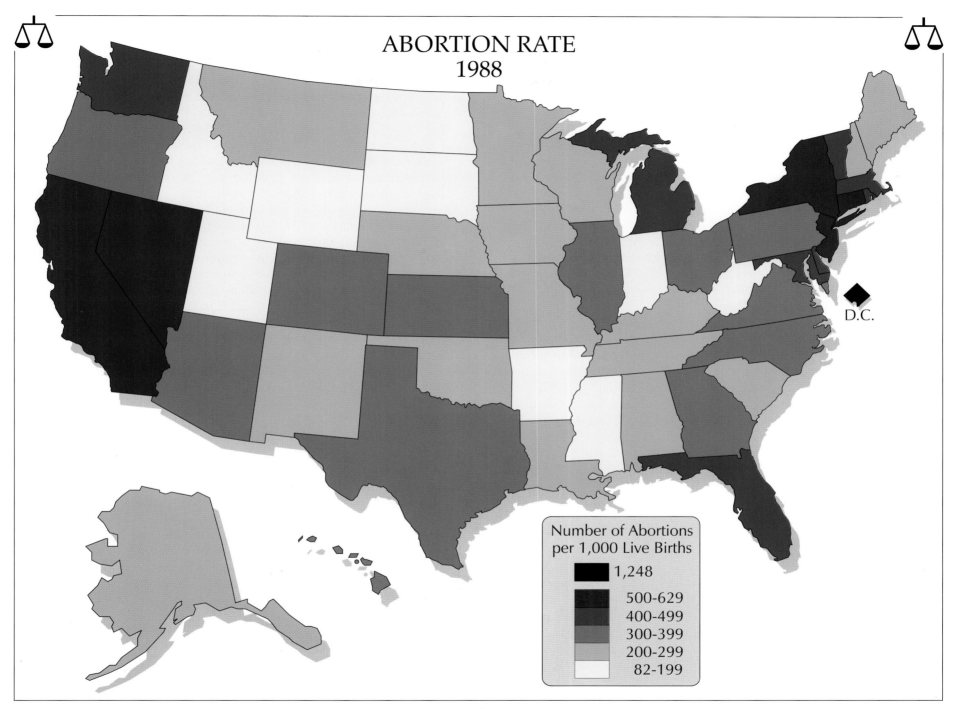

Number of Abortions per 1,000 Live Births

	1,248
	500-629
	400-499
	300-399
	200-299
	82-199

D.C.

MEDICAL MALPRACTICE

While there are many possibilities of medical malpractice, for example among dentists, chiropractors, psychologists, in nursing homes and among practitioners of alternative medicine, the six maps in this section only cover the medical malpractice that occurs in hospitals or in the doctor's office.

According to Jack Schroder in his book, "Identifying Medical Malpractice[1]," in the early 1970s, hospital administrators and their lawyers began to sponsor laws to reduce malpractice lawsuits, not malpractice. According to Schroder, not one new law or regulation passed since the medical crisis of the 1970s was written to reduce malpractice or to protect the patient.

The six maps titled "Medical Malpractice Legislation" consider some of these laws and how the states handle them. The subheading "Statutes of Limitation'" shows that nearly every state has provisions for a statute of limitations stating how long after malpractice occurs a suit can be filed. In seven of those states, the provision was found constitutional by the highest state court. In New Hampshire alone the provision was found unconstitutional.

In 18 states, there are provisions for a special statute of limitations for minors. In Alabama and Indiana, the provisions were found constitutional by the highest state courts, but in Arizona, Nevada, North Dakota and Tennessee, such provisions were found unconstitutional. In Pennsylvania, the provision was allowed to lapse.

A panel to screen litigation before a trial takes place, as the submap "Pretrial Screening Panel" shows, exists in 23 states. In five of those states, the provision was found to be constitutional. Florida and Missouri considered a Pretrial Screening Panel unconstitutional while in Wisconsin the provision was allowed to expire.

In 12 states, as shown by the submap "Limits of Liability," there are caps to the amount someone can sue for in medical malpractice. In Idaho, the provision has been repealed. In California, Indiana and Montana the provision has been found constitutional, but in Illinois, Nevada and North Carolina it was found unconstitutional. In Kentucky, it was unconstitutional because it could not be separated from another unconstitutional act.

A fund to compensate patients could have an effect on medical malpractice suits, but it exists in only ten states. In Indiana, Louisiana and Montana it was found to be constitutional, but was unconstitutional in Kentucky. In North Carolina, it was attached to another unconstitutional law. Hawaii had such a provision, but it was allowed to lapse, while in Colorado, Florida, Illinois and Wisconsin, the provision exists in statutes, but is not implemented.

The final submap, "Arbitration," shows that a provision for arbitration exists in 13 states, and has been found constitutional in Michigan, but in Maine and North Carolina it has been repealed or allowed to expire.

DRIVING AGE

Each state has its own requirements for issuing driving licenses and sets different ages at which a young person can obtain a juvenile license, a restrictive license or a learner's permit.

There are two maps titled "Driving Age." The map subtitled "Regular License" shows that adult or regular licenses are issued at varying ages along with the stipulation that the fledgling driver take a course in driver education. In general for both regular and juvenile licenses, the more congested states of the Northeast set higher minimum ages.

The majority of the states set 16 as the age for an adult license. In Colorado, Vermont and the District of

RESTRICTIONS ON SMOKING IN PUBLIC PLACES
1993

None
Minimal
Moderate
Extensive

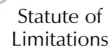

Statute of
Limitations

MEDICAL MALPRACTICE
LEGISLATION

Special Statute
of Limitations
for Minors

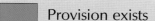 **Provision exists**

Provision found constitutional
by the highest state court

Provision is not separated from an
act found unconstitutional by the
highest state court

Provision exists in statute but is
not implemented

Provision repealed or allowed to expire

Provision found unconstitutional
by the highest state court

Pretrial
Screening

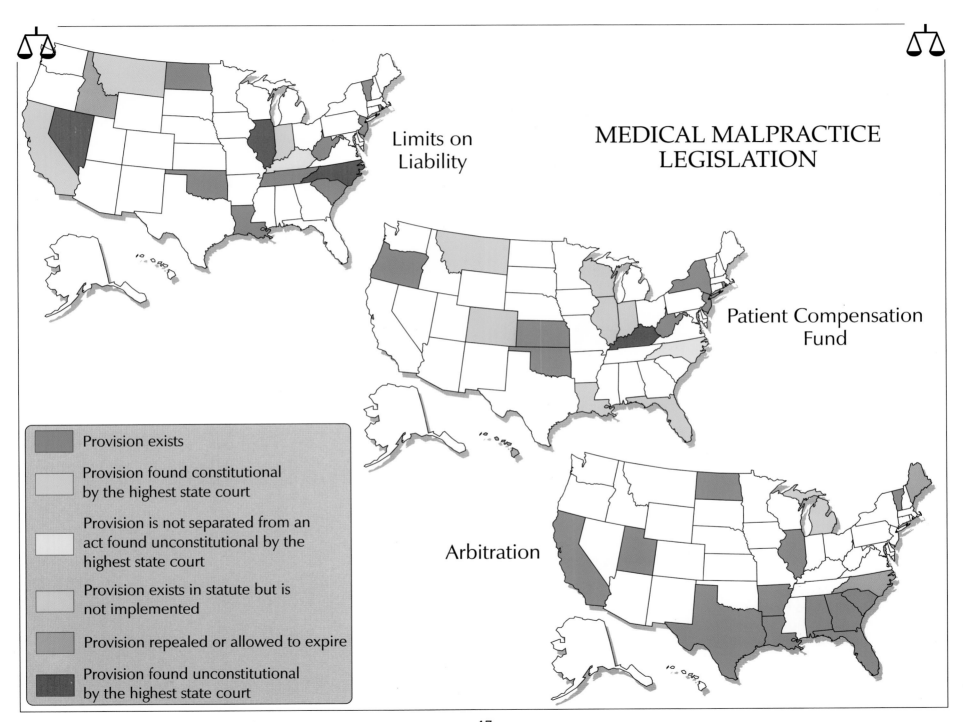

MEDICAL MALPRACTICE LEGISLATION

Limits on Liability

Patient Compensation Fund

Arbitration

Legend:

- Provision exists
- Provision found constitutional by the highest state court
- Provision is not separated from an act found unconstitutional by the highest state court
- Provision exists in statute but is not implemented
- Provision repealed or allowed to expire
- Provision found unconstitutional by the highest state court

Columbia, the age for an adult license is 18, the usual age of majority.

The map subtitled "Juvenile License" shows the minimum age for obtaining a juvenile license with parental consent. The youngest age is 13 years and is found in only one state, Montana. Thirteen predominantly rural states will issue a juvenile license at 14 years, and Texas, Louisiana, South Carolina and Minnesota allow juvenile licenses at age 15. Ten states and the District of Columbia hold 16 to be the minimal age. Massachusetts sets the legal age at 16½. States that do not offer a juvenile license are left blank.

In most states, you can use your out-of-state license for a stated period of time, but there are states that insist that you get a license from the new state at once. Driving licenses are not issued forever. They expire after a specified number of years, and in most states you simply complete a new application form. In some states, you must also take a vision test, and, if you have been involved in auto accidents or violations, you may have to take the driver's test over again.

DRUNKEN DRIVING

The definition of driving while intoxicated (DWI) is linked to the amount of alcohol in a driver's blood. In many states, a blood alcohol level of 0.15 percent or higher is considered drunkenness. Twelve ounces of beer, 4 ounces of wine or 1.5 ounces of 80 proof whiskey, gin or vodka taken during the course of an hour will result in a blood level of .08 to .1 in most people.

Most states consider the granting of a license as implied consent to be tested if the situation justifies it. If a driver refuses, the license could be suspended. Some states allow consultation with an attorney before testing, but a substan-

tive delay will give an incorrect blood level, since the alcohol in the blood is gradually detoxified

The map "Minimal Blood Alcohol Level for DWI Offense" shows that 38 states, located predominately in the central United States, observe the 0.1 rule in adults and 35 states observe it in minors. Only a handful of states drop the minimum level to half of the 0.1 level or lower. In the case of blood alcohol level in minors, six states have lowered their tolerance for determining the minimum level. Of these, four states, Oregon, Missouri, Ohio and most recently Iowa, have enacted a zero tolerance policy, meaning that even if a trace amount of alcohol is detected, a DWI offense can be charged.

The map "Driver License Suspension Terms for Drunk Driving, 1993" shows that, for all but three states and the District of Columbia, there are specific terms of suspension of a driver's license for the first offense of DWI. Of all fifty states only Nevada lacks any suspension terms. With many of the remaining states, an increasing length of license suspension results from subsequent DWI convictions. However, in Idaho, Minnesota and Maryland, the suspension for a second offense can be as little as three to six months. Eleven states and the District of Columbia do not specify the length of suspension for the second offense. For the third offense the number of states without a specified length of suspension increases to 16.

Michigan invokes a permanent suspension of a driver license with the second DWI conviction. Upon a third offense, New Hampshire and West Virginia invoke a permanent suspension.

ARRESTS FOR DRUNK DRIVING

The map "Driving while Under the Influence of Alcohol,

DRIVING AGE
1992

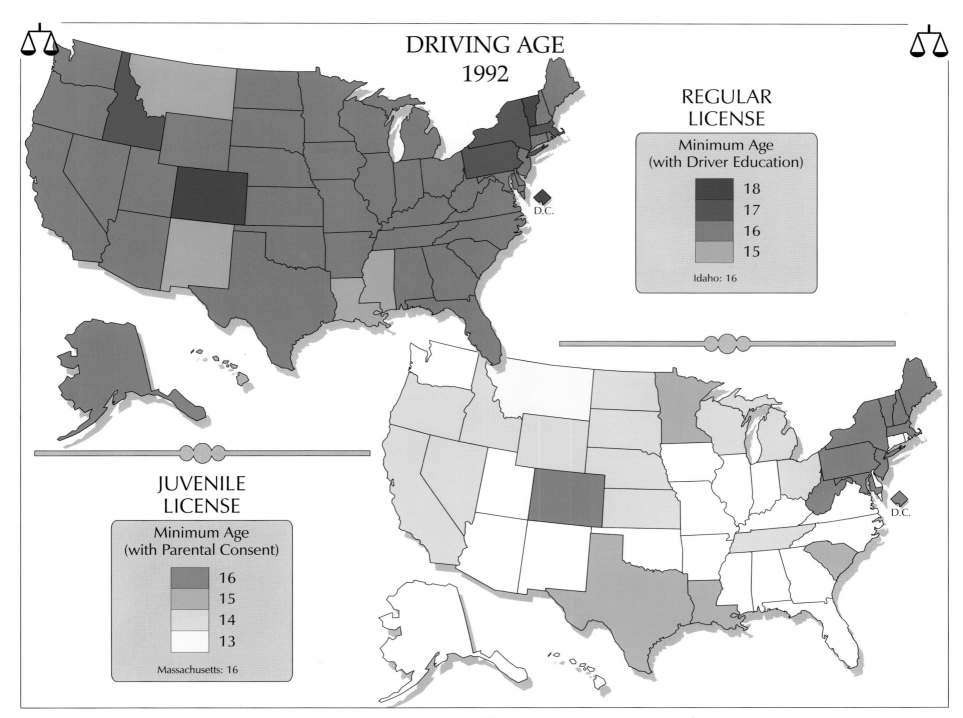

REGULAR LICENSE

Minimum Age
(with Driver Education)

- 18
- 17
- 16
- 15

Idaho: 16

JUVENILE LICENSE

Minimum Age
(with Parental Consent)

- 16
- 15
- 14
- 13

Massachusetts: 16

D.C.

MINIMUM BLOOD ALCOHOL LEVEL FOR DWI OFFENSE

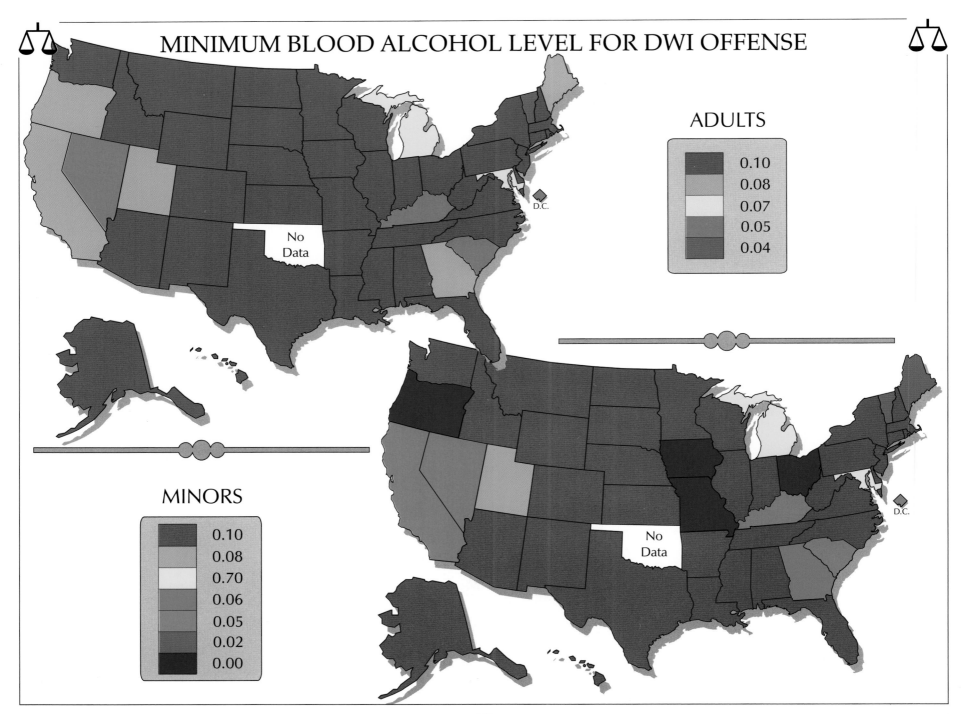

ADULTS

	0.10
	0.08
	0.07
	0.05
	0.04

No Data

D.C.

MINORS

	0.10
	0.08
	0.70
	0.06
	0.05
	0.02
	0.00

No Data

D.C.

DRIVER LICENSE SUSPENSION TERMS
FOR DRUNK DRIVING
1993

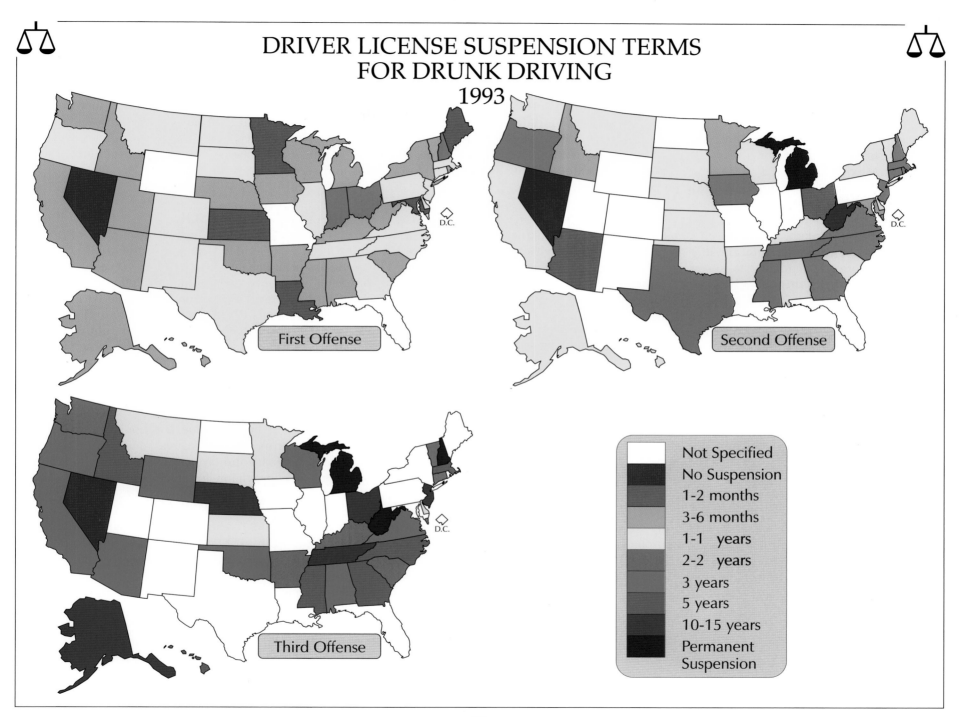

First Offense

Second Offense

Third Offense

Not Specified
No Suspension
1-2 months
3-6 months
1-1 years
2-2 years
3 years
5 years
10-15 years
Permanent Suspension

1991" shows the highest rates for arrests for DWI occur in states west of the Mississippi and in Kentucky. Six states—California, North Dakota, Wyoming, Colorado, New Mexico, Kansas and Kentucky—all have arrest rates of over 1,000 for every 100,000 residents, with New Mexico leading at a rate of 1,546. Most states in the Northeast have relatively low rates of arrest, but Maine, with 800, is an exception.

Just why the Western states have such a high rate is difficult to explain. It may be due to a culture of heavy drinking associated with interminably long stretches of highway where the tendency to speed is overwhelming. Speeding mixed with drinking can lead to arrests.

The punishment for drunken driving can be severe. In most states, a first offense can carry fines of between $100 and $500, plus community service and time in jail.

There was a time, not long ago, when a drunk driving charge could be changed to reckless driving in a plea bargain, but now many states prohibit this plea bargaining and insist that even a first time offender spend at least 48 hours in jail.

JUVENILE DRINKING

No state allows minors under 18 years of age to buy beer, wine or liquor. The map "Legal Age For the Sale of Alcoholic Beverages to Minors" shows that only 46 percent of states set 21 years as a minimum age for purchasing liquor, beer or wine. Six states have lowered the age limit to 20 years, 13 states to 19, and eight states, Hawaii, New Mexico, Louisiana, Kansas, Wisconsin, Tennessee, West Virginia, and Vermont, allow beer, wine and liquor to be sold to 18-year-olds.

Five states, South Dakota, Oklahoma, Tennessee, Ohio and Virginia, restrict hard liquor to 21 year-olds but allow 18-year-olds to buy beer. Two additional states—North and South Carolina—allow 18-year-olds to buy wine and beer. Obviously, beer is considered less likely to cause drunkenness, but in fact the alcohol in beer is no different from the alcohol in wine and hard liquor.

PRAYING IN SCHOOL

One of the hottest legal issues today is prayer in the public schools. This issue has been debated for more than 20 years. In 1962, the Supreme Court of the United States ruled (*Engel et al.* v. *Vitale et al.*) that prayer in the public schools was unconstitutional. State officials could not compose an official state prayer and require that it be recited in the public schools of the state at the beginning of each school day, even if the prayer were denominationally neutral. Religion may be taught in an educational context, but Bible reading and prayer on school premises during school hours are both unlawful.[2]

One side of the argument believes that a school has a legitimate role in fostering moral values. The other side feels that allowing even voluntary prayer in schools violates the constitutional provision for the separation of church and state.

In spite of the Supreme Court decision, the map of "School Prayer in Public Schools, 1993" shows that six states—Montana, Oklahoma, Mississippi, Kentucky, Delaware and New Hampshire—permit prayer. Twenty-three other states attempt to get around the Supreme Court decision by setting aside a daily "moment of meditation" in which students may pray silently if they wish.

The remaining states, located predominately in the West and North Central regions, prohibit prayer in public

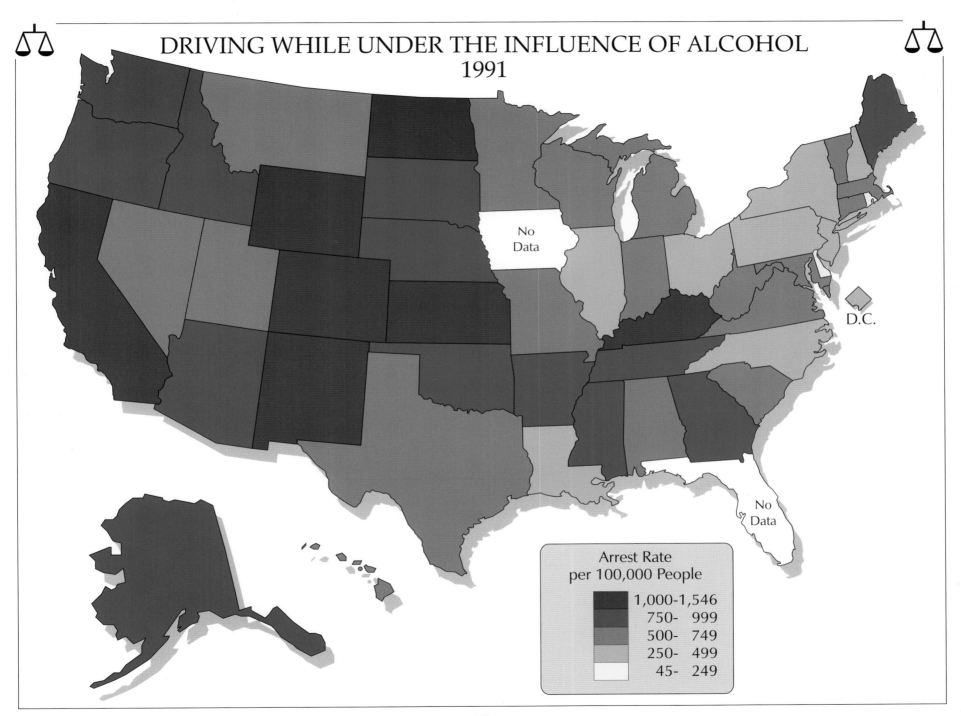

DRIVING WHILE UNDER THE INFLUENCE OF ALCOHOL
1991

No
Data

No
Data

D.C.

**Arrest Rate
per 100,000 People**

1,000-1,546
750-   999
500-   749
250-   499
45-   249

LEGAL AGE FOR SALE OF
ALCOHOLIC BEVERAGES TO MINORS

Minimum Age
for Sale
to Minors

21 — 21
20 — 20
19 — 19
18 — 18

Beer — 19
Beer & Wine — 18
Beer, Wine & Liquor — 18

54

schools. Outside of school hours, the equal access law, passed by Congress in 1984, allows students to meet on school property before or after classes for religious purposes, including prayer.

In 1992, the Supreme Court extended the ban on school prayer to invocations by clergy at public school graduation ceremonies. It ruled that a student could not be required to sit through a religious activity as the price of graduating. A year later, in 1993, two federal court decisions allowed prayer at graduation if led by a student.

Although the laws regarding school prayer seem clear, school prayer has been a political football, with one party launching a strong effort to get prayer back in the schools, and the other resisting. Proponents of the theory of the separation of church and state fight the reintroduction of prayer, pointing out that among other problems there is a difference of religion among students so that no one prayer answers the religious needs of all.

The fight goes on in some of the 23 states where a silent period is allowed, calling it, as Delaware does, "time to voluntarily participate in moral, philosophical, patriotic or religious activity." Other states call this brief period silent time, silent prayer, silent reflection or silent meditation.

CORPORAL PUNISHMENT

The map "Corporal Punishment in Public Schools, 1993" shows that nine states have passed laws prohibiting any form of corporal punishment, such as spanking or paddling. In 16 Southeastern and North Central and Western states, corporal punishment is allowed, but even in these states, restrictions are put on the type of punishment. It must be reasonable, not excessive, in terms of the offense and the child's age.

In addition to the state rules, local rules have differing requirements concerning corporal punishment. Some individual school districts have their own policies and procedures for handling disciplinary problems. It becomes difficult to determine, when corporal punishment is allowed, what constitutes just punishment and what is considered child abuse.

The issue of child abuse is very much on everyone's mind. A few blows with the hand as a spanking may not legally constitute child abuse, but 50 blows with a leather belt do, and so does excessive paddling that necessitates medical attention.

In spite of the national concern over child abuse, nearly half of all states and the District of Columbia do not have statutes concerning corporal punishment.

THE RESPONSIBILITY OF PARENTS

In most cases, a parent's financial responsibility for damage done by his child is regulated by state law. The map "Parental Liability" shows that in Oregon and Louisiana the parent must pay for any damage a child does, no matter what the circumstances. However, in 25 other states, parents can be sued only if their child does deliberate damage through a malicious act or hurts somebody. Even so, there is usually a ceiling on the amount the damaged party can collect. It ranges from $500 to $5,000. In most states the amount is $2,000 or less.

In 14 states, parents can be sued only for destruction done deliberately. Michigan's law is slightly different. There parents can be sued for property destruction, but not for any harm done to another child by an accident their child caused. They are only liable for damage if someone is hurt through the commission of a crime.

If a minor causes an accident in Oklahoma, Iowa, West Virginia or Maryland, which is not deliberate, the minor's

SCHOOL PRAYER IN PUBLIC SCHOOLS
1993

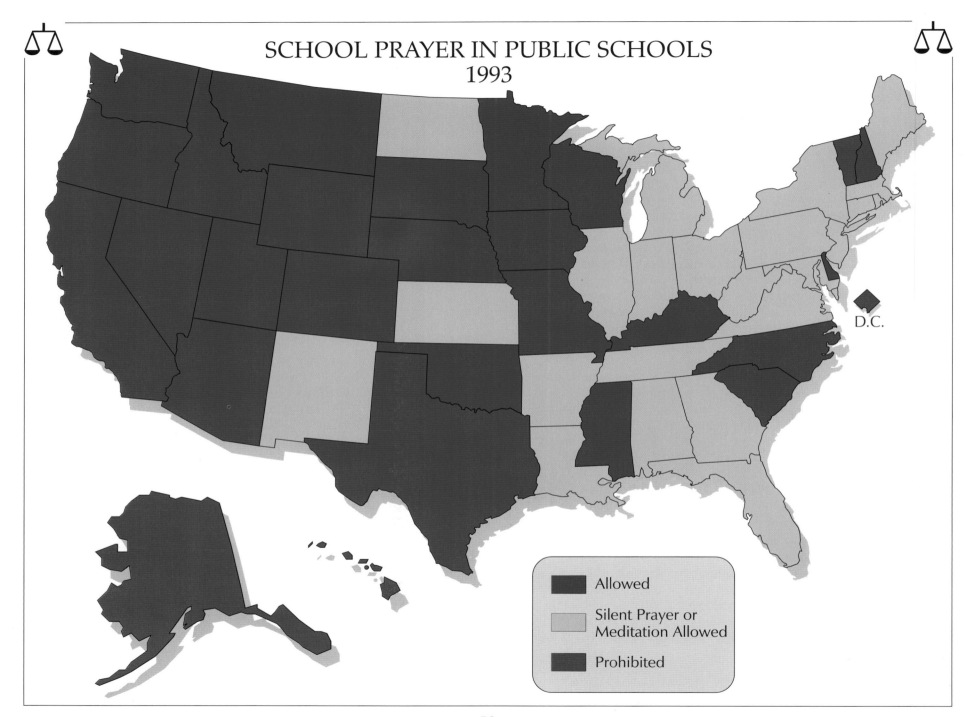

D.C.

Legend:
- Allowed
- Silent Prayer or Meditation Allowed
- Prohibited

CORPORAL PUNISHMENT IN PUBLIC SCHOOLS
1993

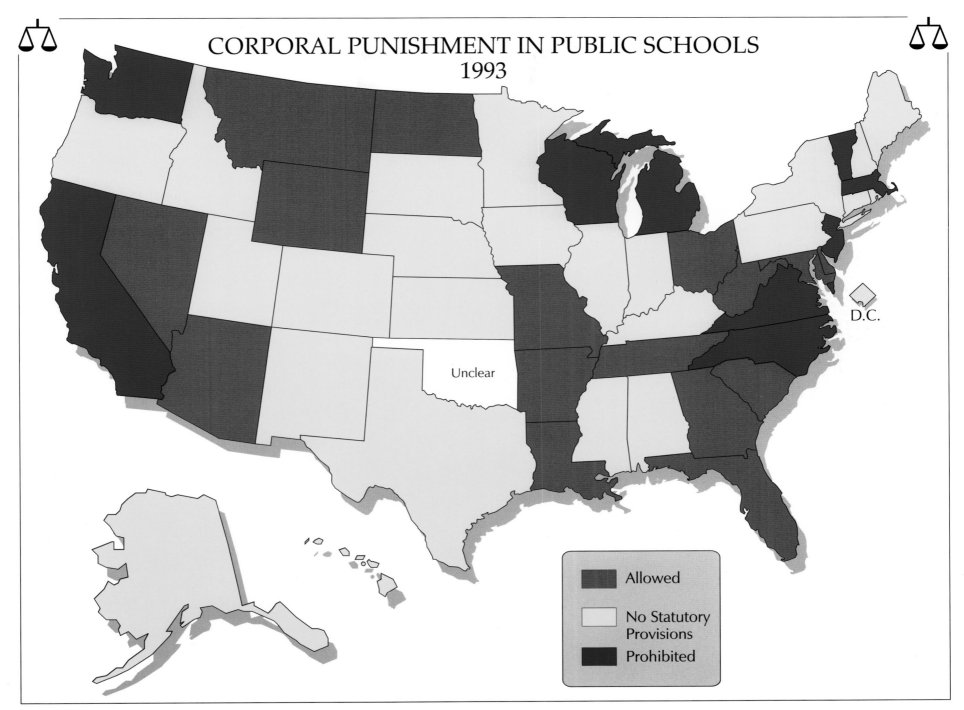

D.C.

Unclear

Allowed

No Statutory
Provisions

Prohibited

parents are not liable. In those states, the parents could be sued only if the damage and injury were done maliciously and willfully. In Florida, Delaware, New Jersey and New York, parents would not be liable if damage were the result of a true accident.

Consider the case of a minor in one of these eight states who decided to rob the local convenience store and, in the course of the holdup, damages the store and injures the storekeeper. In addition to whatever sentence the minor could receive for the crime, the parents could also be sued by the storekeeper for the injury suffered from the robbery as well as the damage to his property. In this case, the parents did nothing wrong, and the injuries and damage to property were completely the fault of minors. It would be an entirely different matter if the parents knew that a crime or an injury were taking place and did nothing to stop it. Then they could be held responsible for any damage or injury done by the minor, whether or not a crime was committed.

PROSTITUTION

In the United States during the 1800s, prostitution existed in almost every town. No attempt to stop it appeared until the end of that century. Through the efforts of James Robert Mann, the Mann Act, or the White Slave Traffic Act was passed. It prohibited the international and interstate transportation of women for immoral purposes.

Nearly all of the states passed laws against brothels and prostitution, but the first World War saw a tremendous increase in prostitution and its resulting venereal disease. With the Second World War in the offing, Congress passed the May Act, making it a federal offense to practice prostitution in areas occupied by the army or navy.

Today, all states but Nevada have laws that make it a crime to operate a house of prostitution. Curiously, the map "Prostitution, 1991" shows that Nevada, the state noted for legalizing prostitution, has the highest arrest rate for the offense. The fact that prostitution is legal in Nevada may account for the large number of arrests. Legalization has allowed the opening of many state-approved brothels. The "legalized" brothels have access to the police, and it is important to brothel owners that "freelance" prostitutes—those not operating in legal brothels—be arrested and discouraged.

In other states, it makes sense to equate the number of arrests with the amount of prostitution that occurs. The District of Columbia has the second highest arrest rate for prostitution, 254 arrests for every 100,000 people, compared to Nevada's rate of 256.

The West Coast and the Southwestern states in general show a high rate of arrests. With the exception of Missouri, Kansas, Georgia and Tennessee, where rates are high, the Deep South, Midwest and the Northern Plains states represent the low end of prostitution arrests. Higher rates seem linked to states with large urban areas.

ARRESTS FOR SEXUAL OFFENSES

According to the Department of Justice, sexual offenses include all sexual offenses except rape and prostitution. Some of these offenses may include seduction, bigamy, pornography, illicit cohabitation, sodomy, incest and indecent exposure. Both Alabama and Tennessee represent the low end of arrest rates for sex offenses, as the map "Sex Offenses, 1991" shows. The highest arrest rates are in Wisconsin and a group of four Western states, Nevada, Utah, Colorado and Arizona. The highest rate in all the states is Utah with 898.

Although the Justice Department does not include rape in

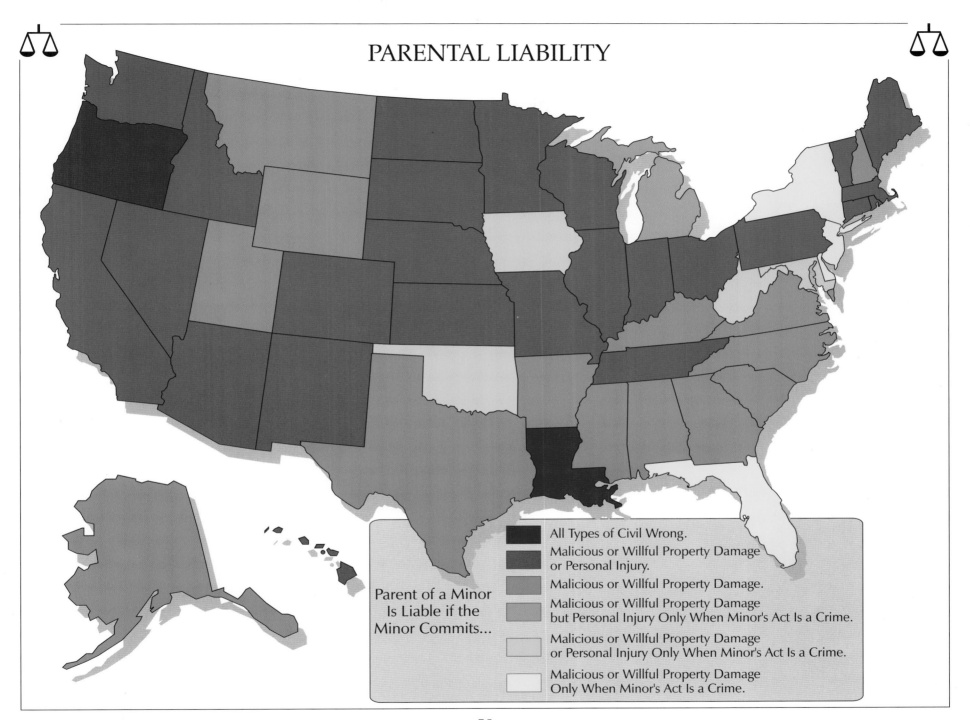

PARENTAL LIABILITY

Parent of a Minor Is Liable if the Minor Commits...

- All Types of Civil Wrong.
- Malicious or Willful Property Damage or Personal Injury.
- Malicious or Willful Property Damage.
- Malicious or Willful Property Damage but Personal Injury Only When Minor's Act Is a Crime.
- Malicious or Willful Property Damage or Personal Injury Only When Minor's Act Is a Crime.
- Malicious or Willful Property Damage Only When Minor's Act Is a Crime.

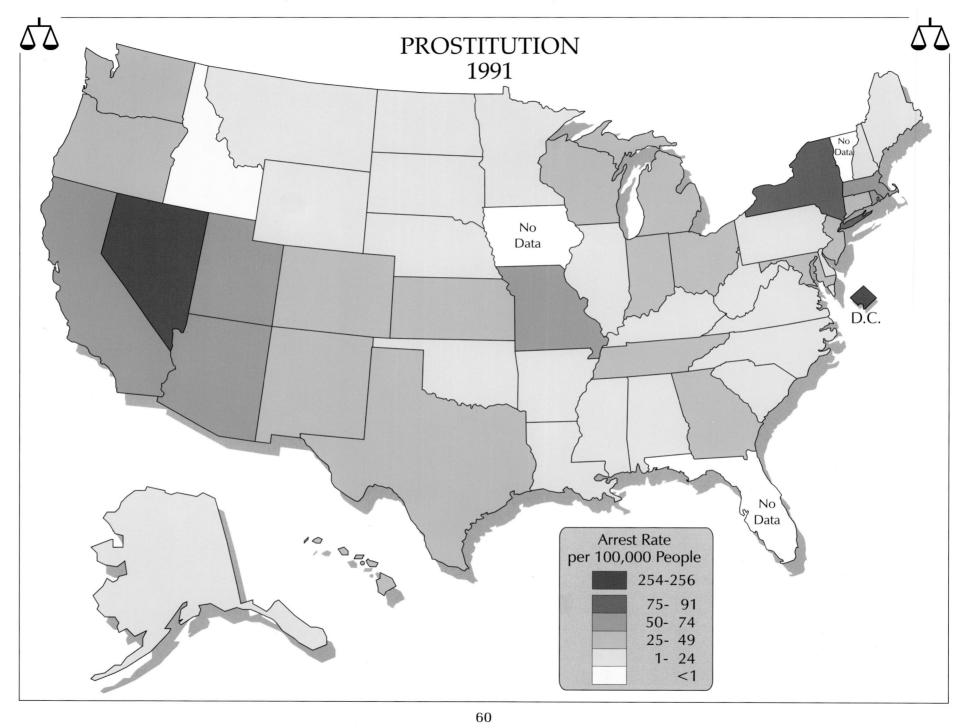

PROSTITUTION
1991

No
Data

No
Data

No
Data

No
Data

D.C.

**Arrest Rate
per 100,000 People**

254-256

75- 91

50- 74

25- 49

1- 24

<1

the classification of sex offenses, the overall pattern is similar to the arrest rate for rape. While only 1.3 percent of rapes are committed by minors, juveniles account for 17.5 percent of sex offense arrests.

GAMBLING

The map "Gambling, 1991" shows an east-west distribution of gambling arrest rates. With the exception of Hawaii, the lowest rates are generally found west of the Mississippi. Lower rates do not mean there is less gambling, but simply that there are fewer arrests. The low arrest rate may be due to legalization, as in Nevada with a rate of three per 100,000, or to a general cultural acceptance of gambling and a reluctance on the part of the police to make arrests for it.

The states east of the Mississippi generally have high arrest rates, with the highest, except for Ohio, New York and the District of Columbia, in the South. In states where casino gambling has been legalized, there has been an impact on personal finances. In Iowa, the second greatest cause for personal bankruptcy has been attributed to gambling.

BUYING AND CARRYING GUNS

State laws vary, but almost all states have restrictions on purchasing and bearing arms. Colorado, Kentucky, South Dakota and Wyoming place no age restrictions on the purchase of a handgun, while other states forbid the sale of a handgun to a minor. These states have ordinances such as the one in Allen Park, Michigan, which stipulate that it is "unlawful for any person under 18 years of age to purchase, carry or transport a firearm on any public street or in any public place. It shall be unlawful to sell a firearm to any person under 18 years of age."

The first of the four maps titled "Gun Control 1992—Purchasing" indicates that 20 states require a waiting period between the request to purchase and the actual purchase. This waiting period gives the police a chance to investigate the purchaser's background, and it also provides a cooling-off period in case the gun is bought in anger with violence in mind.

Thirteen states and the District of Columbia require a license or permit in order to buy a gun, and Nevada, Kansas, Illinois, Michigan, New York and the District of Columbia require registration along with the purchase. In New York, New Jersey, Massachusetts and Illinois, licensing or an ID card is required after the purchase. In 24 states a record of the sale is sent to the state or local government.

The second set of four maps, "Gun Control 1992—Carrying," shows that in 37 states and the District of Columbia, carrying a concealed weapon is prohibited. In Utah, North Dakota, Oklahoma, Texas, Tennessee, Vermont and the District of Columbia, it is against the law to carry a gun openly. In 16 states, a gun can be carried openly if the carrier has a license. In 34 states, a gun can be carried concealed if the carrier has a license.

"Carrying" includes having a gun in hand or in a holster, pocket, purse or briefcase. To be concealed, it must be deliberately hidden from public view. In some states, the law lists weapons, arms or firearms in general. In other states, individual weapons are actually listed, such as machine guns, billy clubs, razors, brass knuckles, sawed-off shotguns.

In these states, if a person carries a weapon the law doesn't list, he is not likely to be convicted. In some states, having the weapon in one's house or place of business doesn't count. Other conditions that permit carrying a

SEX OFFENSES
1991

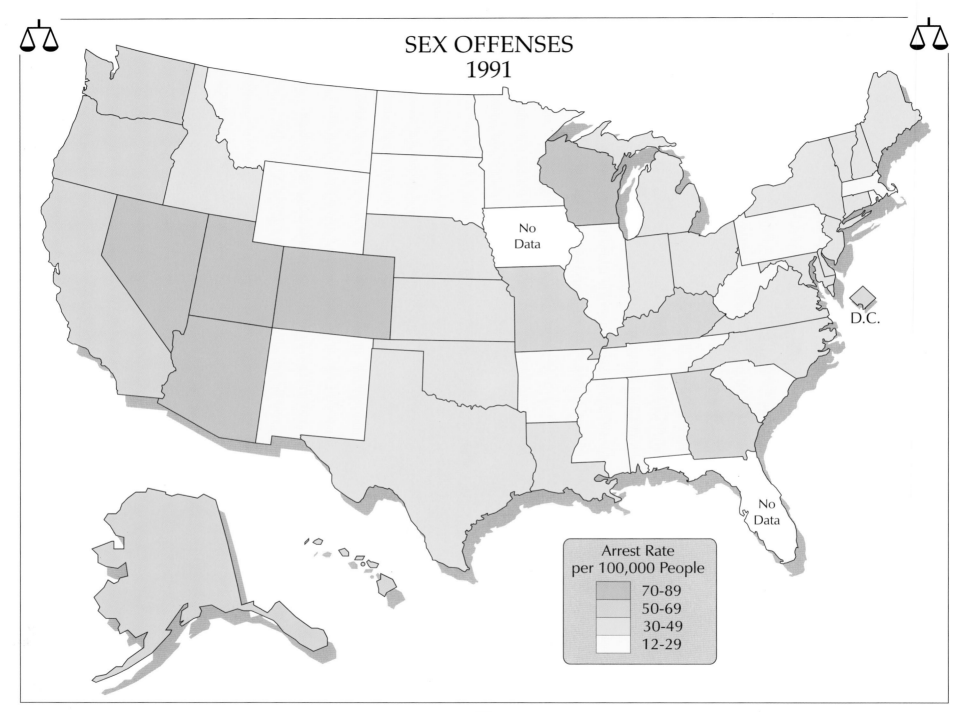

No Data

No Data

D.C.

Arrest Rate
per 100,000 People

70-89
50-69
30-49
12-29

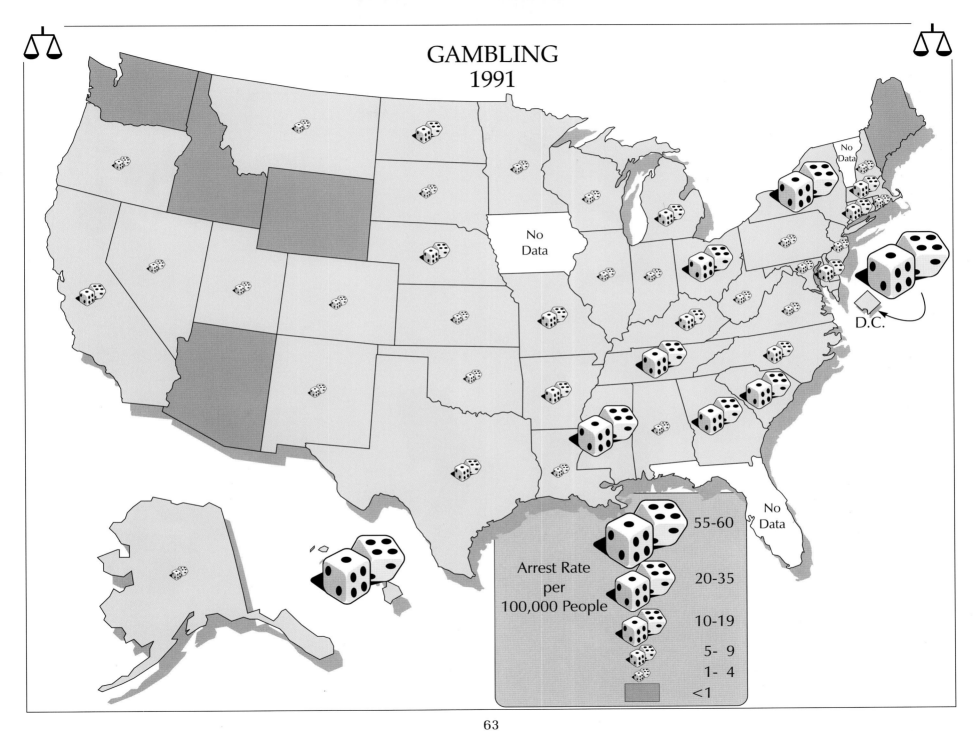

GAMBLING
1991

No Data

No Data

No Data

D.C.

Arrest Rate
per
100,000 People

55-60

20-35

10-19

5- 9

1- 4

<1

63

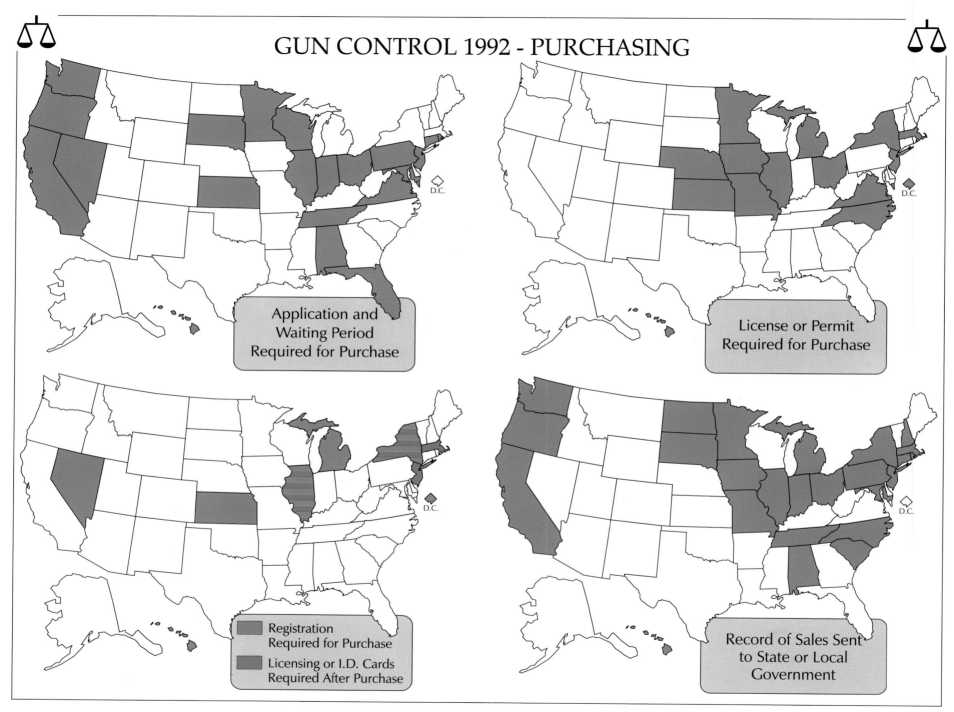

GUN CONTROL 1992 - PURCHASING

Application and
Waiting Period
Required for Purchase

License or Permit
Required for Purchase

Registration
Required for Purchase

Licensing or I.D. Cards
Required After Purchase

Record of Sales Sent
to State or Local
Government

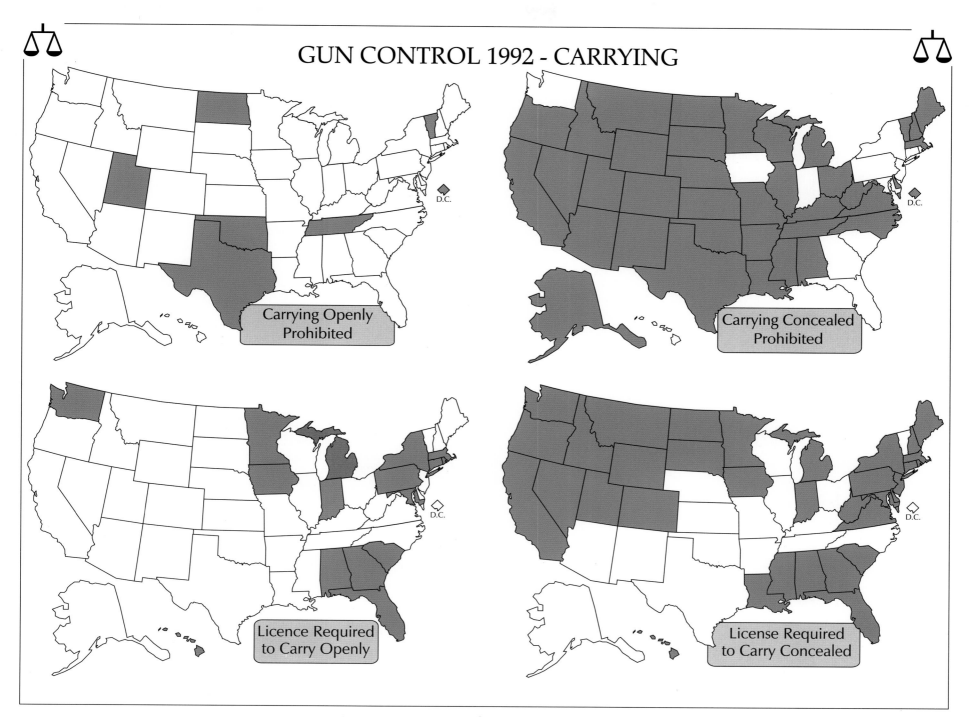

Carrying Openly Prohibited

Carrying Concealed Prohibited

Licence Required to Carry Openly

License Required to Carry Concealed

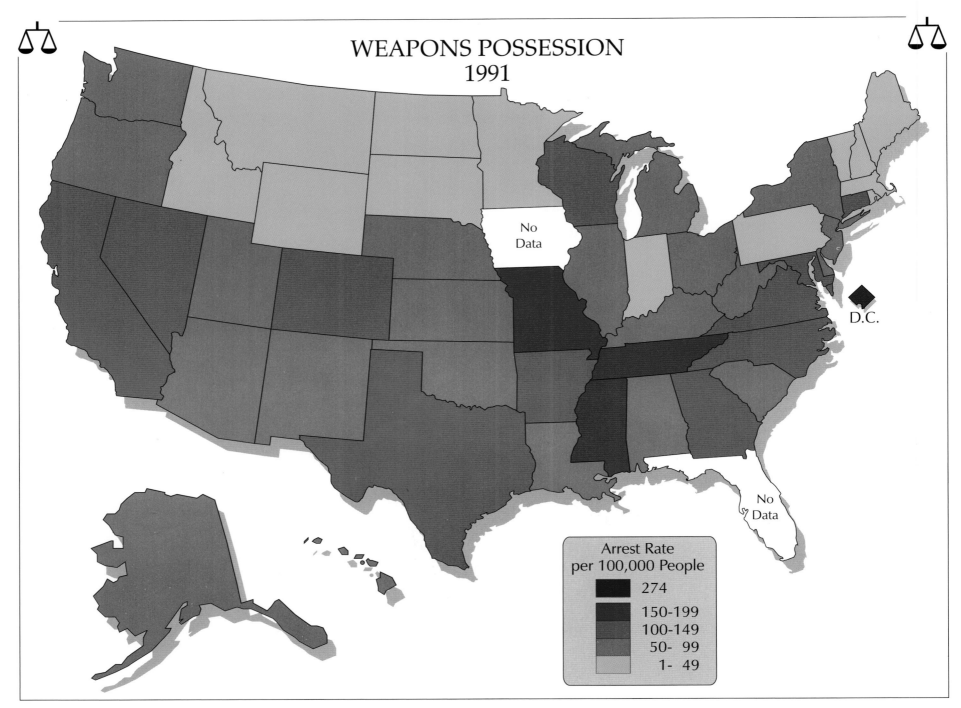

WEAPONS POSSESSION
1991

No
Data

No
Data

D.C.

Arrest Rate
per 100,000 People

274

150-199

100-149

50- 99

1- 49

concealed weapon are the routine carrying of large amounts of cash or jewels, or having received death threats.

Late in 1993, President Clinton signed the Brady Act into law. It nationally mandates a waiting period and a background check before a handgun can be bought. It also requires a reason for the purchase of the gun. Where individual state laws exceed the federal Brady Act, the state law takes precedence.

At the heart of the controversy about gun control and weapons possession is the paradox of responding both to gun crime and the right of citizens to bear weapons. The map "Weapons Possession, 1991" gives the arrest rate per 100,000 people for weapons possession. While not a complete indication of how many citizens carry guns and use them, the arrest rate in this and other crimes gives us some idea of the extent of the problem.

The District of Columbia leads the nation with a rate of 274 arrests per 100,000 people, a rate corresponding to its high rate of violent crime. There is a triad of states, Missouri with a rate of 190, Tennessee with 183 and Mississippi with 154, showing the highest arrest rates among the states.

Usually gun arrests are perceived as an urban problem, but in reality, outside the District of Columbia, this perception does not hold. Of the three states with the highest rates, only Tennessee has a city—Memphis—with a population greater than 500,000.

Other states with high rates—Nevada, Virginia, North Carolina, Delaware and Connecticut—follow a similar pattern of high arrest rates but no large cities with populations greater than 500,000.

Four other states with high arrest rates—California, Texas, Colorado and Wisconsin—contain major urban areas: California with Los Angeles and San Diego and Texas with Dallas, Houston and San Antonio—all five cities having populations close to or well above one million. Milwaukee,

Wisconsin has a population just over 500,000 while Denver, Colorado is just below at 470,000. The three cities generally perceived as high crime centers, Chicago, Detroit and New York, lie in states with arrest rates below 100. In general, states in the southern part of the country and on the West Coast have the highest arrest rates for weapons possession. The Northern states, with the exception of Wisconsin and Connecticut, have relatively low arrest rates.

Although no exact statistics are available for Florida, it not only shows a high arrest rate for weapons possession, but also, in Miami, a high rate of violent crime.

ARRESTS FOR DRUG POSSESSION

The severity of the legal sanctions against drugs depends on whether the drugs are being used or being sold. Arrests for drug possession refer to those arrested for drug abuse, the use of illegal drugs such as marijuana, heroin and cocaine, as well as legal drugs such as codeine, demerol and diazepam (Valium).

The map "Drug Possession" shows the District of Columbia leading the nation with a staggering rate for drug arrests of 1,762 per 100,000 people, a rate more than double that of the next highest state, California.

Arizona (with the fourth highest rate) and California border Mexico, making these states ideal for smuggling drugs into the U. S. The remainder of the states west of the Mississippi, with the exception of Nevada, have comparatively low rates of drug arrests. In general, the Southern states and the Northeast have higher rates. Although statistics are unavailable for Florida, it too has a very high drug arrest rate because of the large flow of drug traffic from the Caribbean and South America.

PARAMILITARY GROUPS

As a result of the bombing of the Federal building in Oklahoma City and its possible connection to paramilitary groups, such organizations and the state laws about them are coming under the scrutiny of officials throughout the country. Although laws in 41 states ban or regulate armed paramilitary groups, militia organizations are on the rise.

The map "State Laws Banning or Restricting the Activities of Paramilitary Groups" shows that 24 states (shown in green and dark green) have anti-paramilitary laws that ban paramilitary training with weapons, and 25 states (shown in blue and dark green) have anti-militia laws that prohibit drills and parades by military organizations other than the government and school units. Out of those states, only seven—Idaho, Illinois, Florida, Georgia, North Carolina, New York and Rhode Island—have both anti-militia and anti-paramilitary laws.

However, some experts who check on the various extremist groups around the country claim that even states that have anti-military laws are lax about enforcing them. The Southern Poverty Law Center of Montgomery, Alabama, which follows hate groups and paramilitary activity, estimates that 190 paramilitary groups now operate in 36 states, and at least 37 of those groups have ties to white supremacist organizations. In the Center's view, this amounts to an armed, private army. Some state officials point out that even though groups call themselves militia, they are not necessarily private armies or threats to the public safety.

According to the *New York Times*,[3] experts know of no instance in which the current groups calling themselves militias have been prosecuted under paramilitary laws. Some legal experts, such as Attorney General Frank J. Kelley of Michigan, point out that such groups are legal unless they are organized to commit unlawful acts. Robert Sedler, a law professor at Wayne State University, is quoted in the *Times* article as saying that just because an organization uses the term militia does not mean that it is one.

TO HATE ANOTHER

According to law, any crime committed because of the victim's sex, race, nationality, religion, politics or sexual persuasion is considered a hate crime. Hate crimes can vary from graffiti markings on a synagogue or church to threats and physical violence.

The map "Hate Crime Laws" shows that 28 states clustered in the West, northern Midwest and the Northeast, along with the District of Columbia, have laws concerning bias crimes. Bias crimes include defacement of schools, tombstones, places of worship and community centers, where vandalism is motivated by hatred or bias against a particular group. These crimes carry higher penalties than straight vandalism. The same standard applies to acts of intimidation and assault motivated by bias. Sentences can range from community service to fines and imprisonment, depending on the severity of the crime.

Of the 28 states that have bias crime laws, 14 include crimes committed because of sexual orientation, such as crimes against homosexuals. Sixteen states have laws against vandalism to religious burial sites, cemeteries and specific acts of intimidation.

Six states have no laws against hate crimes. Three of these states, Texas, Arizona and Utah, collect data about hate crimes, however.

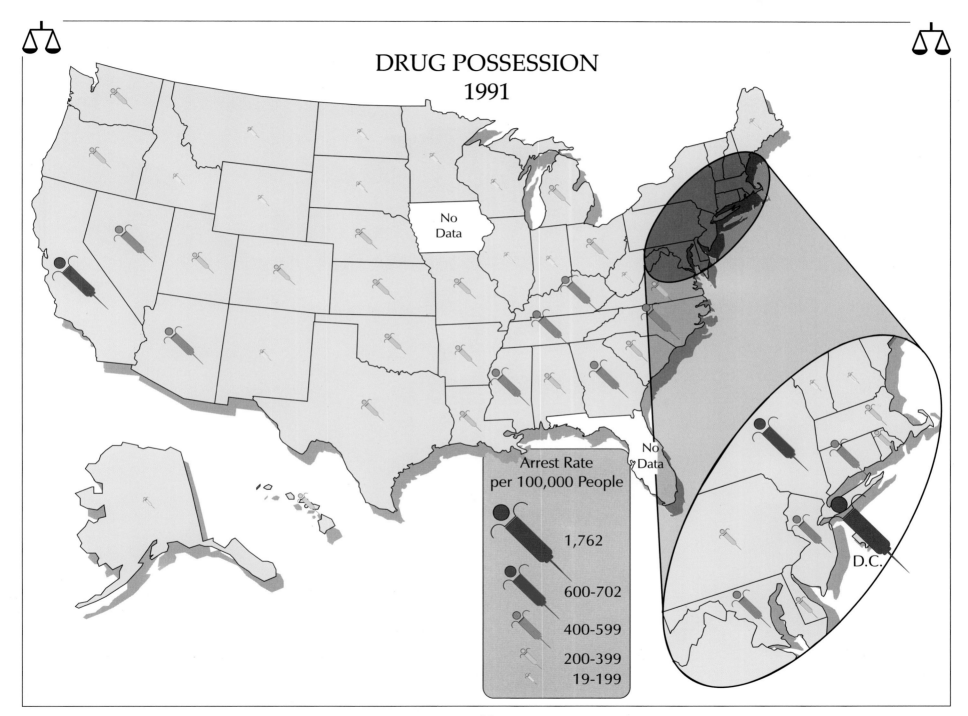

DRUG POSSESSION
1991

No Data

No Data

Arrest Rate
per 100,000 People

1,762

600-702

400-599

200-399

19-199

D.C.

STATE LAWS BANNING OR RESTRICTING THE ACTIVITIES OF PARAMILITARY GROUPS
1995

Anti-Militia and Anti-paramilitary Laws[1,2]

Anti-Paramilitary Laws[1]

Anti-Militia Laws[2]

No Law

[1] Bans paramilitary teaching or training with weapons and can ban groups if state can show their intent is to create civil disorder.

[2] Generally prohibits drills or parades by military organizations other than government or school units. State does not have to show group's intent to create civil disorder to ban them.

HATE CRIME LAWS
1993

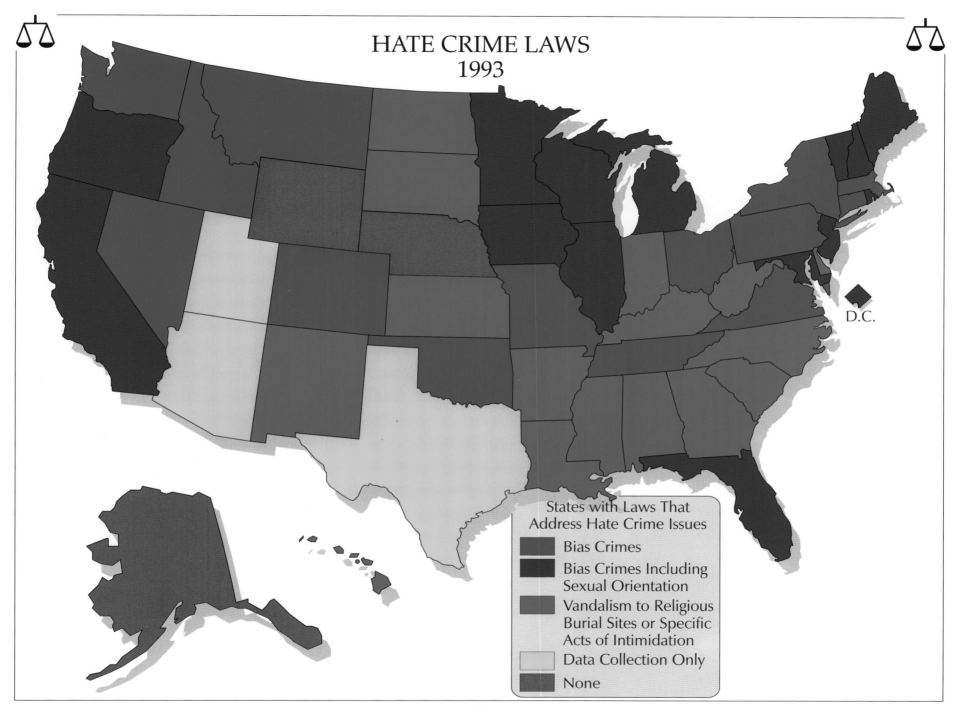

D.C.

States with Laws That Address Hate Crime Issues

- Bias Crimes
- Bias Crimes Including Sexual Orientation
- Vandalism to Religious Burial Sites or Specific Acts of Intimidation
- Data Collection Only
- None

VIOLENT CRIME

The circumstances leading to a crime often have a large impact on the severity of that crime. For instance, a "simple" robbery escalates into aggravated assault when the victim resists. An argument between friends turns deadly when one gets a gun and shoots the other. These circumstances often help determine the legal definition of the crime and ultimately the punishment if someone is convicted.

The legal definition of violent crime includes: murder, rape, robbery and aggravated assault. Each of these is a crime against a person. The most serious is murder. There is a connection among all four crimes. Aggravated assault can lead to murder. Robbery and rape can lead to aggravated assault, depending on the circumstances and the reaction of the victim.

MURDER

Homicide is a crime when it is labeled murder or manslaughter, whether it is voluntary or involuntary. When someone kills another intentionally, or kills another through a beating intended only to injure, this is considered to be murder. When someone is killed during a dangerous felony, it is also considered murder. When there is no "malice aforethought," no plan to kill, the killing may be classified as manslaughter. Voluntary manslaughter is an intentional killing, but without malice aforethought, in other words, a killing done on the spur of the moment. Involuntary manslaughter is an unintentional killing, a killing due to negligence, without the intent to kill.

A killing is also considered murder when someone undertakes an act carrying a high risk of death—for example, a killing that occurs because someone shoots into a crowd or at a car. This type of killing is called a "depraved heart" killing. Killing a police officer while resisting arrest is murder, even if the killer did not intend to kill.

Legally, it is important to differentiate between murder and homicide. In the book *Everybody's Guide to the Law*,[1] the authors point out that homicide occurs when one person kills another, but such a killing may not always be criminal. An accidental killing can occur with no blame attached. Additionally, if a homicide occurs as a result of self-defense, it is not considered murder.

In most states, there are two degrees of murder, first and second degree. When the intent is to kill, and the intention is carried out willfully, deliberately or with premeditation, it is considered murder in the first degree. A homicide is also considered first degree murder if it is committed by the use of poison, explosive, torture or ambush. First degree murder also applies to killings committed during certain felonies such as arson, burglary, robbery, rape or beating.

Second degree murder, which usually receives a lighter sentence, is defined as a homicide not planned in advance, or occuring although the intent was to harm but not to kill. A "depraved heart" killing is usually considered second degree murder. Killings committed in the course of a felony, other than those listed previously, are usually classed as murder in the second degree.

The map "Murder Rate" depicts the number of murders per 100,000 people. The District of Columbia, with a rate close to 78 homicides for every 100,000 residents, ranks far above all other states. Because the District of Columbia is entirely urban, one would expect that the high rate might be misleading. However, the map "Murder in Major Cities" indicates that the District of Columbia has the highest rate of murder when compared to other major cities of the United States.

There is a sharp drop to the murder rate in Louisiana, the state with the second highest rate. Comparing overall murder rates with those in the map "Murder in Major Cities," it becomes clear that large metropolitan areas are major contributors to a state's high murder rate.

Several regional patterns emerge when looking at the nation's murder rate. A large portion of the Southwest, the Deep South, along with New York State and a few scattered states in the North Central and the Northeast, have the highest murder rates. In most cases, this is a function of large cities in those states. In the South, New Orleans, Atlanta, Dallas, Miami and Memphis all boost their states' overall murder rates. However, the high rate found in Nevada, which has no large urban areas, and California, with several large cities and a relatively low urban crime rate, seem to contradict this.

North Dakota has the lowest murder rate, about one in every 100,000 people. In general, the lowest rates are clustered in the Northern High Plains states and portions of the Midwest and Rocky Mountain states, where there are fewer urban areas.

The map "Murder in Major Cities" shows a similar pattern to the overall state distribution of murder rates in the states. Those cities with a high murder rate are also associated with states with high murder rates. The notable exception is New York City with a low murder rate among cities, while New York State has the third highest rate among states. California also exhibits a discrepancy between the relatively low murder rate in the cities and high state murder rate. In the majority of states, their metropolitan areas are a prime contributor to the state's murder rate.

The map and chart "Murder Rate Through Time" gives us a different view of murder rates. Although the murder rate for the entire nation increased steadily from 1965 to 1980, the Midwest, Rocky Mountain and Western states have shown a decrease in the percentage of murders during the last decade. However, many of the states that currently have a low murder rate have shown an increase in the murder rate during the last ten years, an increase that matches the national increase. The greatest increases are in Vermont, 64 percent, Rhode Island, 50 percent and Wisconsin, 35 percent.

The chart gives us an idea of the national situation since 1960. In 1970, there was a sharp increase in the national murder rate which continued to peak until 1980. There was a drop in 1985, but the rate picked up again in 1990, although it did not run as high as it did in 1980.

DEADLY FORCE

The use of deadly force is a violent crime, a crime that can

CHILD ABUSE - GENERAL PROVISIONS
1987

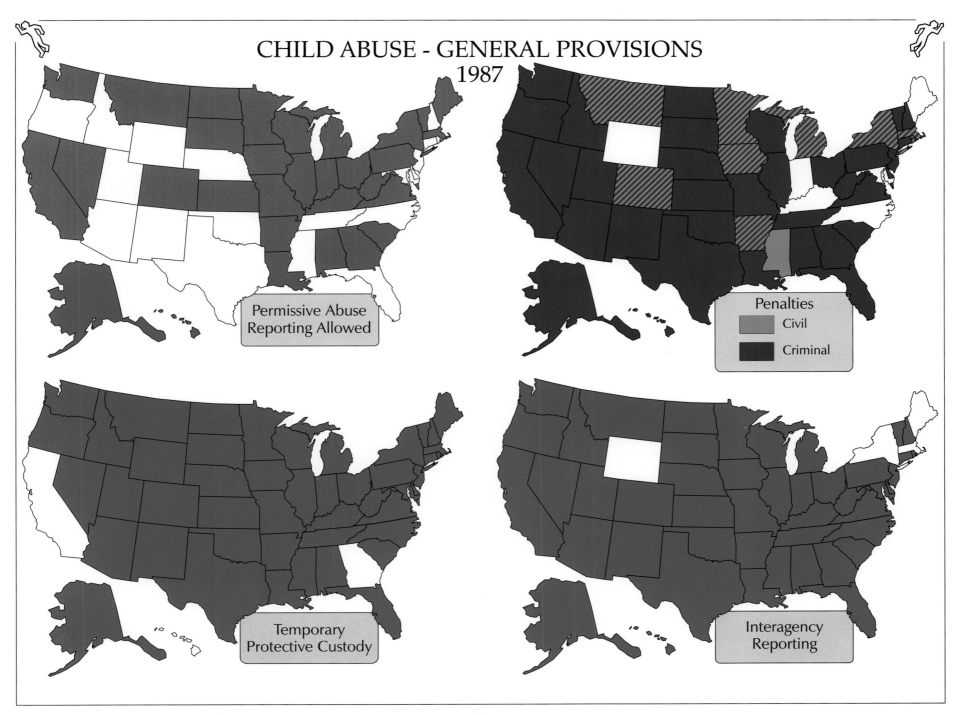

Permissive Abuse Reporting Allowed

Penalties
Civil
Criminal

Temporary Protective Custody

Interagency Reporting

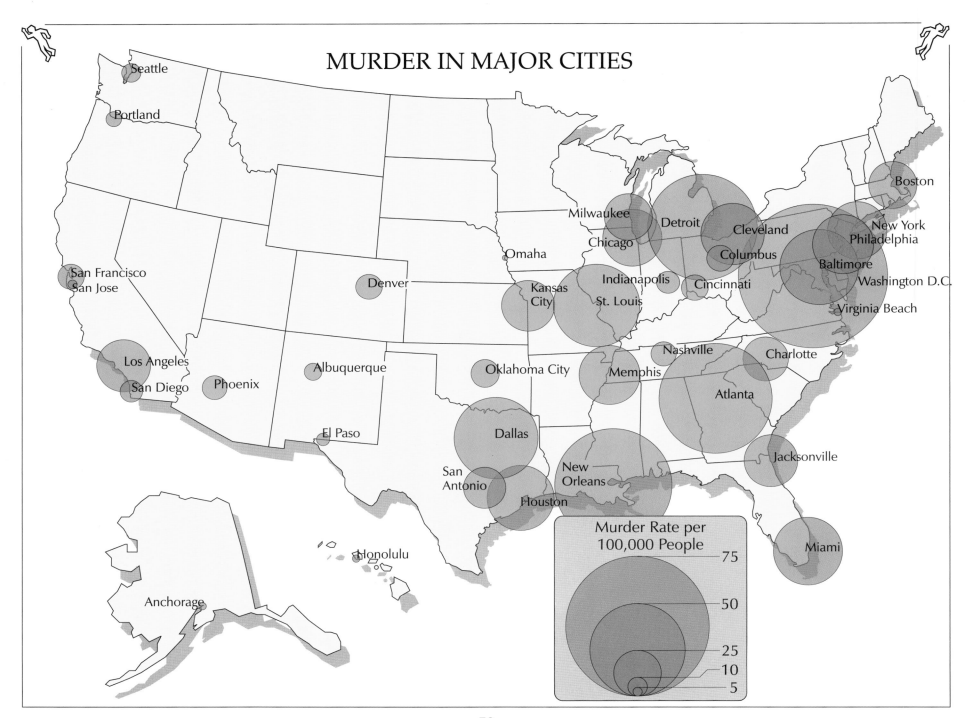

MURDER IN MAJOR CITIES

Seattle
Portland
San Francisco
San Jose
Los Angeles
San Diego
Phoenix
El Paso
Anchorage
Honolulu
Denver
Albuquerque
Oklahoma City
San Antonio
Dallas
Houston
New Orleans
Omaha
Kansas City
St. Louis
Milwaukee
Chicago
Indianapolis
Detroit
Cleveland
Columbus
Cincinnati
Memphis
Nashville
Atlanta
Charlotte
Jacksonville
Miami
Boston
New York
Philadelphia
Baltimore
Washington D.C.
Virginia Beach

Murder Rate per
100,000 People
75
50
25
10
5

MURDER RATE THROUGH TIME

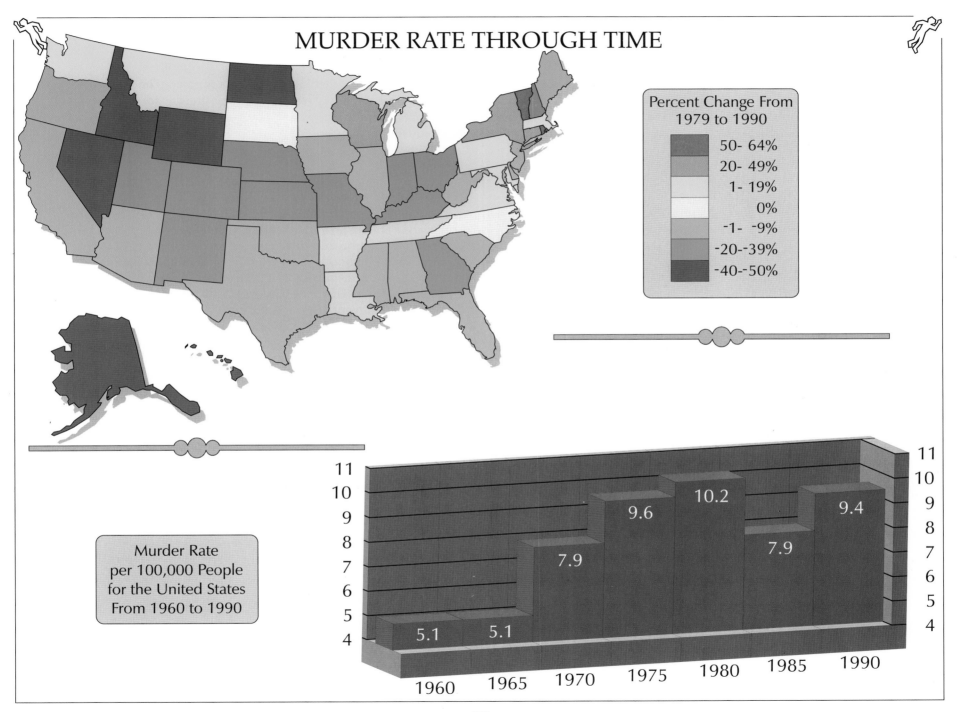

Percent Change From
1979 to 1990

50- 64%
20- 49%
1- 19%
0%
-1- -9%
-20- -39%
-40- -50%

Murder Rate
per 100,000 People
for the United States
From 1960 to 1990

5.1 5.1 7.9 9.6 10.2 7.9 9.4

1960 1965 1970 1975 1980 1985 1990

result in murder. However, if deadly force is used as a means of self-defense, and the result is murder, it is not considered a crime. But self-defense is not the only situation in which deadly force justifiably may be used.

In 24 states and the District of Columbia, deadly force can be used to defend oneself against rape. See the map "Violent Crimes against Which Deadly Force Is Justified." In two additional states (Arizona and New York), deadly force can be used as a defense against kidnapping. In 27 states and the District of Columbia, it can be used against robbery.

Texas and New Jersey, two states that do not allow the use of deadly force as a defense in rape or kidnapping, permit it as a defense against robbery—a curious situation implying property seizure is to be defended against more strenuously than personal violation.

In 23 states and the District of Columbia, deadly force can be used against aggravated assault. This law seems logical, since aggravated assault can result in death.

There are 18 states in which the use of deadly force is not legally justified in any situation. Many of these states are located on the West Coast or in the North Central region of the country. In Michigan alone, the use of deadly force is judged according to each particular situation.

WHO KILLS WHOM

Most murders are committed by someone who is related to or who knows the victim, as the chart "Percentage of Murders by Relationship to Victim, 1991" shows. Only about 25 percent of murders are committed by someone who is a stranger. Of the remaining 75 percent, 44 percent of homicides are carried out by acquaintances of the victims. Twenty percent of all murders are committed by some

member of the immediate family or a relative. The police are well aware of these facts, and in any murder investigation, the first people suspected are family members and then friends of the family.

MURDER WEAPONS

The map "Type of Weapons Used in Murders, 1991" shows firearms are the principle murder weapons. In only 13 states is the use of a firearm in the minority. Not only are firearms used in the majority of murders in this country, handguns alone are responsible for over 50 percent of all homicides in 19 states. In the District of Columbia, handguns are involved in over 75 percent of all murders.

In every state except Montana, North Dakota and Vermont, and in the District of Columbia, hands and fists have been used to kill, more frequently in the Midwest and the Rocky Mountains. In every state except North Dakota, knives or cutting instruments have also been used.

If we compare the states where handguns are most frequently used in murders, we see that these are also states with large metropolitan areas. The exceptions are Alabama, Mississippi, Arkansas and Utah.

AGGRAVATED ASSAULT

Aggravated assault is a reckless attack with the intent of causing serious injury. It also includes assault with a deadly weapon. The map "Aggravated Assault" shows that the District of Columbia leads the nation with a rate of 1,117 assaults for every 100,000 people.

Florida, with a rate of 764, and South Carolina, with 759, have the highest assault rates among the states. The high rate

VIOLENT CRIMES AGAINST WHICH DEADLY FORCE IS JUSTIFIED

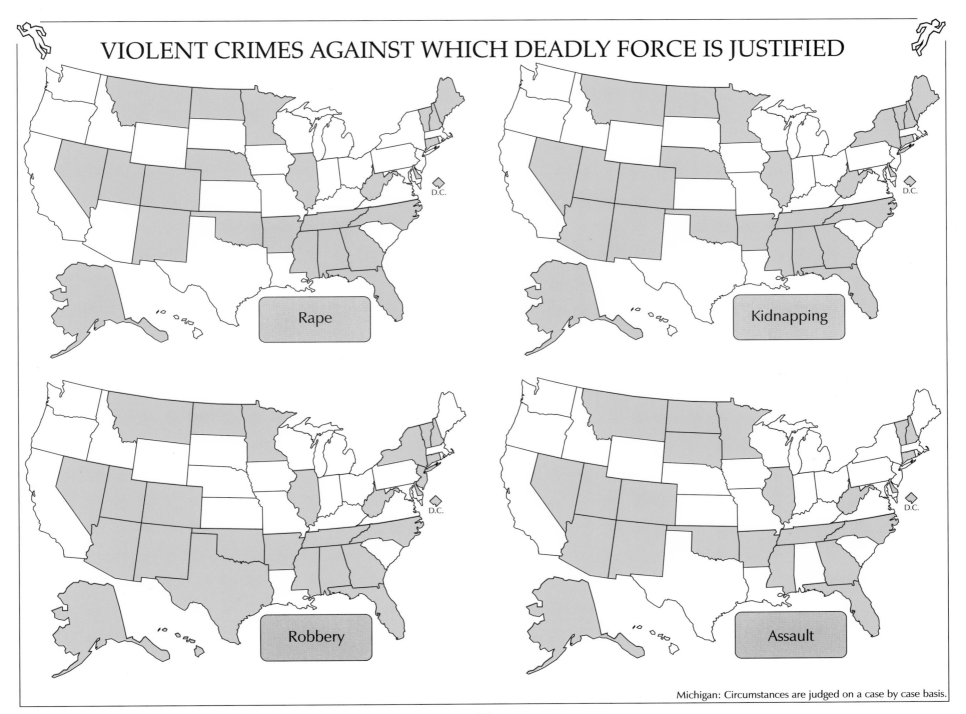

Rape

Kidnapping

Robbery

Assault

Michigan: Circumstances are judged on a case by case basis.

PERCENTAGE OF MURDERS BY RELATIONSHIP TO VICTIM
1991

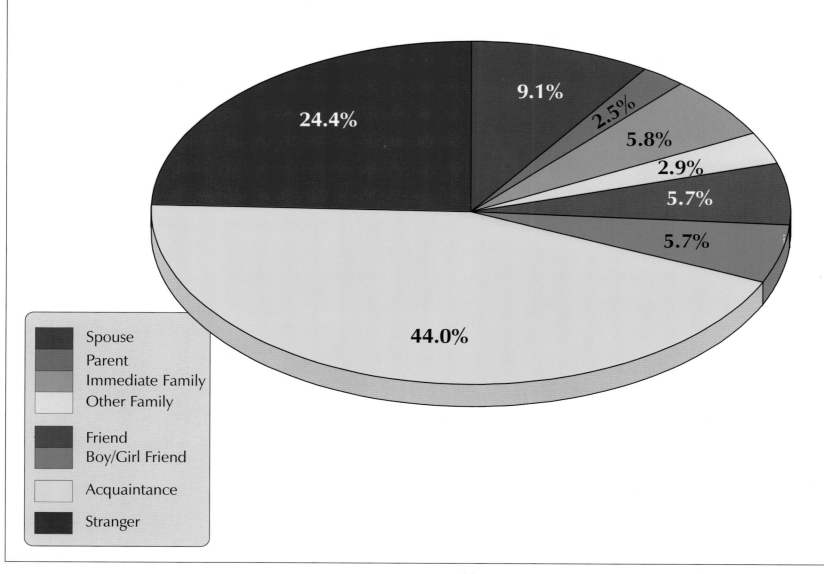

9.1%

2.5%

5.8%

2.9%

5.7%

5.7%

24.4%

44.0%

Spouse
Parent
Immediate Family
Other Family

Friend
Boy/Girl Friend

Acquaintance

Stranger

TYPES OF WEAPONS USED IN MURDERS
1991

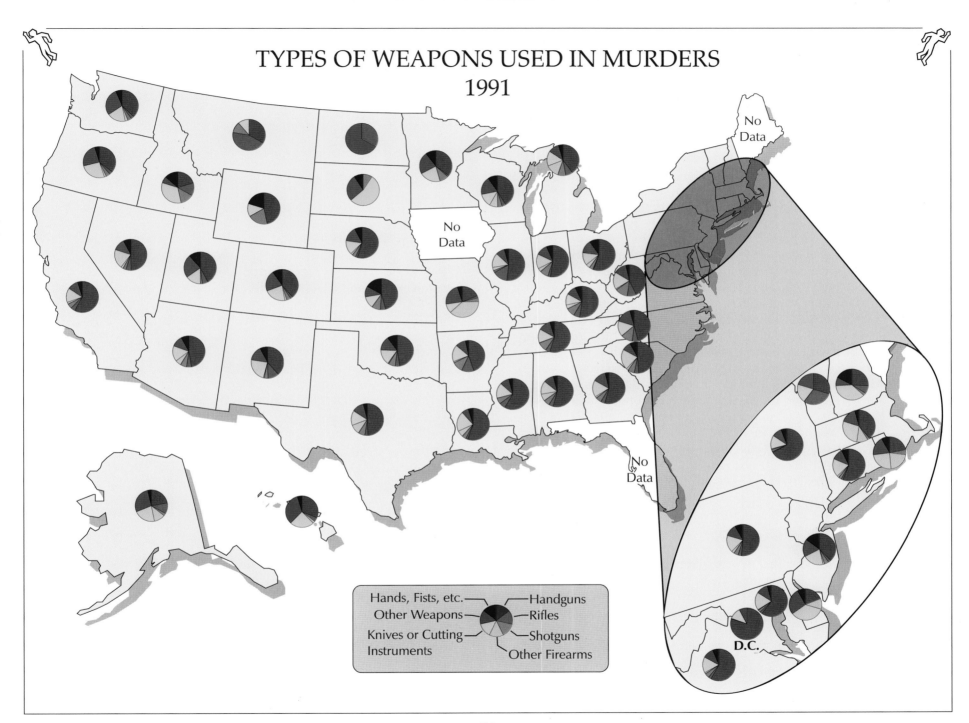

Legend:
- Hands, Fists, etc.
- Other Weapons
- Knives or Cutting Instruments
- Handguns
- Rifles
- Shotguns
- Other Firearms

No Data

D.C.

in Florida may be attributed to both Jacksonville and Miami, cities which have high rates of aggravated assault, as seen on the map "Aggravated Assault in Major Cities." However, the high rate in South Carolina is puzzling, since there are no large metropolitan areas in that state.

With the exception of predominantly rural northern New England where rates are low, the highest rates of assault occur along both coasts and the southern half of the United States. A pattern of low assault rates typically occurs in states that are predominantly rural, although there are a few notable exceptions. Wyoming, Arkansas, Nevada and Alaska are all states which lack large metropolitan areas; however, they exhibit high assault rates.

Although high assault rates are often associated with states that have large metropolitan areas, the map "Aggravated Assault in Major Cities" shows that some of the largest cities do not have the highest rates. Atlanta, with 2,134 assaults per 100,000 residents, St. Louis, with 2,300, and Miami, with 1,954, are the three cities with the highest assault rates, but they are not among the largest metropolitan areas. New York, which is often perceived as a crime capital, has a relatively low assault rate of 941 per 100,000 residents.

The chart, "Aggravated Assault Rate through Time," shows that, unlike the murder rate, the assault rate has climbed steadily since 1960, from 86 per 100,000 residents to 424 per 100,000 in 1990. There was a leveling off during the early 1980s, but the greatest increase occurred during the latter half of the decade.

 The accompanying map shows the highest increase in percent of assaults in the past ten years took place in Kentucky, 126 percent, a state where the murder rate decreased by 24 percent. Increases in the assault rate have occurred in the states around Kentucky, in Tennessee, Illinois, Iowa, Indiana, Alabama and Nebraska. There have been moderate increases in California, Texas, Minnesota,

Georgia and Massachusetts.

Decreases in the assault rate are clustered among the states in northern New England, portions of the Pacific Northwest and the Northern High Plains.

RAPE

Rape, according to the law, is sexual intercourse with a woman without her consent. However, the definition of rape can vary from state to state. In rape, physical force does not have to be used; threats are sufficient. In addition, the woman does not have to resist, especially if threatened physically or with a weapon, where resistance means danger. It is rape even if the man does not ejaculate. Any penetration of a woman's vagina is rape. A rape using any foreign object is "rape by artifice."

In looking at the map "Rape Rate," Delaware and Michigan can be seen to be the states with the greatest number of rapes—88 per 100,000 people in Delaware and 78 in Michigan. The map "Rape in Major Cities" shows that the rate of rapes in Detroit—134 per 100,000 inhabitants—contributes to Michigan's overall high rate. However, there is no corresponding major city with a high rate in Delaware. Its high rape rate remains puzzling. Alaska and Washington with their high rape rates both have cities, Seattle and Anchorage, with equally high rates. With the exception of Pennsylvania, Connecticut and Rhode Island, the lowest rates occur in predominantly rural states.

The map "Rape in Major Cities" dispels some widely held beliefs about rape. It is usually thought that the more populous cities have the highest rape rates, but New York City and Los Angeles have among the lowest rates, while Atlanta, Detroit and Cleveland have the highest. Washington, Miami, St. Louis and New Orleans are all cities

AGGRAVATED ASSAULT

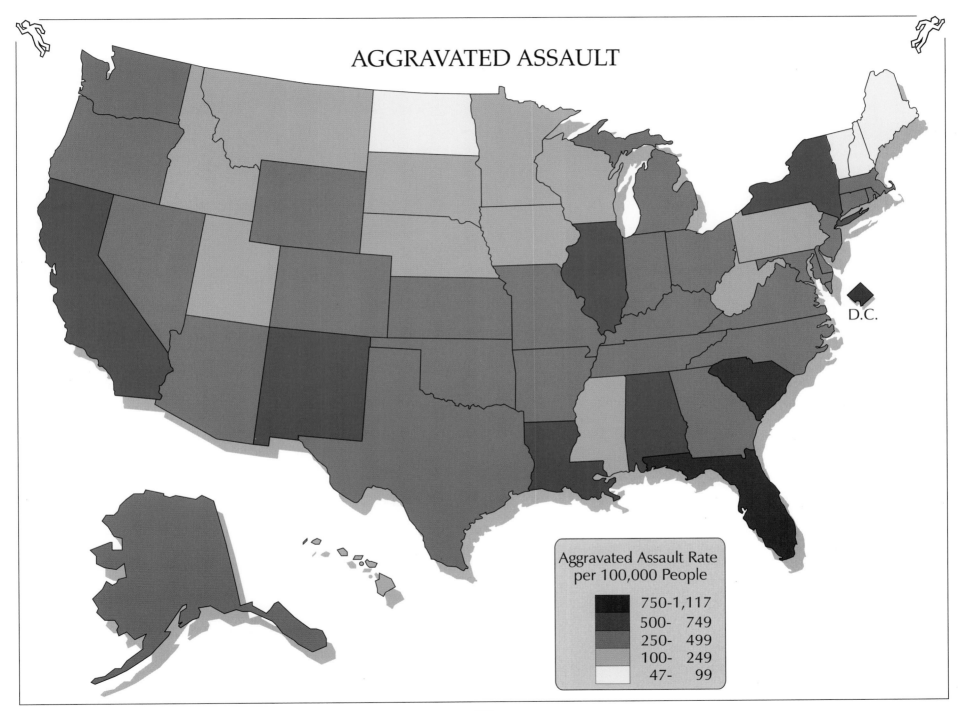

D.C.

Aggravated Assault Rate
per 100,000 People

750-1,117
500- 749
250- 499
100- 249
47- 99

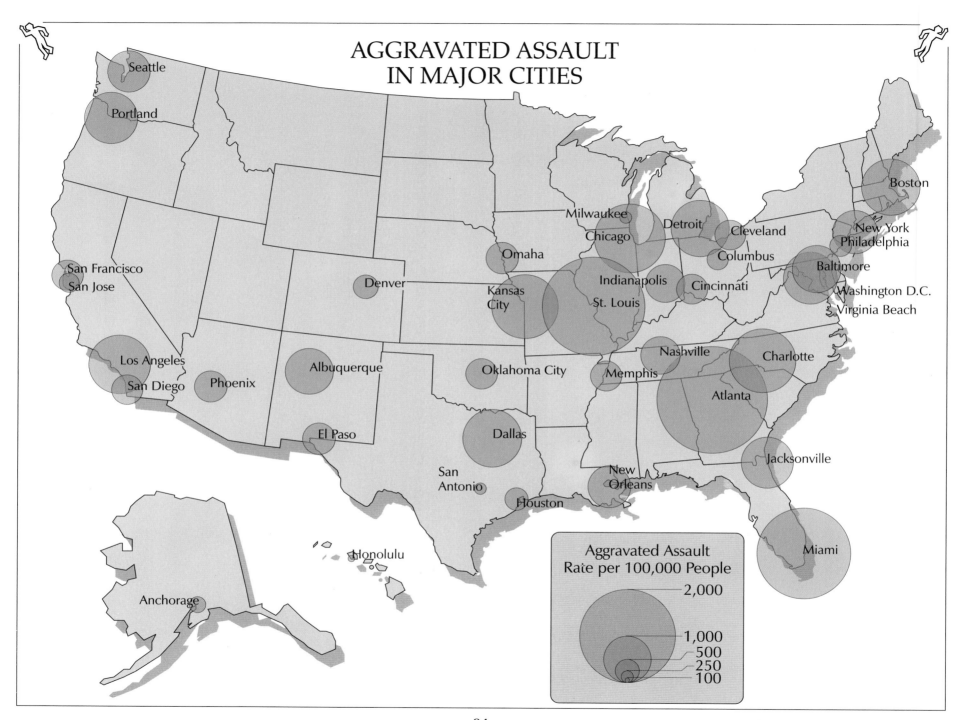

AGGRAVATED ASSAULT IN MAJOR CITIES

Seattle
Portland
San Francisco
San Jose
Los Angeles
San Diego
Phoenix
Albuquerque
El Paso
Denver
Oklahoma City
Dallas
San Antonio
Houston
Omaha
Kansas City
Milwaukee
Chicago
St. Louis
Indianapolis
Memphis
New Orleans
Nashville
Atlanta
Detroit
Cincinnati
Columbus
Cleveland
Charlotte
Jacksonville
Miami
New York
Philadelphia
Boston
Baltimore
Washington D.C.
Virginia Beach
Honolulu
Anchorage

Aggravated Assault
Rate per 100,000 People

2,000
1,000
500
250
100

84

AGGRAVATED ASSAULT RATE THROUGH TIME

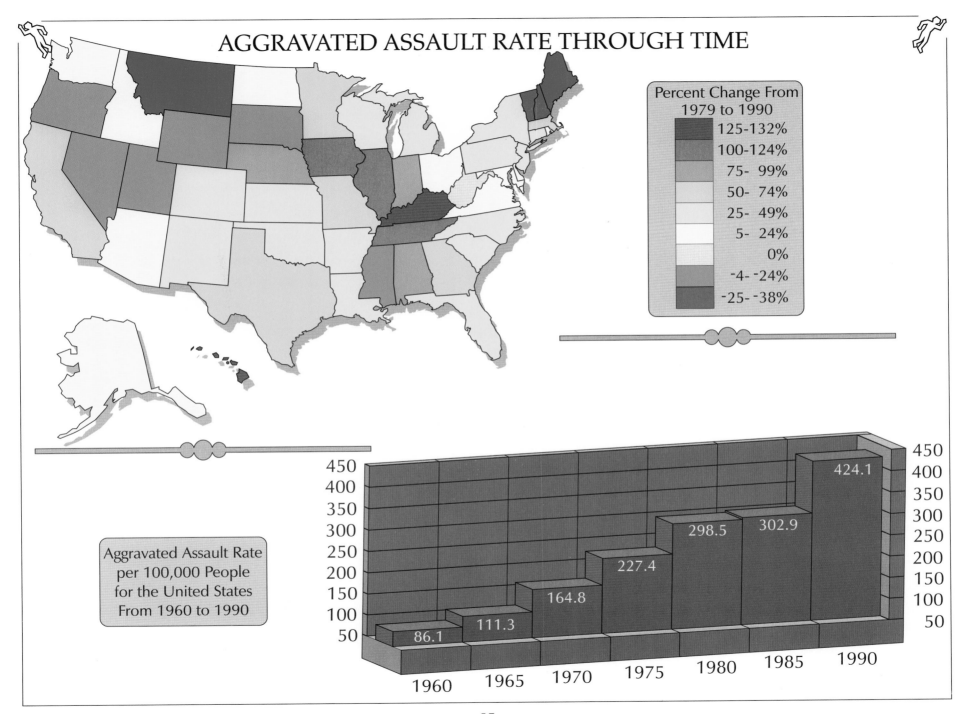

Percent Change From
1979 to 1990

125-132%
100-124%
75- 99%
50- 74%
25- 49%
5- 24%
0%
-4- -24%
-25- -38%

Aggravated Assault Rate
per 100,000 People
for the United States
From 1960 to 1990

Year	Rate
1960	86.1
1965	111.3
1970	164.8
1975	227.4
1980	298.5
1985	302.9
1990	424.1

RAPE RATE

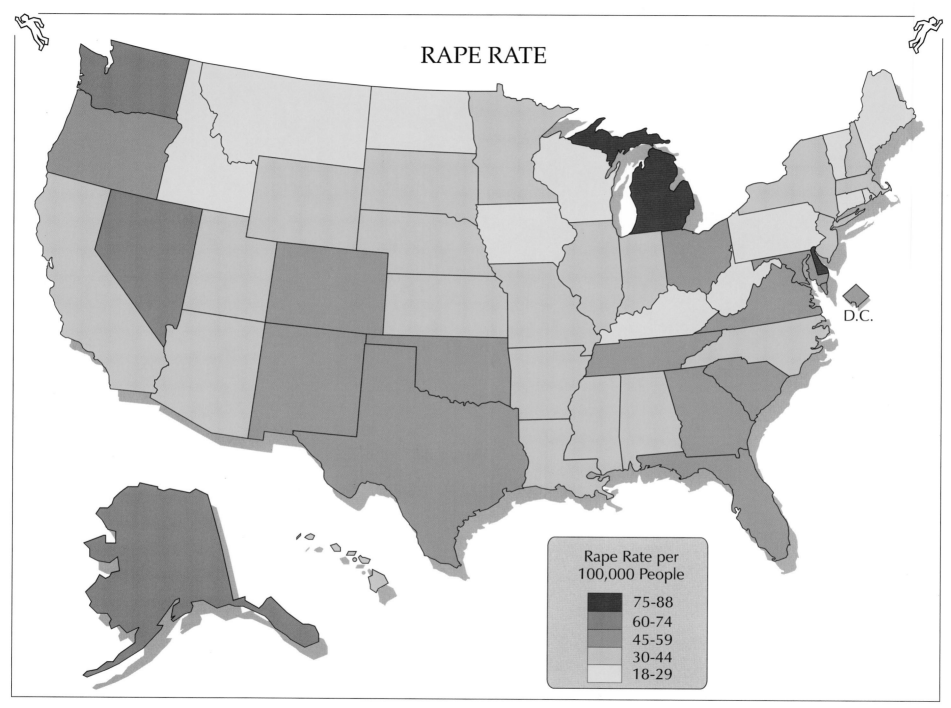

Rape Rate per
100,000 People

75-88
60-74
45-59
30-44
18-29

D.C.

RAPE IN MAJOR CITIES

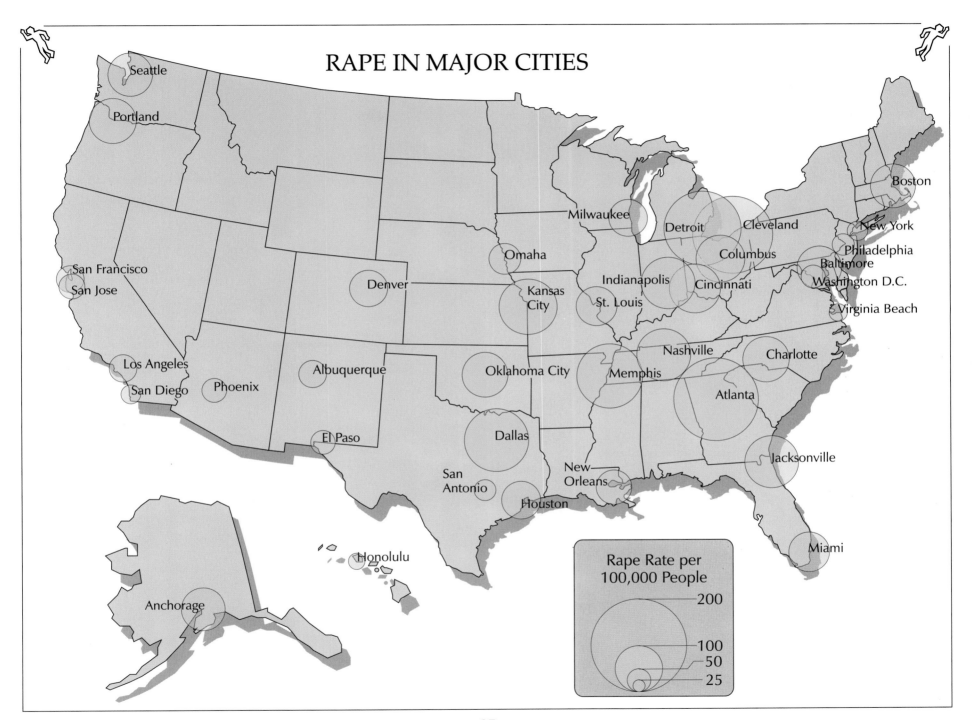

Rape Rate per
100,000 People

200

100

50

25

RAPE RATE THROUGH TIME

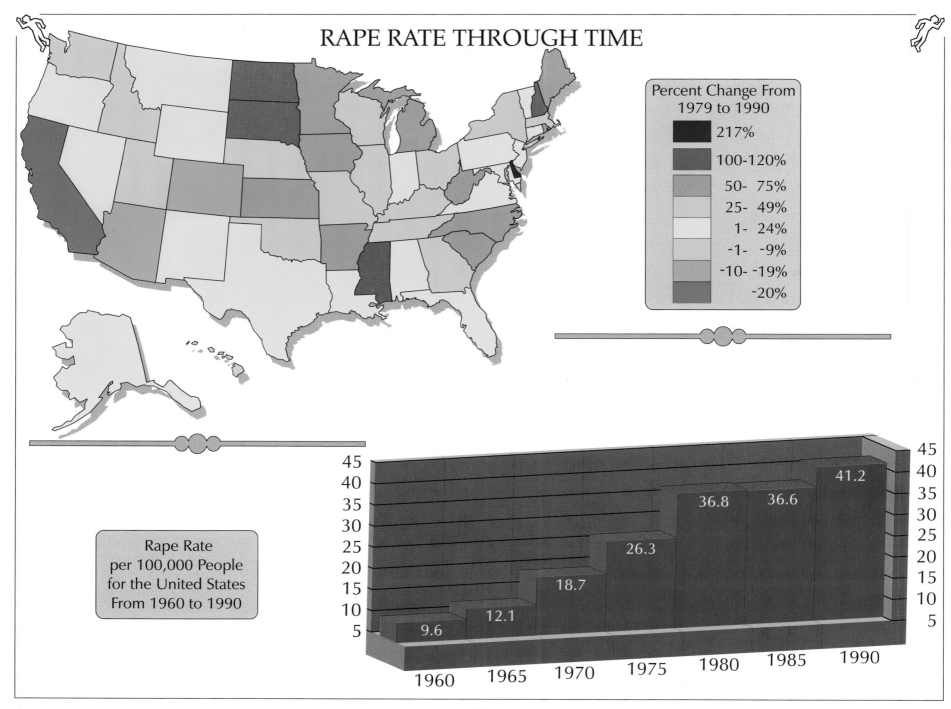

Percent Change From 1979 to 1990

- 217%
- 100-120%
- 50- 75%
- 25- 49%
- 1- 24%
- -1- -9%
- -10- -19%
- -20%

Rape Rate per 100,000 People for the United States From 1960 to 1990

9.6 — 1960
12.1 — 1965
18.7 — 1970
26.3 — 1975
36.8 — 1980
36.6 — 1985
41.2 — 1990

with high rates of other violent crimes, but surprisingly, their rape rates are not. Kansas City seems to have a disproportionately high rate, as do Dallas and Memphis.

The chart "Rape Rate through Time" shows that, although there has been a steady climb in rape rates, since 1980 there has been a slowdown in the rate of increase. From 1979 to 1990 only six states, California, Arizona, Colorado, Hawaii, Missouri and New York, have shown a drop in the rape rate. Of the remaining 44 states, six principally rural states jumped over 100 percent, with Delaware exhibiting an increase of over 200 percent.

MARITAL RAPE

In a marriage, when a husband forces an unwilling wife to have sex, it is considered marital rape. However, the map "Marital Rape Laws, 1987" shows that in eight states, Georgia, Arkansas, Illinois, Alabama, Kentucky and West Virginia, a husband cannot be charged for the rape of his wife. In Alabama and West Virginia, neither a husband nor someone living with a woman in "cohabitation" can be charged with rape. Five of these states are also considered politically conservative. Illinois, however, is something of a surprise. It is one of the more populous and less conservative states, with a number of large cities. These factors might lead us to expect that the state would be tougher in marital rape laws.

In four other states, Montana, Nevada, Delaware and Pennsylvania, cohabitants cannot be charged with rape, but in these states, as well as in 21 other states, a husband can only be charged with marital rape if the couple are legally separated. In Wyoming, Oklahoma, Louisiana, Ohio, Virginia and Maryland, a husband can be charged with rape if the couple are living apart. They do not have to be legally separated.

There are only 12 states in which a husband can be charged with marital rape. Three are Pacific Coast states, two are part of the Midwest, one is Florida and the others are clustered in the Northeast and New England. These are states that have traditionally shown concern for women's issues.

CHILD ABUSE

There is no simple definition of child abuse, as definitions vary from one parent to another. One may feel that spanking is abuse, while another sees it as a necessary discipline.

"If my child runs out into the street, I'll give him a smack on the behind!" Most parents consider this statement appropriate. National Family Violence Surveys have found that at least 97 percent of parents with children under three had slapped or spanked their child at some time in the past year. Indeed, in most states parents can use corporal punishment as long as it is not excessive. Is spanking excessive if the parent uses a belt and leaves marks? At what point does discipline become abuse?

The official definition of abuse tries to sort these problems out, but even the government definition changes with each agency. The Department of Health and Human Welfare[2] defines physical abuse as inflicting physical injury by punching, beating, kicking, biting, burning or otherwise harming a child. A lack of intent to harm the child does not matter.

The Department characterizes child neglect, a form of abuse, as failure to provide for the child's basic needs. Neglect can be physical, such as refusing to provide health care or adequate supervision by abandoning or turning a child out of the house or by not allowing a runaway child to return. The neglect can be educational, by permitting chronic truancy or not attending to preschool educational needs. It can be emotional, by allowing spousal abuse in the child's presence, permitting alcohol or drug use by the child or refusing to provide psychological help. Lest all these prove overwhelming, the Department makes a distinction between willful neglect and neglect due to poverty or cultural bias.

Sexual abuse ranges from fondling a child's genitals to incest, rape, intercourse, sodomy and exhibitionism. Legally, to be held child abuse, any of these acts must be committed by a parent or a childcare worker responsible for the care of the child. Any of these acts committed by a stranger would be sexual assault.

Sexual abuse may be a difficult thing to call. While outright sexual acts seem obvious, there is always the question, "When does normal hugging and kissing cross over the line?"

The maps "Definitions of Child Abuse" show the states which consider five conditions reason for bringing charges of child abuse. Neglect is a reason in every state except the six mostly Southern states of Arizona, Texas, Tennessee, Georgia, Maryland and Massachusetts. Emotional injury is considered a reason in all but seven states and medical neglect in all but eight.

Tighter guidelines are held for physical and sexual abuse. Colorado, Tennessee, Georgia and Massachusetts do not recognize physical abuse, and only Arizona and Georgia will not recognize sexual abuse as child abuse.

Georgia does not recognize any of the five provisions as abuse. Massachusetts recognizes only sexual abuse, and Tennessee, surprisingly, in view of the three conditions it does not accept, accepts emotional injury, a rather difficult definition.

The four maps "Child Abuse—General Provisions, 1987" explain how child abuse is handled in the states. Reporting permissive abuse is allowed in all but 19 states, and in all states except Hawaii, California and Georgia, children who are abused can be taken into temporary protective custody.

One agency is allowed to report abuse to another agency in every state but Wyoming, New York, Massachusetts and Maine. Six states have neither criminal nor civil penalties for child abuse. Wyoming, which allows temporary protective custody for child abuse, resists the other three provisions.

The maps "Child Abuse" address two aspects of the problem of abuse. The top map shows reported cases as a percentage of children under 18 years of age. The lower map shows the number of deaths from child abuse per 100,000 children. Montana, which allows all provisions for reporting child abuse and has both civil and criminal penalties for it, has next to the highest number of deaths. Delaware, which accepts all the general provisions except the reporting of permissive abuse, has the highest rate of abuse—7.93.

The map, "Offenses against Family and Children, 1991" includes not only child abuse, but abuse of other members of the family. The distribution of the states that fall into both the high and low end are interesting. Hawaii, normally low in crime rates, has the highest arrest rate of all the states at 244 per 100,000 people. California, the most populous state, has an arrest rate of only two per 100,000 residents, and is the lowest of all the states. The District of Columbia, high in other types of crime, has an equally low arrest rate.

ROBBERY

Using force or the threat of force to take money or property from someone is robbery. It doesn't matter who the force is directed against—a friend, a relative, a child—it is still robbery. However, stealing from an unconscious person is not robbery, but larceny, since no force or threat was used.

Just under 25 percent of all robberies are committed by

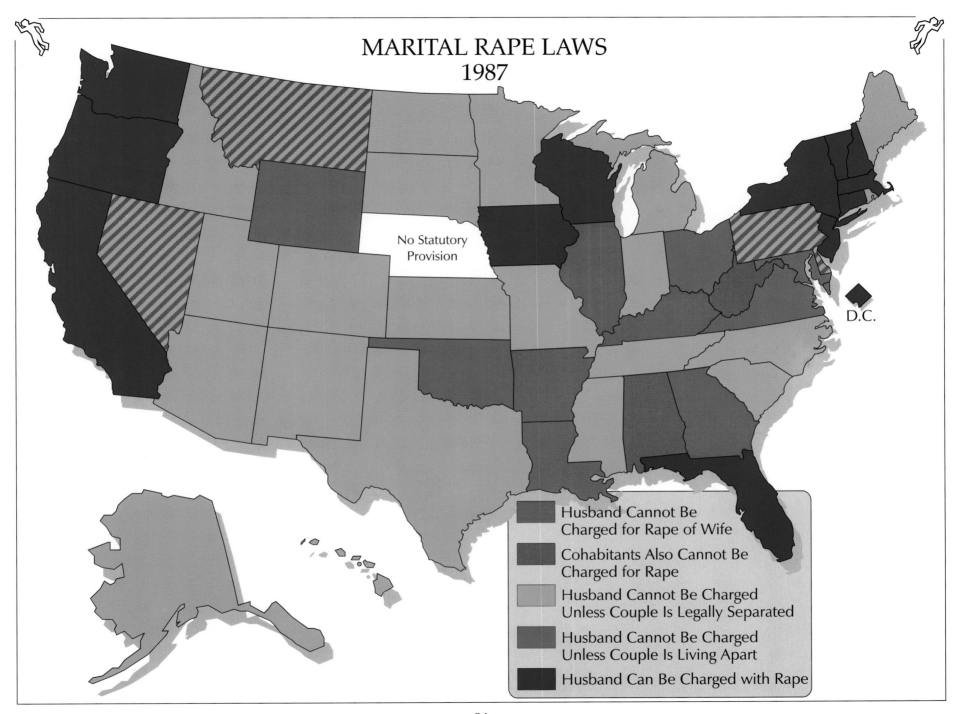

MARITAL RAPE LAWS
1987

No Statutory Provision

D.C.

Husband Cannot Be Charged for Rape of Wife

Cohabitants Also Cannot Be Charged for Rape

Husband Cannot Be Charged Unless Couple Is Legally Separated

Husband Cannot Be Charged Unless Couple Is Living Apart

Husband Can Be Charged with Rape

DEFINITIONS OF CHILD ABUSE

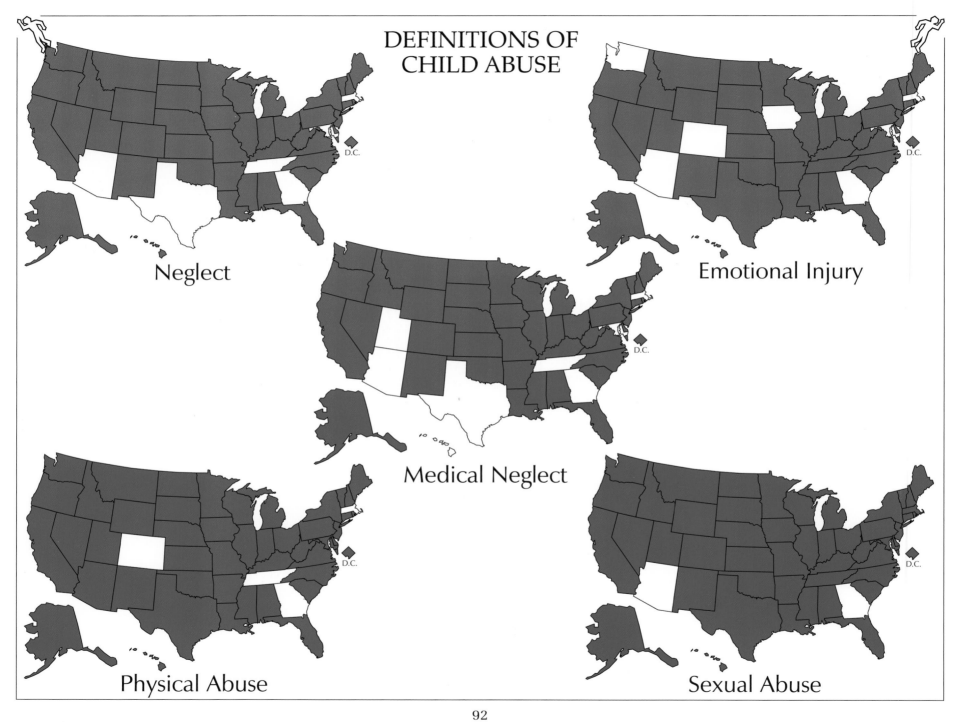

Neglect

Emotional Injury

Medical Neglect

Physical Abuse

Sexual Abuse

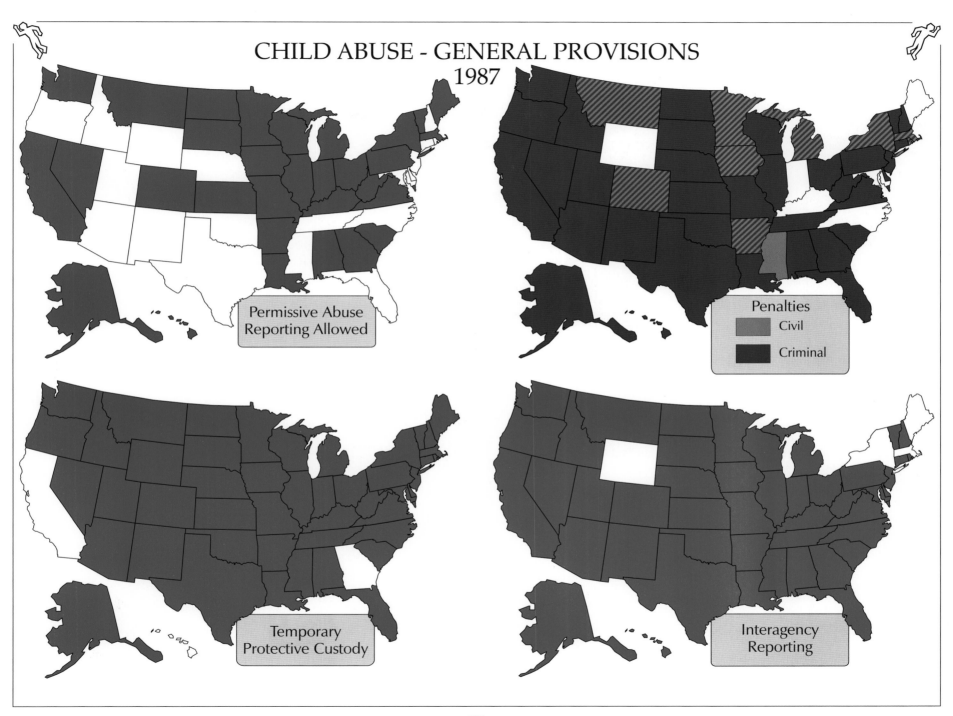

CHILD ABUSE - GENERAL PROVISIONS
1987

Permissive Abuse Reporting Allowed

Penalties
Civil
Criminal

Temporary Protective Custody

Interagency Reporting

CHILD ABUSE

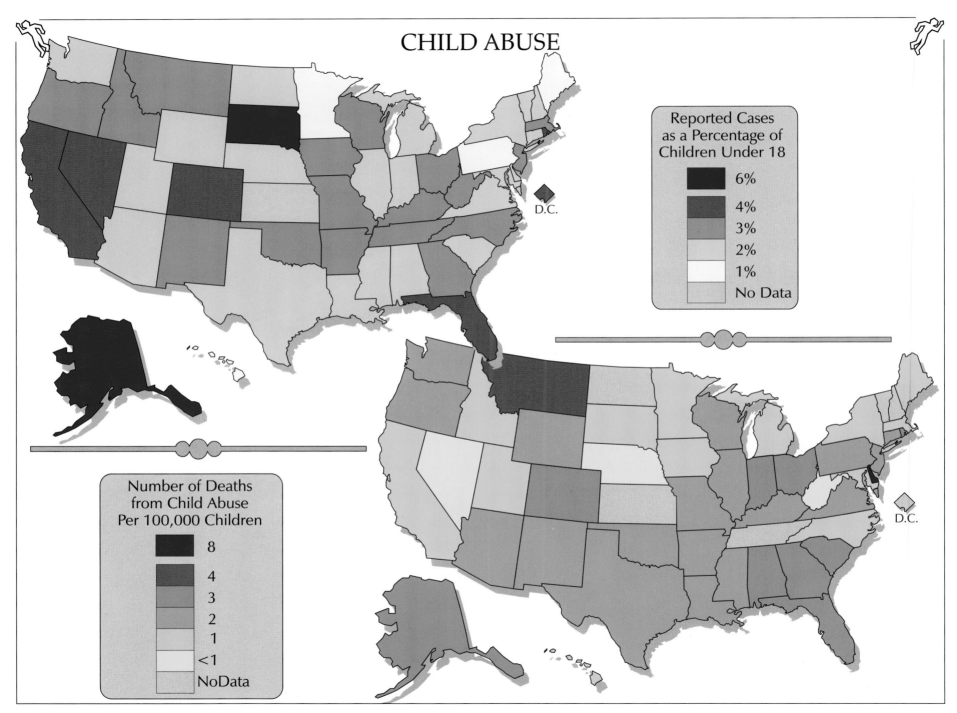

Reported Cases as a Percentage of Children Under 18

- 6%
- 4%
- 3%
- 2%
- 1%
- No Data

D.C.

Number of Deaths from Child Abuse Per 100,000 Children

- 8
- 4
- 3
- 2
- 1
- <1
- NoData

D.C.

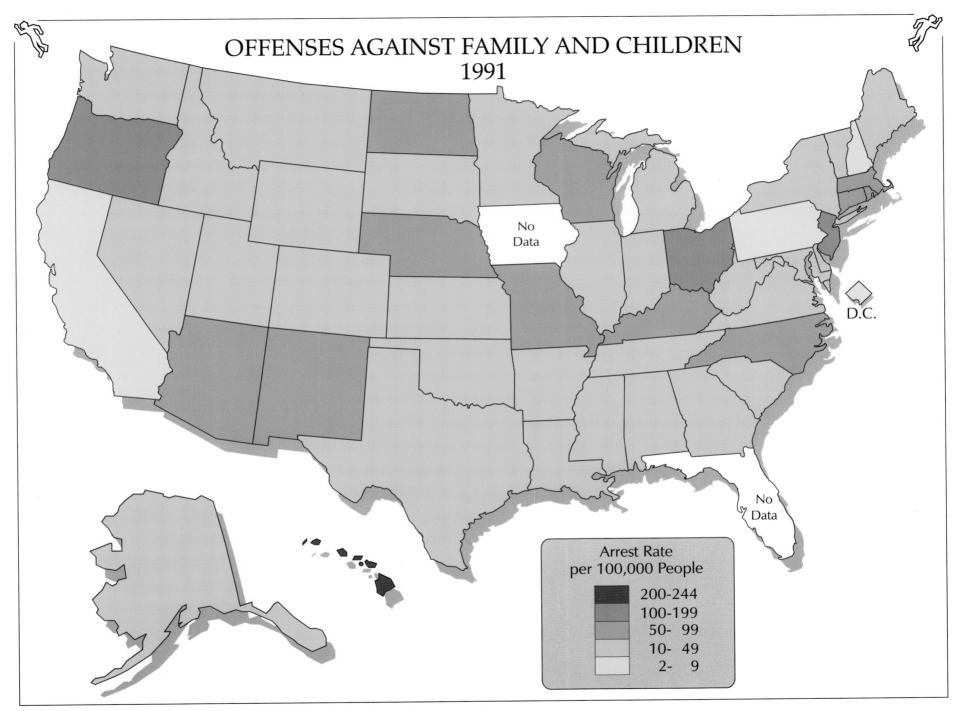

OFFENSES AGAINST FAMILY AND CHILDREN
1991

No Data

No Data

D.C.

Arrest Rate
per 100,000 People

200-244
100-199
50- 99
10- 49
2- 9

juveniles, a higher percentage than commit rape, murder or assault. Contributing factors may be the need for drug money or juvenile gang influence.

The map "Robbery" shows that in a large northern region of the country and northern New England robbery rates are low. This area is predominantly rural, with few large metropolitan areas. Alaska, Hawaii, Kentucky, West Virginia and Alabama, all rural states, also exhibit low robbery rates. Several states with large metropolitan areas located in the Northeast, along with California, Texas, Nevada, Illinois, and the District of Columbia, all have high robbery rates.

The influence of the urban population on robbery rates is shown in the map "Robbery in Major Cities." Some of the large cities—New York, Chicago, Detroit, Dallas, Baltimore, Los Angeles and Miami—all have rates well over 1,000.

In the chart "Robbery Rate from 1960 to 1990" that accompanies "Robbery Rate through Time," we see that the rate for the United States dropped in 1985, but rebounded sharply in 1990. The sudden upswing may have been linked to the general downturn in the American economy in the late 1980s.

The map "Robbery Rate through Time" gives some interesting insights. With the exception of the Northeast, the pattern for rate of change in robbery rates parallels the present rate—that is, states with low rates for robbery have shown a steady decrease, while those states which presently have a high rate have been increasing during the past decade. This pattern is in contrast to that of rape and assault, where states with low rates have shown the greatest increase in the past ten years.

EXTORTION

Extortion occurs when someone is forced to give up money or possessions by threats of fear, force or authority of office.

The threat may be physical or emotional.

It is extortion if a storekeeper is told he will have his legs broken unless he pays protection money. It is extortion if a homosexual is threatened with exposure unless he pays the blackmailer. Blackmail is a form of extortion. Extortion differs from robbery because the damage entails future threat. In robbery, the threat occurs at the time the person is robbed.

When it comes to extortion, the map "Extortion, 1992" shows Wyoming as having the highest rate among the states, 2.1 per 1,000,000. The heaviest rates for extortion are to be found in states lying in a band across the center of the West, a puzzling phenomenon for a rural area. We tend to think of extortion as a big city crime, involving gangs and mobs demanding protection money from stores; however, those states with big cities are either free of extortion arrests or have low arrest rates. The high arrest rate for extortion in the District of Columbia is understandable; in Wyoming, it is baffling.

JUVENILE CRIMINALS

The map "Juvenile Criminals, All Arrests, 1992" shows juvenile arrests as a percentage of all arrests in each state. The Deep South and some Mid-Atlantic states show the smallest percentage of juvenile arrests, while over 30 percent of all arrests in Idaho, Utah are of juveniles. These states, along with most of those in the 20 percent range, all lie in a band along the northern part of the United States.

The District of Columbia, while leading in murder, aggravated assault and robbery, is among the lowest in juvenile arrests, matched only by Kentucky, both with juveniles arrests slightly over seven percent of all arrests.

When we begin to break down juvenile crime, as the four maps "Juvenile Criminals, 1992" show, we see that South

Dakota leads in murder with a juvenile arrest rate of one third of all homicide arrests; however it has one of the lowest percentages of juvenile arrests for robbery.

One quarter of homicide arrests in Vermont are juveniles, but in arrests for robbery, assault and rape, Vermont ranks among the lowest states. These percentages must be compared with the overall low state rates for these crimes.

In addition to South Dakota, the Southwest and West show high juvenile arrest rates for murder. Iowa, North Dakota and New Hampshire reported no juvenile arrests for murder in 1992.

When it comes to rape, the distribution differs. Utah takes the lead with 32.4 percent, yet the overall rape rate for the state is relatively low. North Dakota and Illinois are in the 25 to 30 percent range, yet North Dakota has the lowest overall rate, and Illinois is relatively low.

Robbery yields another picture. In general, the Deep South and portions of the Northern High Plains are regions of low juvenile robbery arrests. Wyoming and Vermont have the lowest rates, and they are also extremely low in adult robbery rates.

The states with high juvenile robbery arrest rates are scattered throughout the West and Northeast. Within these regions, Utah leads, with juveniles accounting for over 39 percent of all robbery arrests. Nebraska, Minnesota and Wisconsin follow, with rates greater than 30 percent. Again, these percentages should be compared with the map "Robbery" to see their place in the overall rates for the states.

States with high juvenile arrest rates for aggravated assault are clustered in the Southwest, the Pacific Northwest and in the northern Midwest. As with robbery, Utah leads in aggravated assault with 35 percent. Idaho and Minnesota are close, with about 26 percent. Lower rates can be found in the Deep South and New England.

ROBBERY

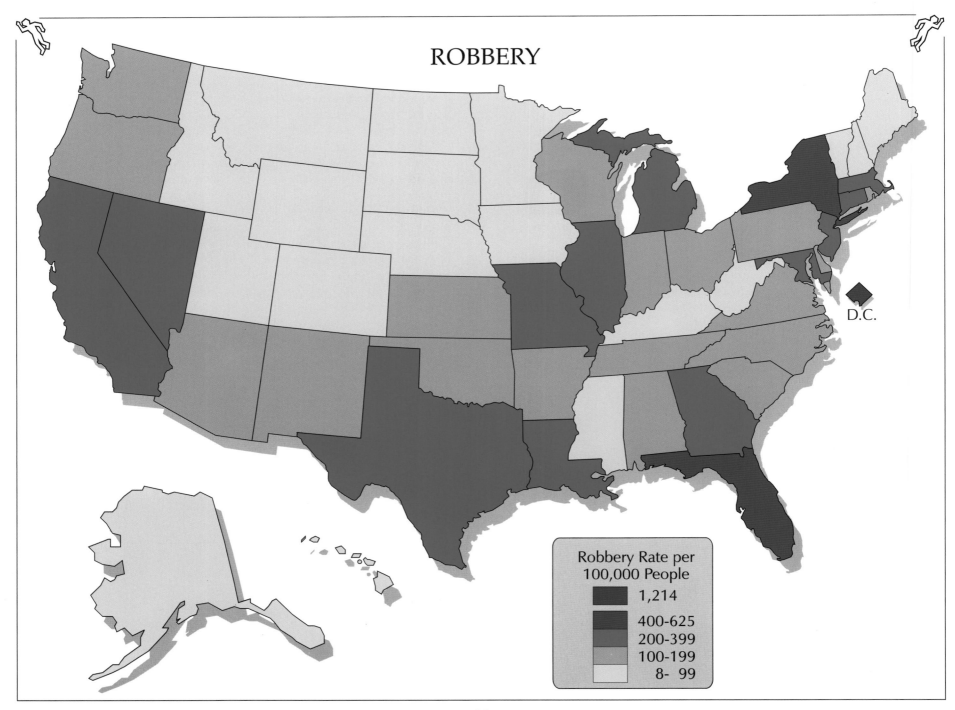

Robbery Rate per
100,000 People

	1,214
	400-625
	200-399
	100-199
	8- 99

D.C.

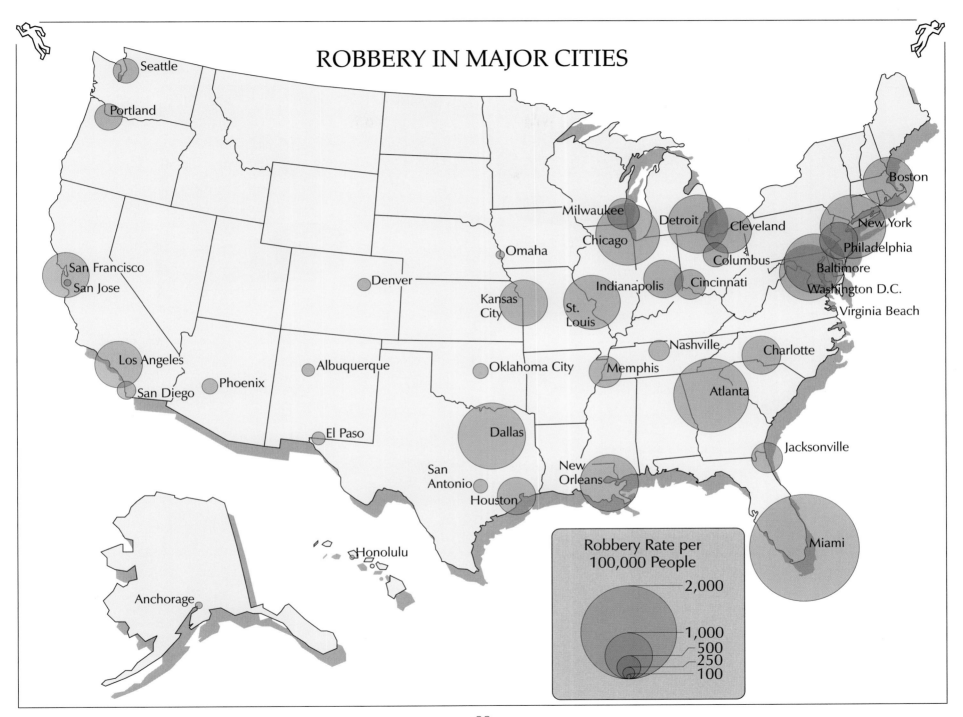

ROBBERY IN MAJOR CITIES

Seattle
Portland
San Francisco
San Jose
Los Angeles
San Diego
Phoenix
Honolulu
Anchorage

Milwaukee
Chicago
Omaha
Denver
Kansas City
St. Louis
Indianapolis
Albuquerque
Oklahoma City
Memphis
Nashville
El Paso
Dallas
San Antonio
Houston
New Orleans

Detroit
Cleveland
Columbus
Cincinnati
New York
Philadelphia
Baltimore
Washington D.C.
Virginia Beach
Boston
Charlotte
Atlanta
Jacksonville
Miami

Robbery Rate per 100,000 People

2,000
1,000
500
250
100

ROBBERY RATE THROUGH TIME

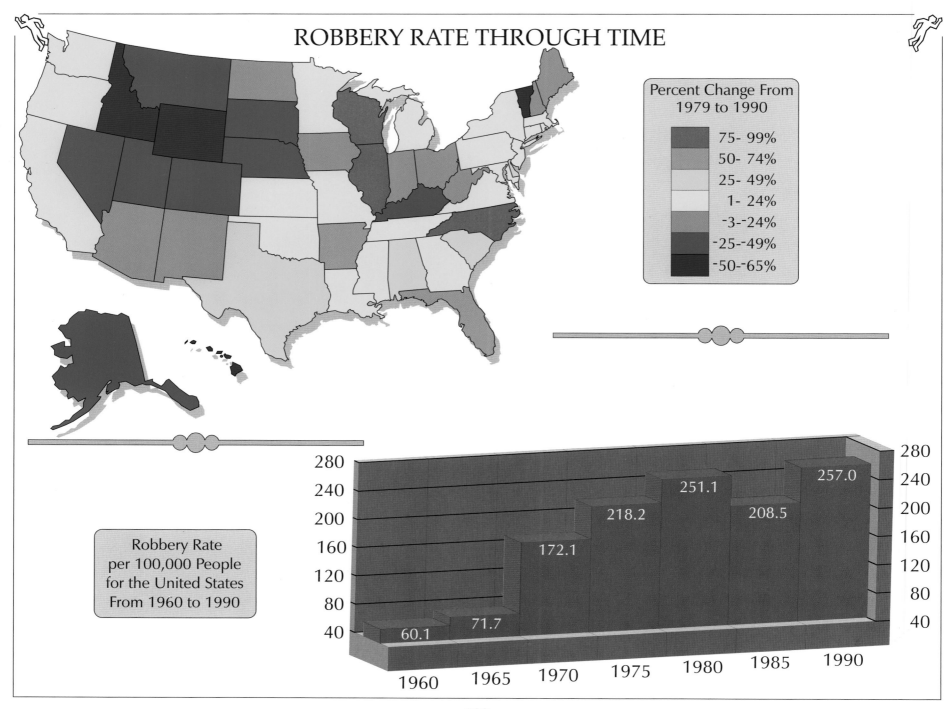

Percent Change From
1979 to 1990

75- 99%
50- 74%
25- 49%
1- 24%
-3--24%
-25--49%
-50--65%

Robbery Rate
per 100,000 People
for the United States
From 1960 to 1990

280
240
200
160
120
80
40

257.0
251.1
218.2
208.5
172.1
71.7
60.1

1960 1965 1970 1975 1980 1985 1990

EXTORTION
1992

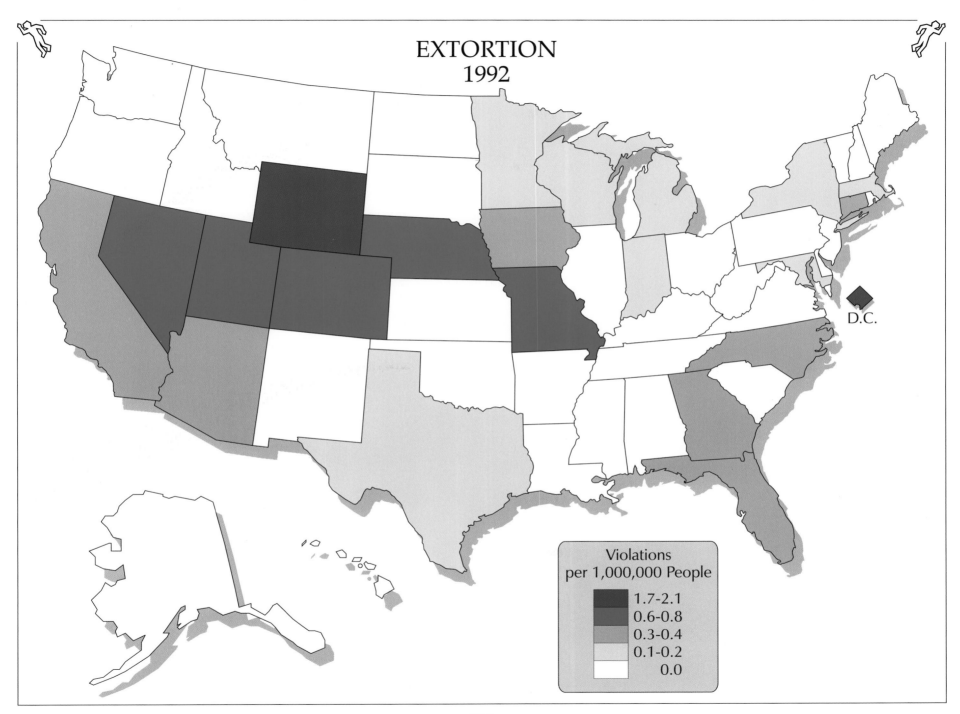

D.C.

Violations
per 1,000,000 People

1.7-2.1
0.6-0.8
0.3-0.4
0.1-0.2
0.0

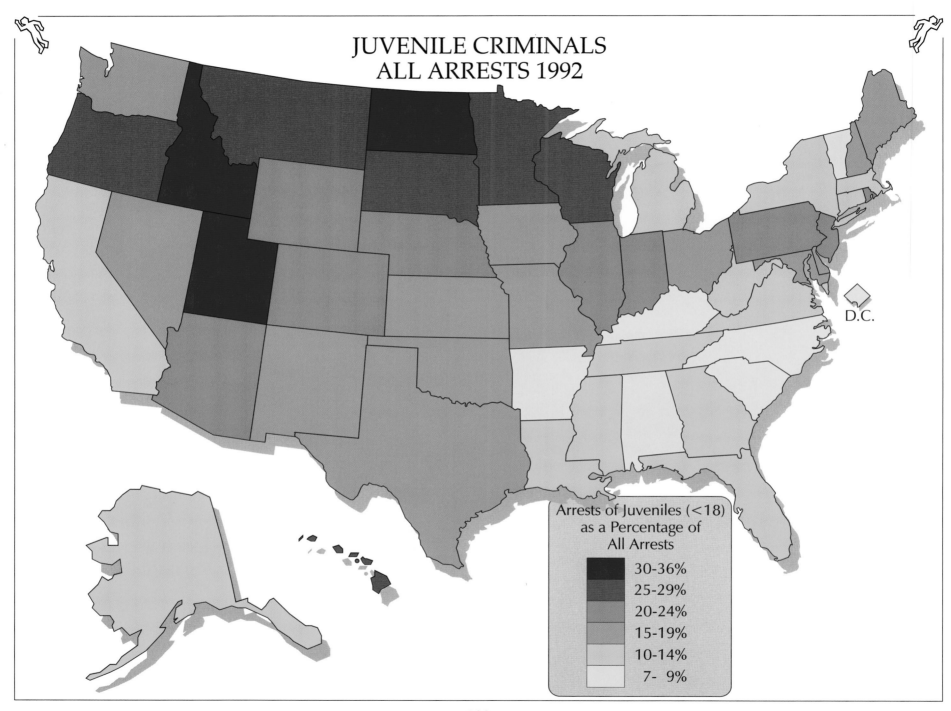

JUVENILE CRIMINALS
ALL ARRESTS 1992

**Arrests of Juveniles (<18)
as a Percentage of
All Arrests**

- 30-36%
- 25-29%
- 20-24%
- 15-19%
- 10-14%
- 7- 9%

D.C.

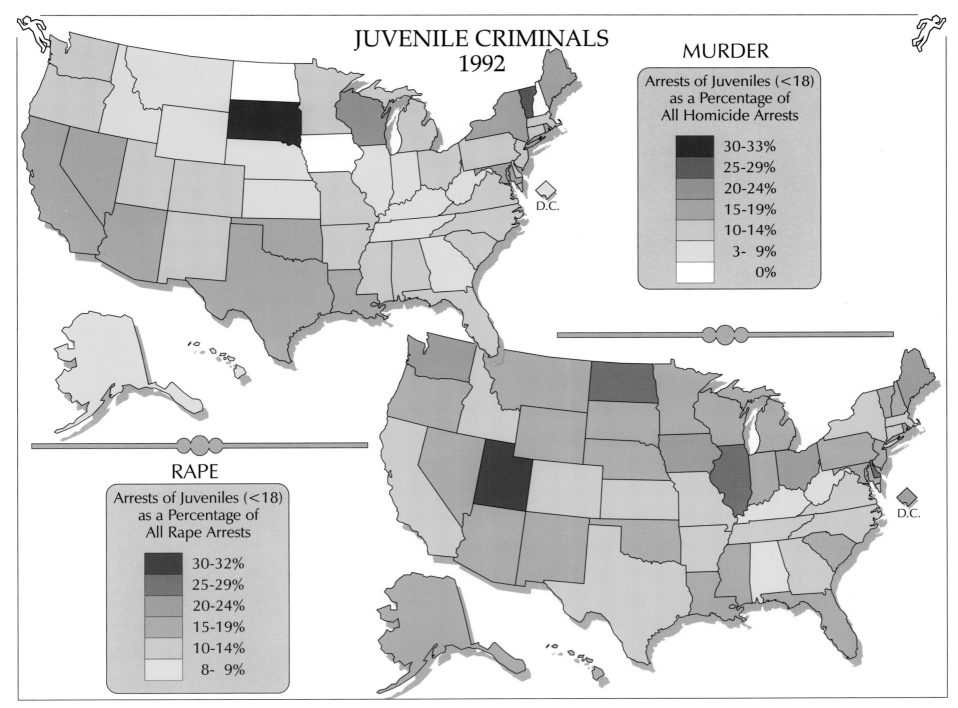

JUVENILE CRIMINALS
1992

MURDER

Arrests of Juveniles (<18)
as a Percentage of
All Homicide Arrests

30-33%
25-29%
20-24%
15-19%
10-14%
3- 9%
0%

D.C.

RAPE

Arrests of Juveniles (<18)
as a Percentage of
All Rape Arrests

30-32%
25-29%
20-24%
15-19%
10-14%
8- 9%

D.C.

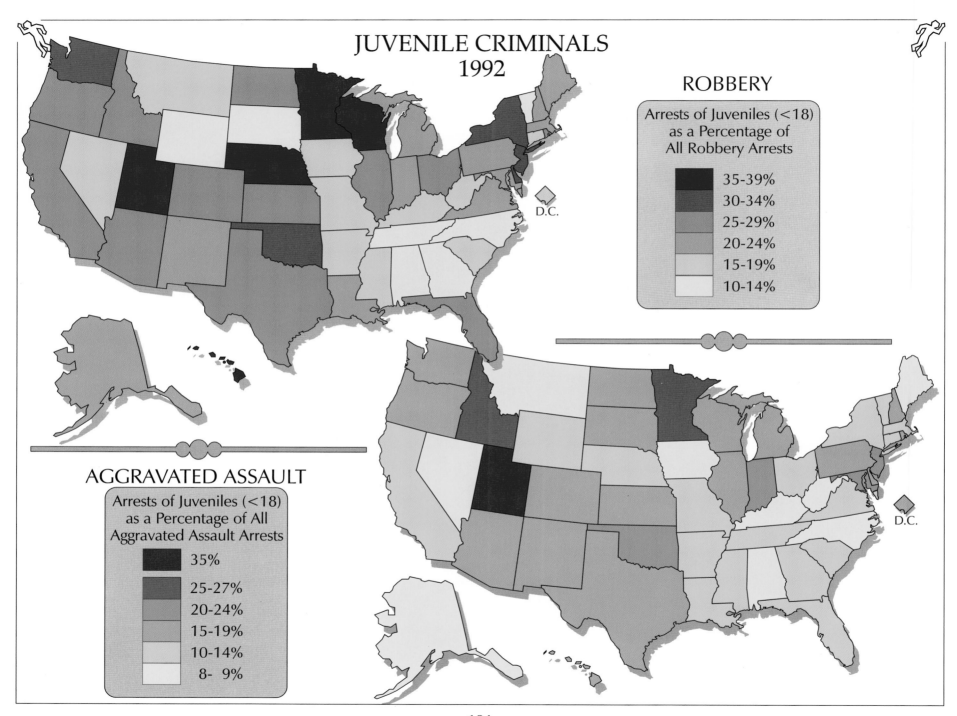

JUVENILE CRIMINALS
1992

ROBBERY

Arrests of Juveniles (<18)
as a Percentage of
All Robbery Arrests

- 35-39%
- 30-34%
- 25-29%
- 20-24%
- 15-19%
- 10-14%

D.C.

AGGRAVATED ASSAULT

Arrests of Juveniles (<18)
as a Percentage of All
Aggravated Assault Arrests

- 35%
- 25-27%
- 20-24%
- 15-19%
- 10-14%
- 8- 9%

D.C.

PROPERTY CRIME

Crimes that do not involve violence but result in the loss or destruction of property are legally described as "property crimes." These crimes include burglary, larceny, theft and arson. A separate division of theft involves motor vehicles. It is important to define the various property crimes and distinguish them from violent crimes.

BURGLARY

Burglary is defined by the Uniform Crime Reporting Program of the Federal Bureau of Investigation as unlawful entry into a structure to commit a felony or a theft. To commit a burglary, the criminal must enter a building with the intention of stealing something. If a suspect were to break open a door and enter a house without intending to steal or commit a crime, and left without doing so, he would not be guilty of burglary, but could be found guilty of trespassing.

The map "Burglary" depicts a north-south distribution of burglary in the country, with the heaviest concentration of burglaries in the southern half of the country. Of the Southern states, Florida exceeds all others with a rate of 2,171 burglaries for every 100,000 people. Arizona, New Mexico Texas, Georgia, North Carolina and Virginia come

next, with 1,500 to 1,999 burglaries per 100,000 people.

At the other end of the spectrum, the Northern High Plains states, along with some of the Northeastern states, have low burglary rates, all falling below 750 per 100,000 people. With a few exceptions, the burglary rate throughout the country parallels the robbery rate, which can be seen in the previous section on violent crime.

As with the state burglary map, the map "Burglary in Major Cities" shows a high concentration of burglary rates in Southern cities, with Atlanta in the lead with 3,939 per 100,000 inhabitants. Miami is not far behind with 3,767. Although the Southern cities hold the lead in burglaries, several Midwestern and North Central cities rank high. They include Kansas City, St. Louis, Detroit and Columbus. The large metropolitan areas of New York, Chicago and Los Angeles, with bad reputations as centers of urban crime, all have burglary rates below 2,000.

The chart in "Burglary Rate through Time" shows that, until 1980, the overall burglary rate for the United States had been steadily rising. Following a sharp drop in 1980, the burglary rate has remained fairly steady around 1,200 per 100,000. Recently released figures for 1991 show only a one percent gain in the burglary rate, to 1,252 per 100,000 people nationwide. During 1991, a total of 3,157,150 burglaries

BURGLARY

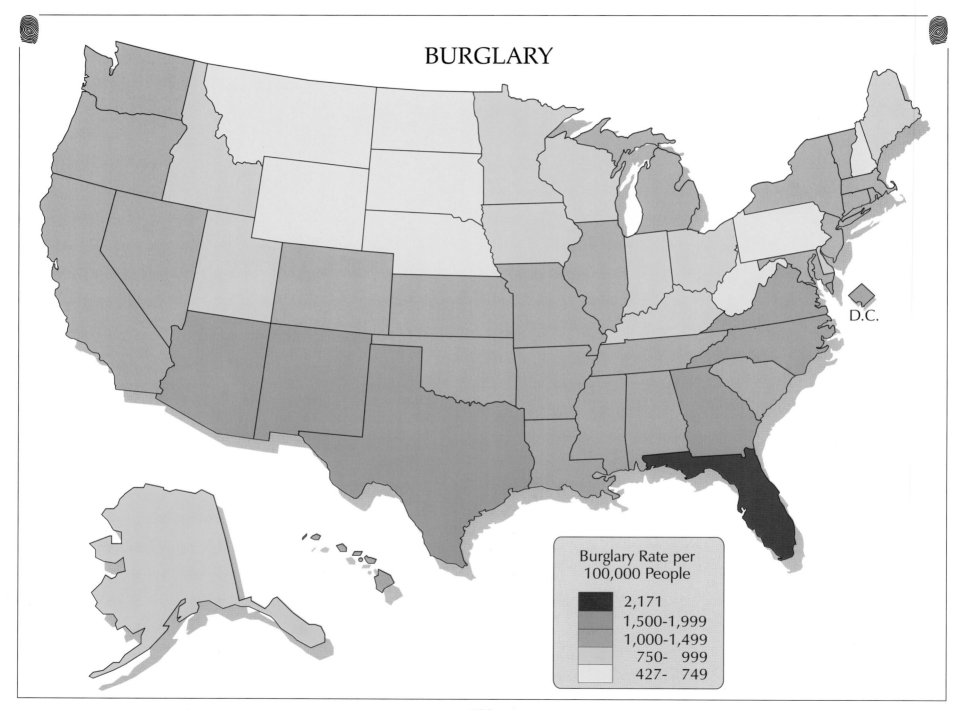

Burglary Rate per
100,000 People

- 2,171
- 1,500-1,999
- 1,000-1,499
- 750- 999
- 427- 749

D.C.

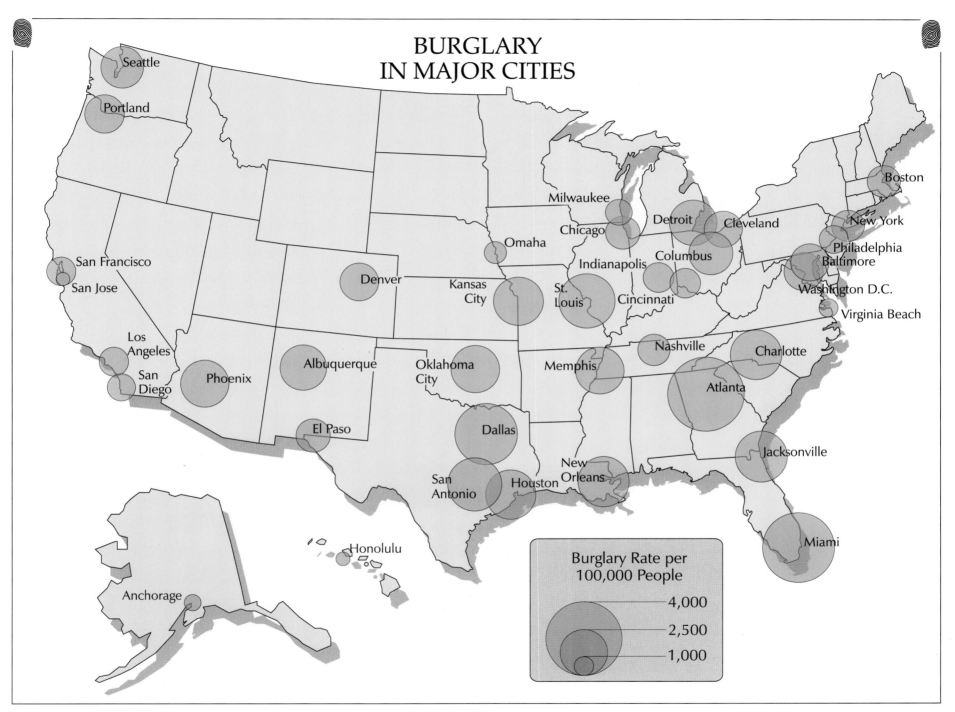

BURGLARY
IN MAJOR CITIES

Seattle
Portland
San Francisco
San Jose
Los Angeles
San Diego
Phoenix
El Paso
San Antonio
Honolulu
Anchorage
Denver
Albuquerque
Oklahoma City
Dallas
Houston
New Orleans
Omaha
Kansas City
St. Louis
Memphis
Nashville
Milwaukee
Chicago
Detroit
Indianapolis
Cincinnati
Columbus
Cleveland
Atlanta
Charlotte
Jacksonville
Miami
New York
Boston
Philadelphia
Baltimore
Washington D.C.
Virginia Beach

Burglary Rate per 100,000 People

4,000
2,500
1,000

BURGLARY RATE THROUGH TIME

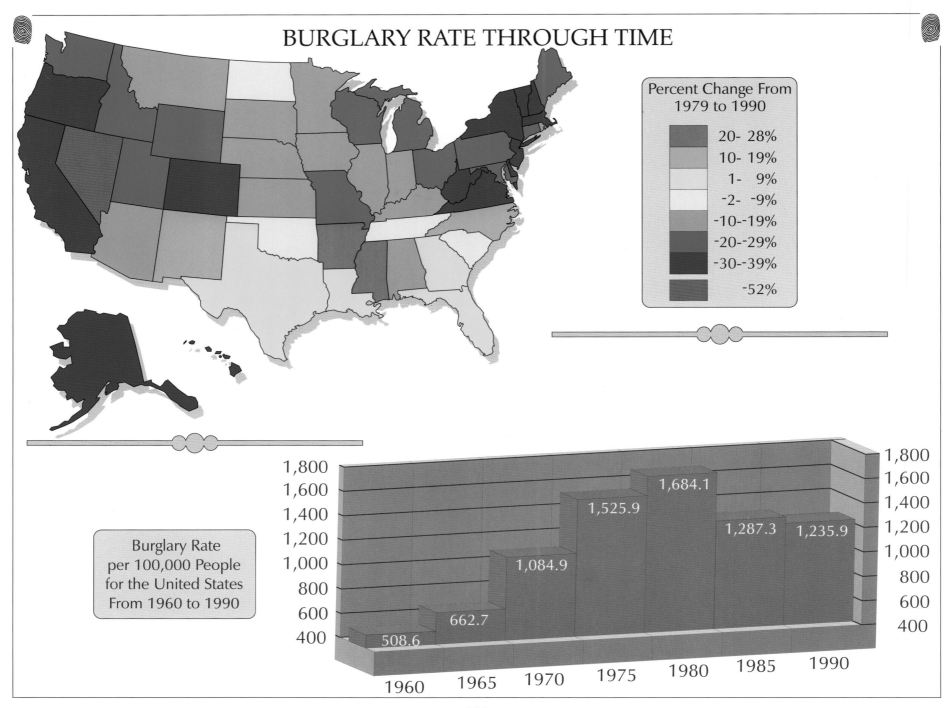

Percent Change From
1979 to 1990

20- 28%
10- 19%
1- 9%
-2- -9%
-10--19%
-20--29%
-30--39%
-52%

Burglary Rate
per 100,000 People
for the United States
From 1960 to 1990

508.6
662.7
1,084.9
1,525.9
1,684.1
1,287.3
1,235.9

1,800
1,600
1,400
1,200
1,000
800
600
400

1960 1965 1970 1975 1980 1985 1990

occurred in the United States, accounting for 24 percent of all property crimes.

In the accompanying map, only the Southern states show increases in burglary rates for the past decade. Mississippi, with a 28 percent increase, and Arkansas, with a 23 percent increase, were the highest. Alabama and South Carolina are the only two Southern states that have shown a drop in the burglary rate. With the exception of the Southern states, the majority of states have shown a drop in the burglary rate. Slightly over one-quarter of all the states (13 states) had declines greater than 30 percent.

LARCENY

Closely related to robbery and burglary, larceny is a crime that involves taking property from another person unlawfully. It includes a host of minor crimes, such as shoplifting, pocket picking, purse snatching, thefts from motor vehicles, bicycle theft, etc. The distinguishing element of larceny is that neither violence nor the use of force occurs. Embezzlement, con games or bouncing worthless checks are usually excluded from larceny. Stealing motor vehicles is also treated as a separate crime category.

There are two types of larceny, each defined by the value of whatever is stolen. Below a certain monetary amount, theft is considered petty larceny; over that amount, the theft is grand larceny. In the following maps and charts, petty and grand larceny are lumped together.

Thirty-eight percent of all larceny occurs in Southern states, 23 percent in the Midwest, and another 23 percent in the West. The map "Larceny/Theft" shows that Arizona, with nearly 5,000 larcenies and thefts per 100,000 people, has the highest rates of larceny and theft. The lowest rates are to be found in the Appalachian states of Kentucky, West Virginia and Pennsylvania.

The District of Columbia, with 4,997 larceny arrests for every 100,000 people, has a higher rate than any state, but it ranks about average when compared with other major cities, as seen in the map "Larceny/Theft in Major Cities." There, as with burglary, Atlanta leads with a rate of 8,380, followed by Miami, with 8,237. Low larceny and theft rates also parallel burglary rates.

When we consider larceny and theft over the past ten years, the chart "Larceny Rate through Time" shows a constant rise in larceny nationwide until 1985. As with burglaries, the rate dropped slightly during the 1980s. The accompanying map shows that in the Deep South, Texas and Oklahoma, rates increased from 20 to 40 percent. Florida, unlike the rest of the South, had an increase of only seven percent. Overall, the West, New England and scattered states in the North Central and Rocky Mountains have experienced a drop in larceny rates. Nevada experienced the greatest decline of 22 percent.

The average value of the property stolen through larceny during 1991 was $478, and the national loss to victims totaled $3.9 billion. However, these figures may be conservative, since many larcenies are not reported to the police and thus never find their way into crime statistics—especially if the value of the stolen goods is small. In 24 percent of the thefts reported in 1991, the value of objects stolen ranged from $50 to $200.

Thefts of greatest value were those from buildings, with an average loss of $788. Thefts from motor vehicles averaged $544, while pocket picking yielded an average loss of $366, purse snatching $280 and shoplifting $104.

The chart "Trends in Larceny & Theft" shows the five year trends for the six major types of larceny and theft. The more personal crimes of pocket picking and purse snatching showed a consistent decrease. The less personal crimes of

LARCENY/THEFT

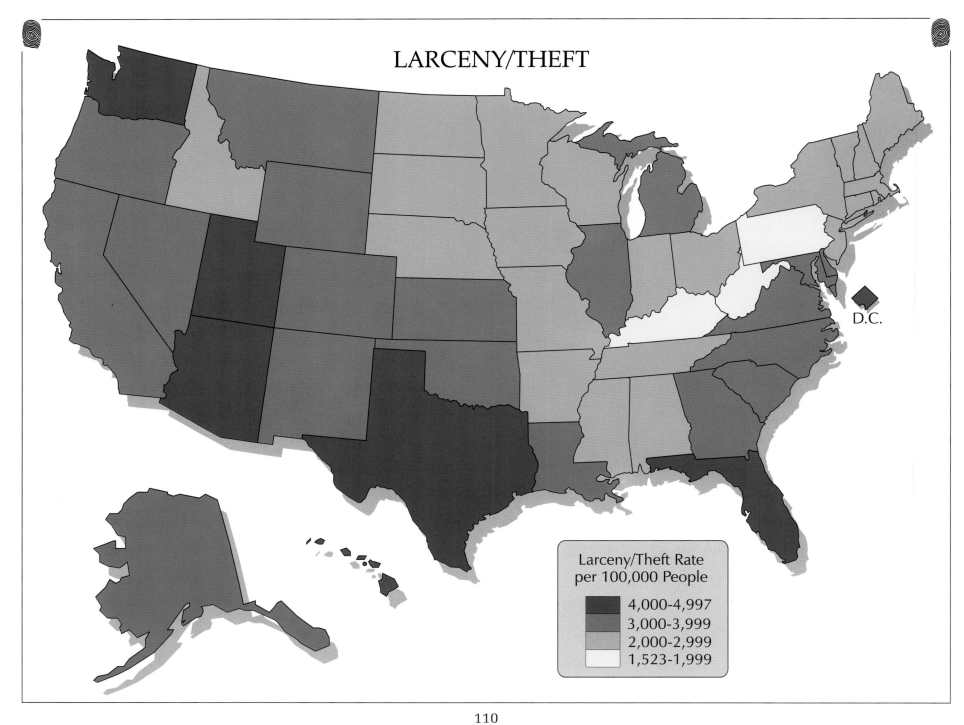

D.C.

Larceny/Theft Rate
per 100,000 People

4,000-4,997
3,000-3,999
2,000-2,999
1,523-1,999

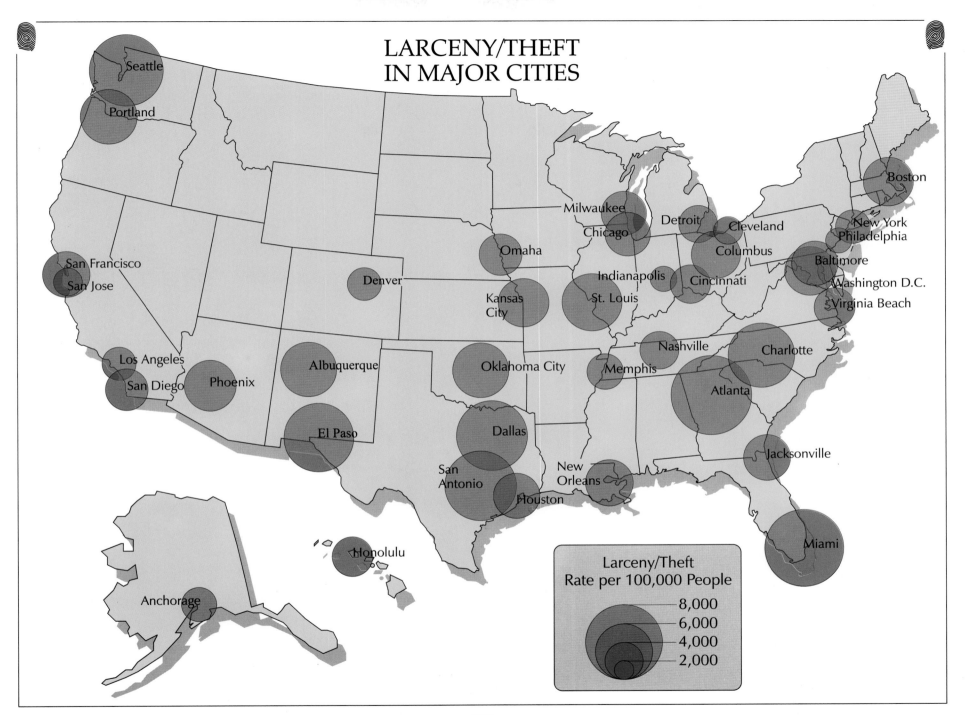

LARCENY/THEFT IN MAJOR CITIES

Larceny/Theft
Rate per 100,000 People

8,000
6,000
4,000
2,000

LARCENY RATE THROUGH TIME

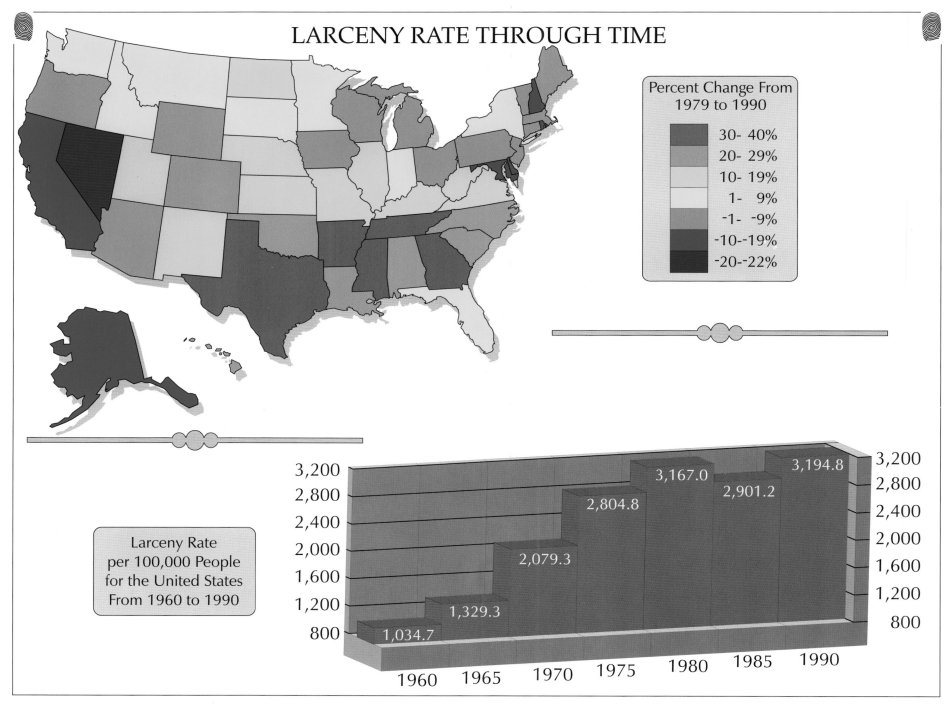

Percent Change From
1979 to 1990

30- 40%
20- 29%
10- 19%
1- 9%
-1- -9%
-10--19%
-20--22%

Larceny Rate
per 100,000 People
for the United States
From 1960 to 1990

3,200
2,800
2,400
2,000
1,600
1,200
800

1,034.7
1,329.3
2,079.3
2,804.8
3,167.0
2,901.2
3,194.8

1960   1965   1970   1975   1980   1985   1990

TRENDS IN LARCENY & THEFT

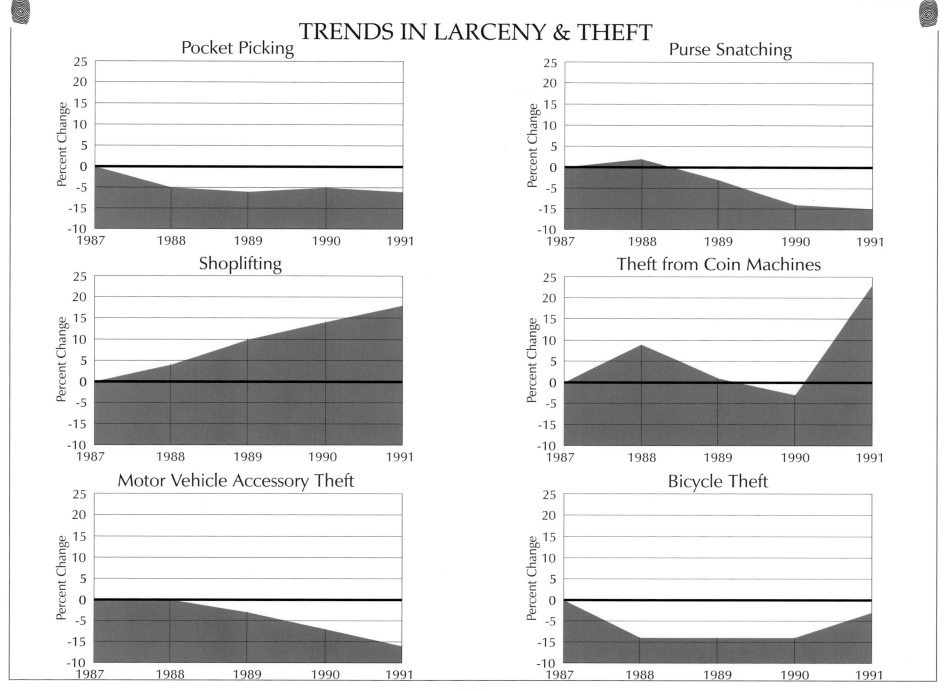

shoplifting and theft from coin machines have shown a dramatic increase.

MOTOR VEHICLE THEFT

Although theft from a motor vehicle is considered larceny, the theft of the car itself is classed separately by the Justice Department as motor vehicle theft. The definition of motor vehicle theft covers theft or attempted theft of automobiles, trucks, buses, motorcycles, motor scooters and snowmobiles.

The map "Motor Vehicle Theft" shows that the two states which have the highest rate of motor vehicle theft are California with 1,106 per 100,000 residents, and New York with 1,043. Within both of these states, the highest rates are concentrated in the metropolitan areas of New York City, Los Angeles and San Diego.

The states with the lowest rate of motor vehicle theft are South Dakota with 110 per 100,000, and North Dakota with 133. Both states are located in the largest region of low motor vehicle theft rates, the predominately rural Northern Plains states. The other area of low rates is located in rural, northern New England.

A total of 1.6 million thefts of motor vehicles occurred in the United States during 1991, which accounted for 13 percent of all property crime. It is estimated that, nationally, one out of every 117 registered motor vehicles was stolen during 1991. The rate was highest in the Northeast, where one out of every 84 registered motor vehicles was stolen. That motor vehicle theft is not a minor property crime is shown by the fact that during 1991 the total value of motor vehicles stolen was estimated to be about $8.3 billion. Of all the vehicles stolen, 80 percent were automobiles, 15 percent trucks, and the remainder all other types of vehicles.

The highest rates of theft did not always take place in the most heavily populated cities, as the map "Motor Vehicle Theft in Major Cities" shows. Detroit had the highest rate—2,955 per 100,000 people. Atlanta, Miami, Boston and Houston are all hot spots for motor vehicle theft. The lowest rate of motor vehicle theft, 330, occurred in Virginia Beach.

The chart in "Motor Vehicle Theft Rate through Time" shows that the overall motor vehicle theft rate has been on the rise since 1960. The rate leveled off during the 1970s and 1980s but it suffered a dramatic increase in 1990. The map details the increase that took place between 1979 and 1990. The greatest increases was in Florida, with a 91 percent rise from 1979 to 1990. Arizona also showed as sizable increase of 75 percent. Texas, Wisconsin, Tennessee and Georgia all showed a rise in the theft rate of over 50 percent. Although there is no clear pattern to the states which have shown an increase in motor vehicle theft, those states which have shown a decrease are concentrated in the Northern Plains, Rocky Mountains and northern New England, along with West Virginia, Alaska and Hawaii.

ARSON

Arson is the act of intentionally setting fire to a building or other property. There are different definitions of arson in different states, but the general definition is the deliberate burning of any structure, whether owned by yourself or another person. In some states, it is arson to burn a bridge, a boat, a forest or even an open field. Burning an abandoned building or one under construction is a crime, although it may not be considered arson. How bad must the fire be to consider it arson? In some states the entire building must be destroyed by fire, in others only a small portion suffices.

The map "Arson" shows that Oregon and North Dakota

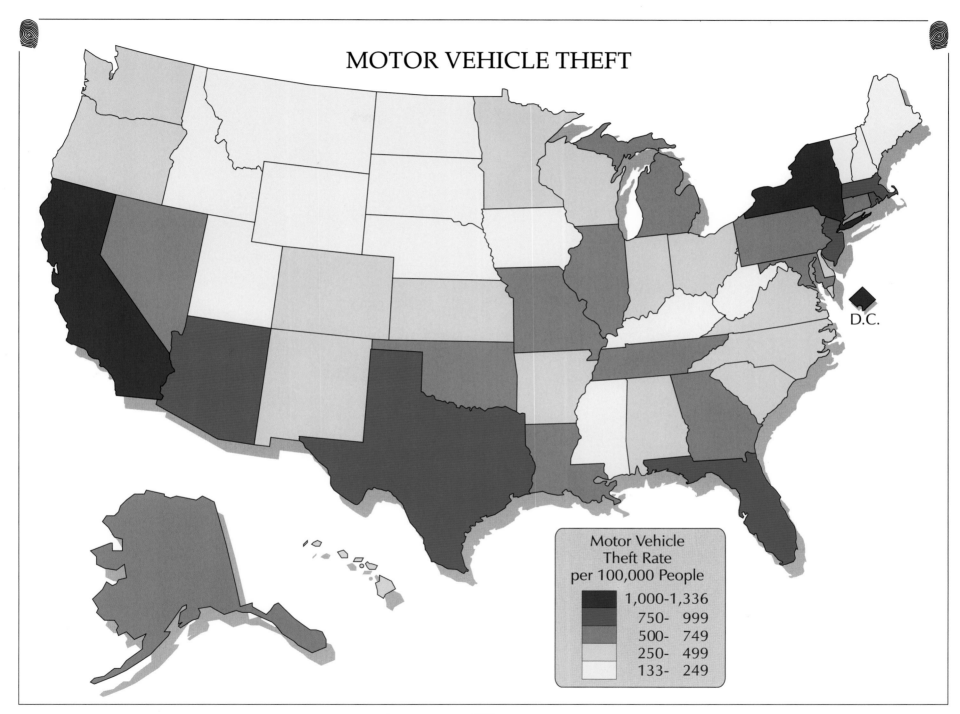

MOTOR VEHICLE THEFT

D.C.

Motor Vehicle Theft Rate per 100,000 People

- 1,000–1,336
- 750– 999
- 500– 749
- 250– 499
- 133– 249

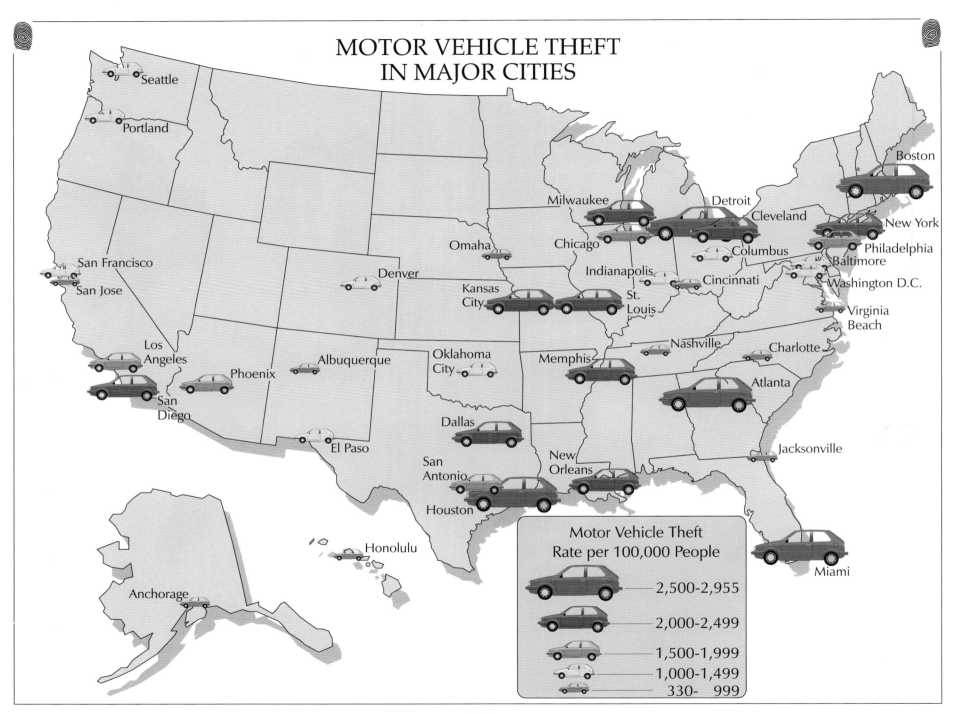

MOTOR VEHICLE THEFT IN MAJOR CITIES

Seattle
Portland
San Francisco
San Jose
Los Angeles
San Diego
Phoenix
Albuquerque
El Paso
San Antonio
Houston
Dallas
Oklahoma City
Denver
Omaha
Kansas City
Memphis
New Orleans
Milwaukee
Chicago
Indianapolis
Detroit
Cleveland
Columbus
Cincinnati
St. Louis
Nashville
Atlanta
Jacksonville
Charlotte
Virginia Beach
Washington D.C.
Baltimore
Philadelphia
New York
Boston
Miami
Honolulu
Anchorage

Motor Vehicle Theft Rate per 100,000 People

2,500–2,955
2,000–2,499
1,500–1,999
1,000–1,499
330– 999

MOTOR VEHICLE THEFT RATE THROUGH TIME

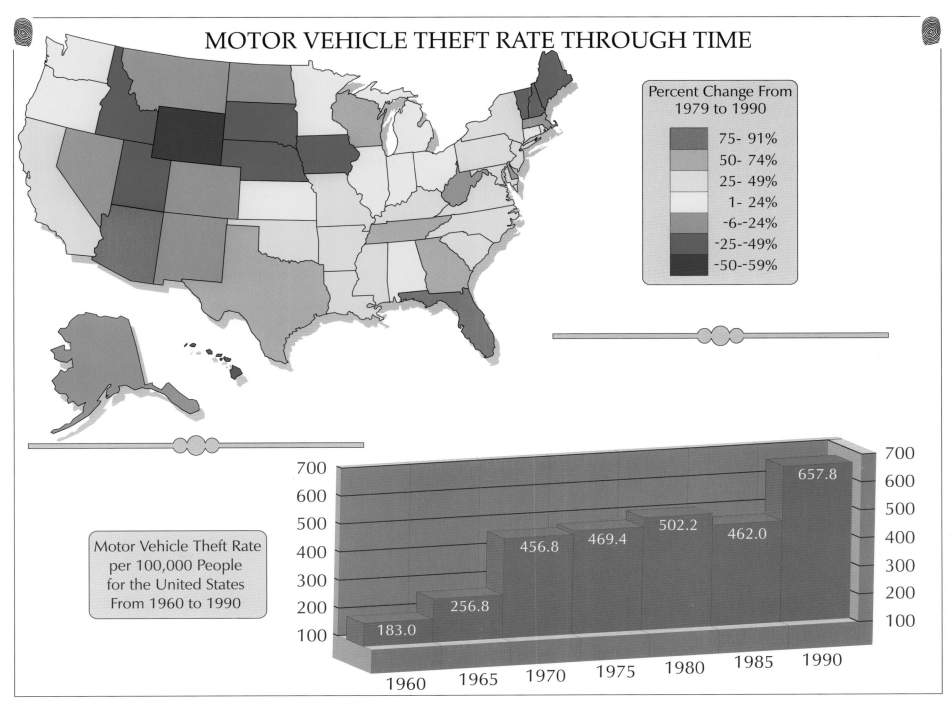

Percent Change From
1979 to 1990

75- 91%
50- 74%
25- 49%
1- 24%
-6--24%
-25--49%
-50--59%

Motor Vehicle Theft Rate
per 100,000 People
for the United States
From 1960 to 1990

700
600
500
400
300
200
100

183.0
256.8
456.8
469.4
502.2
462.0
657.8

700
600
500
400
300
200
100

1960 1965 1970 1975 1980 1985 1990

hold records for the highest arrest rates for arson—17 people arrested for arson for every 100,000 residents in 1990. At the other end of the spectrum, Alaska has the lowest incidence of arson arrests, at only three arrests, along with Nevada, Alabama and Massachusetts, each with a rate of four arrests per 100,000 residents.

The arrest rates for arson in cities are nearly ten times greater than the overall rates for the states. The map "Arson in Major Cities" shows that Los Angeles has the highest rate at 162 incidents of arson per 100,000 people. Cleveland, with a rate of 160, Detroit with 150 and St. Louis with 151 are the three cities with the next highest rates. Anchorage, with an arson rate of 17 per 100,000 inhabitants, and San Diego with 22, represent the low end of the scale.

Buildings were the most frequent targets of arsonists, accounting for 54 percent of reported incidents. Twenty-seven percent of arson incidents involved motor vehicles and trailers, while 19 percent involved damaged crops, timber, etc.

FRAUD

Fraud occurs when someone tells you something he or she knows is false, intending you to act on the falsehood. For example, if you are buying a used car and the used car salesman tells you the car has never been in a wreck, when in truth the car was damaged by a collision and repaired, then the salesman is being fraudulent. Your decision to buy the car is based on your belief that it is free of the damage a collision can cause. However, if the salesman tells you he believes the car is in perfect condition and a good buy, he is only giving you his opinion, and that is not fraud.

The map "Fraud, 1991" shows that the state with the greatest number of arrests, at the rate of 1,710 per 1,000,000

residents, is North Dakota. Three other states with high arrest rates for fraud are Arkansas and the Carolinas, with rates over 800.

In general, the Western states, with the exception of Nevada, have low rates of arrests for fraud, while the Southern states seem to have the highest rates. In general, a high incidence of fraud arrests occurs in predominantly rural states.

EMBEZZLEMENT

Embezzlement occurs when someone takes something that was entrusted to him or her. The embezzler must have legal possession of what is taken. For example, a lawyer is entrusted with the estate of his client, an elderly man. The lawyer, over the years, siphons off parts of the estate for his own use. He is committing embezzlement. A banker who takes part of the money he legally handles for the bank is embezzling. If a postmaster, clerk or letter carrier steals letters, it is considered embezzlement under an act of Congress.

While the arrest rates for fraud are low, the arrest rates for embezzlement are even lower. The map "Embezzlement, 1991" shows Nevada and Mississippi with the highest rates, at only 29 and 34 per 1,000,000 people, respectively. In general, the majority of states have embezzlement arrest rates that fall below 10 per 1,000,000. Higher incidence of embezzlement occurs in a band running east to west through the south-central United States.

FORGERY

Forgery is the crime most removed from its victim. It occurs

ARSON

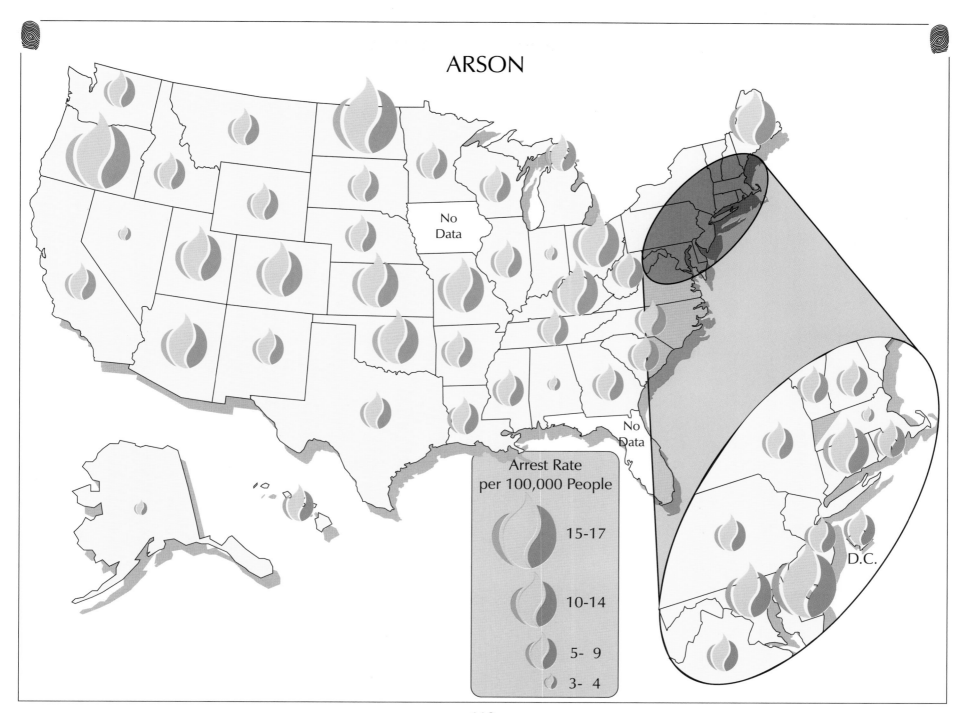

Arrest Rate per 100,000 People

15-17

10-14

5- 9

3- 4

No Data

No Data

D.C.

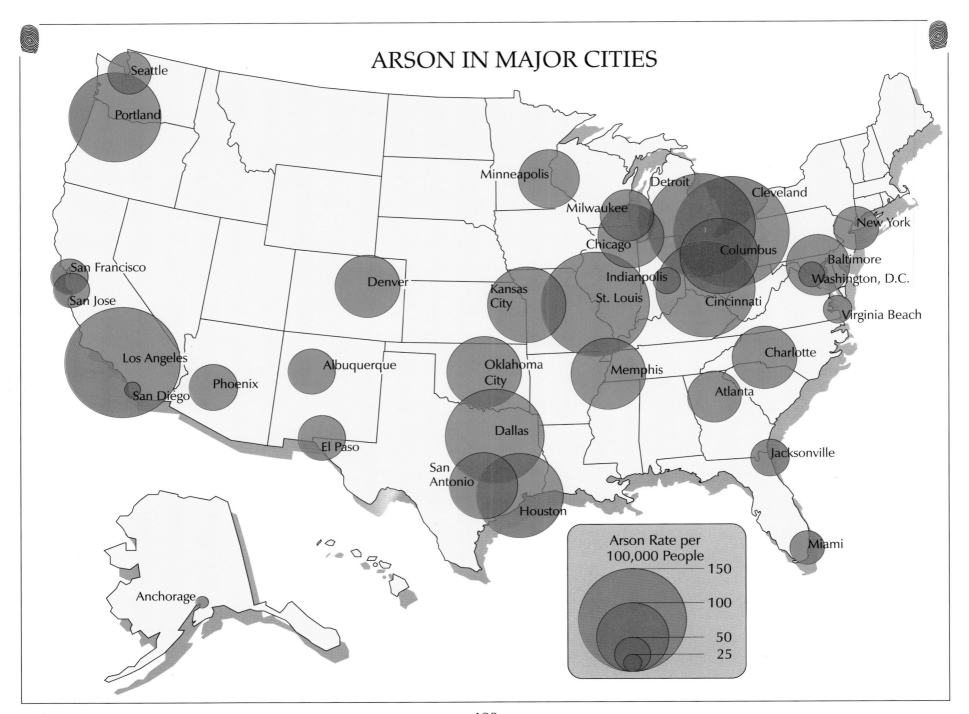

ARSON IN MAJOR CITIES

Arson Rate per 100,000 People

150
100
50
25

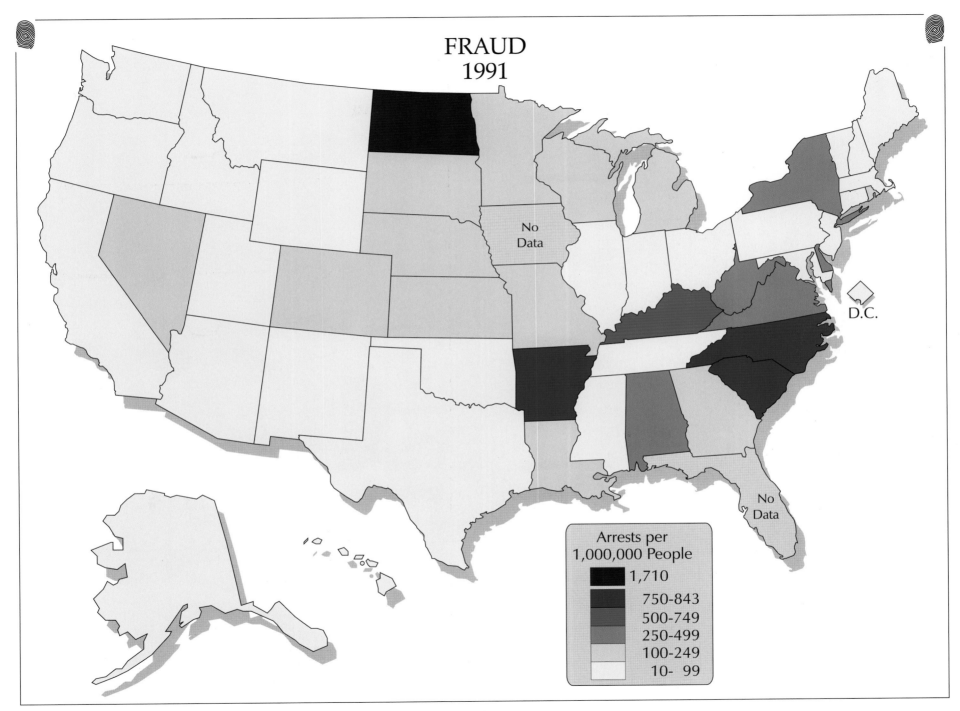

FRAUD
1991

No Data

No Data

D.C.

Arrests per
1,000,000 People

1,710

750-843

500-749

250-499

100-249

10- 99

EMBEZZLEMENT
1991

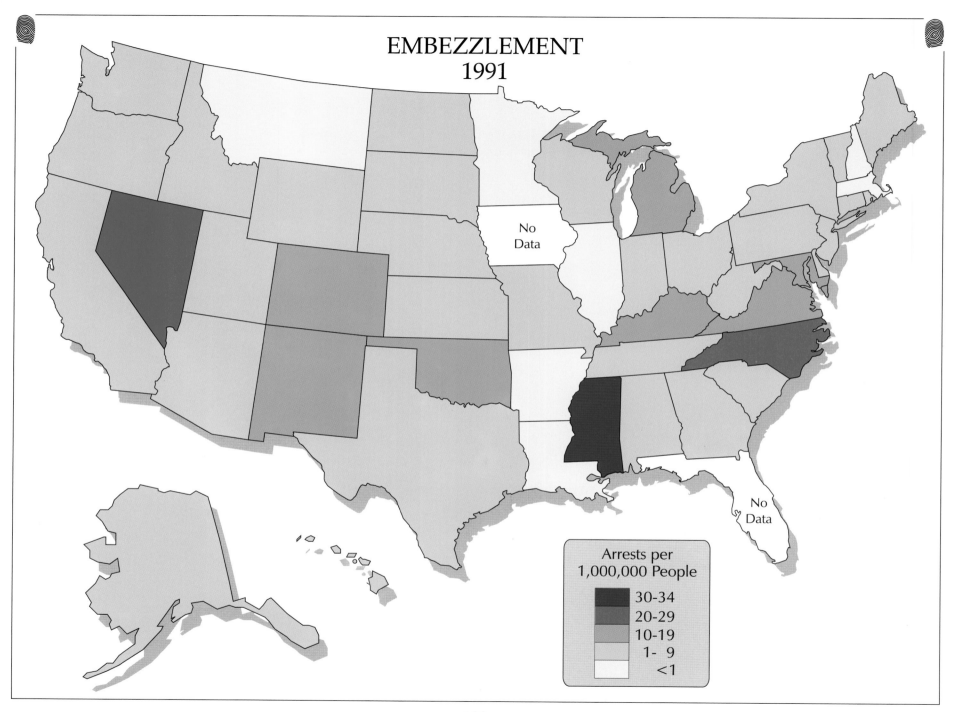

No Data

No Data

Arrests per
1,000,000 People

30-34
20-29
10-19
1- 9
<1

when someone willfully alters or creates a document that has legal significance. It is forgery to sign someone else's name to a check or to a contract. It is forgery if one makes an insertion or alteration in any legal document without the signer's permission. It is not forgery if one signs someone else's signature with their permission, as long as there is no intent to defraud that person or embezzle something from him or her.

Forgery is most frequently with checks or other means of obtaining money, but it can also be applied to documents of title, deed, marriage or birth certificates. Ordinarily, forgery is a state crime, but sending a forged document through the mail can make it a federal offense.

The map "Forgery, 1991" shows the Southeastern states with high rates of arrest. States in the Northeast, with the exception of Delaware, have rather low arrest rates, along with portions of the North Central and Northern High Plains states. New Mexico, Wyoming and Montana have the lowest forgery rates in the country.

WHEN DEADLY FORCE IS JUSTIFIED

In a normal situation, deadly force is justified only when it seems necessary to prevent immediate death or serious injury, or to prevent the commission of a violent crime, but there are other situations involving property when the user of deadly force is justified. In some states, deadly force can be used to protect against arson, burglary, criminal trespass or to protect a dwelling.

In all but ten states, deadly force can be used to protect your home even when your life is not threatened, because in those states, the home is considered to be inviolate. The map "Justifiable Use of Deadly Force When Life Is Not Threatened" shows the majority of states allow you to use deadly force when your home is threatened.

In six states deadly force can be justified if it is used to protect your property. Deadly force, it is generally accepted, can be used to prevent a serious crime. For this reason, these states allow it to be used to protect property, since a person taking property is almost always committing a crime.

In general, the use of deadly force is a thorny legal issue because, in choosing between a home or property and someone's life, the law will usually come down on the side of life. Nevertheless, in many states, a case can be made to justify the use of deadly force even when the victim's life is not in danger.

The map "Property Crimes against Which Deadly Force Is Justified" narrows the field. In preventing arson, 19 mostly Southern and Northeastern states, along with the District of Columbia, consider the use of deadly force justified. In eight states, deadly force can be used against burglary, although the amount or value of the property stolen is considered in justifying it. Deadly force is not permissible, however, when the owner or occupant of the house knows the intruder only intends to use the house temporarily, to make a phone call or to take shelter. The "perception" of the homeowner is vitally important.

In eight other states deadly force can be justified when it is used against unlawful entering or breaking and entering, and in Pennsylvania and Maine, deadly force is justified in cases of criminal trespass.

Since Pennsylvania does not justify deadly force against arson, burglary or breaking and entering, it is unusual that it would justify it in criminal trespass. Maine justifies it in arson and protecting a dwelling, but not in burglary or breaking and entering.

JUVENILE CRIMINALS

In general, as we examine crimes that are not violent, the

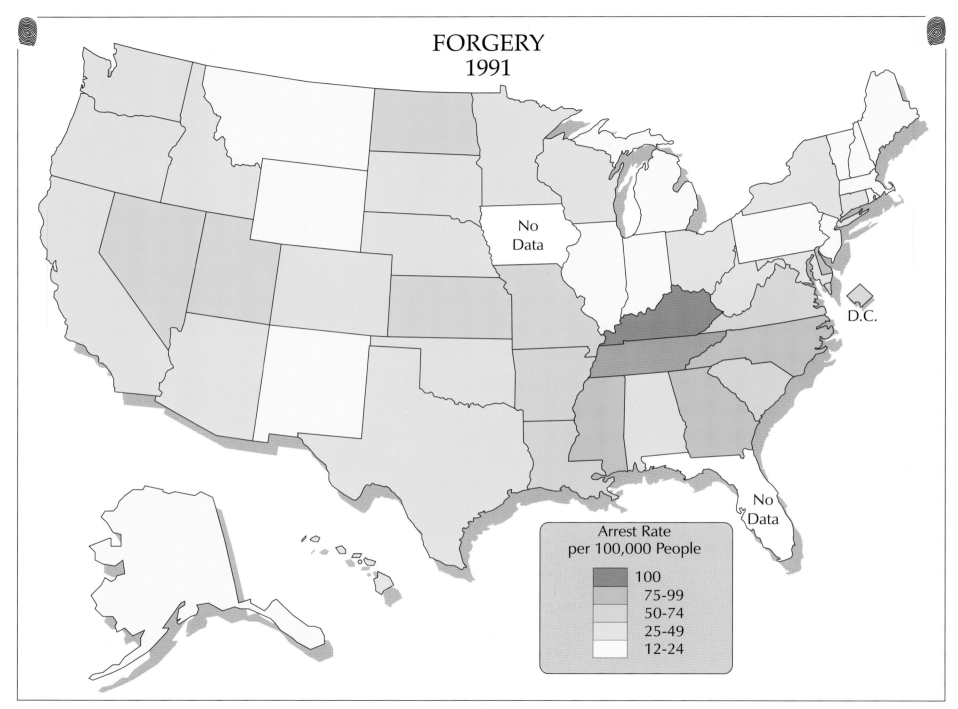

FORGERY
1991

No Data

No Data

D.C.

No Data

**Arrest Rate
per 100,000 People**

100
75-99
50-74
25-49
12-24

JUSTIFIABLE USE OF DEADLY FORCE WHEN LIFE IS NOT THREATENED

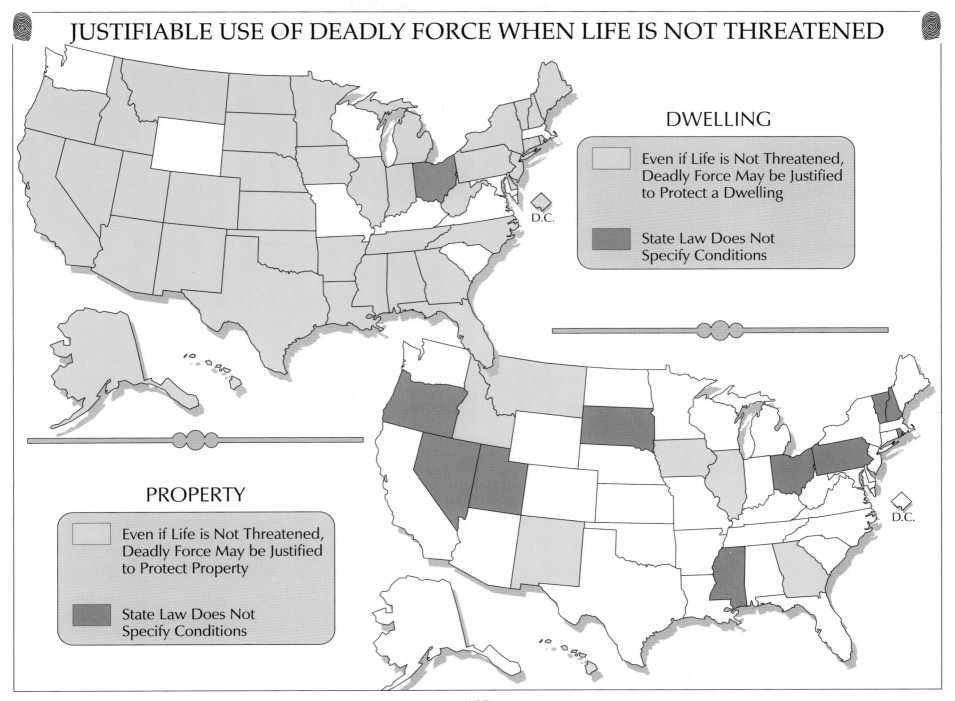

DWELLING

Even if Life is Not Threatened, Deadly Force May be Justified to Protect a Dwelling

State Law Does Not Specify Conditions

PROPERTY

Even if Life is Not Threatened, Deadly Force May be Justified to Protect Property

State Law Does Not Specify Conditions

PROPERTY CRIMES AGAINST WHICH DEADLY FORCE IS JUSTIFIED

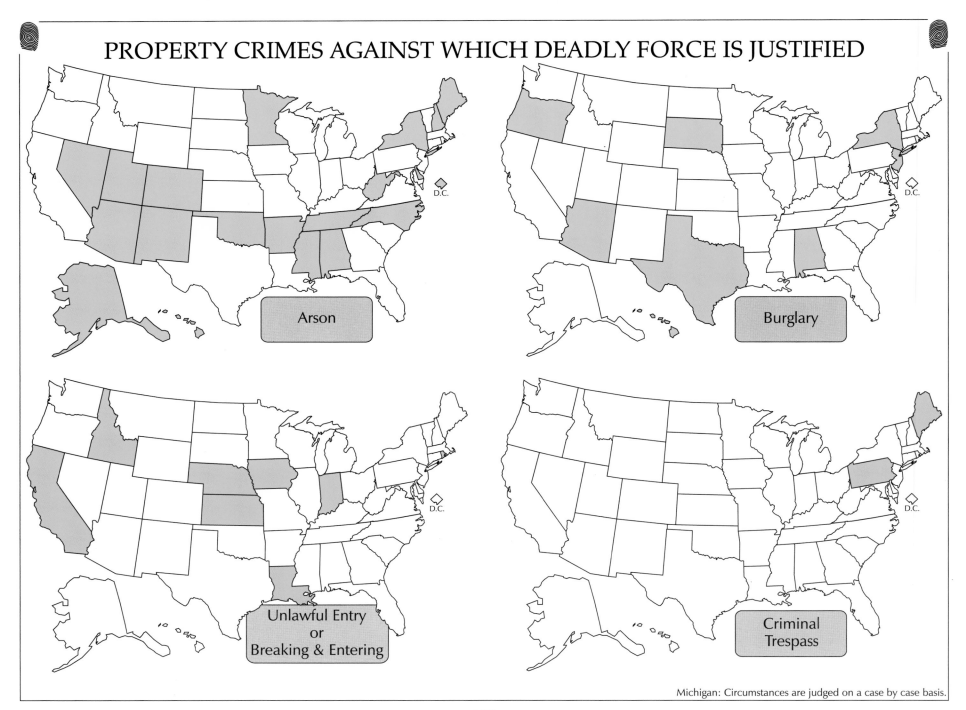

Arson

Burglary

Unlawful Entry
or
Breaking & Entering

Criminal
Trespass

Michigan: Circumstances are judged on a case by case basis.

involvement of juveniles increases. During 1991, about one third of the burglaries in the nation were committed by juveniles. As for larceny, some 30 percent of offenders were under 18 years of age. Over 40 percent of the arrests for motor vehicle theft were juveniles, as were about 46 percent of those arrested for arson.

The map "Juvenile Criminals, 1992" under "Larceny and Theft," shows that there was no state in which the arrest of juveniles for burglary or larceny was less that 17 percent. The heaviest percentage of juvenile burglary is in Idaho and Utah. Juvenile larceny was heaviest in these states and in Wyoming and the Dakotas. In these five states, the majority of all burglary and larceny arrests are of juveniles. The Deep South exhibited the lowest rates for juvenile arrests for these crimes.

Of all the states, Utah shows the highest rate of juvenile crimes of robbery, assault, burglary and larceny. The state with the lowest percentage of juvenile larceny is Massachusetts. In the District of Columbia, juveniles comprised only four percent of all larceny arrests, along with low percentages for burglary, motor vehicle theft and arson.

The map "Juvenile Criminals, 1992" under "Motor Vehicle Theft," notes that the highest percentage of juvenile arrests for motor vehicle theft was in Idaho at 77.4 percent, and in Utah at 72.5 percent. In general, the Northern states, from Washington across to Wisconsin, had the highest percentages. New York, Alabama and the District of Columbia showed the lowest percentages.

The Northern High Plains, the Rocky Mountain states and the Northern Midwest define a region where juveniles account for three-quarters of arson arrests. In North Dakota alone, 88.2 percent of all arson arrests are of juveniles. The Southern states have low percentages, running between 25 and 40 percent of all arson arrests.

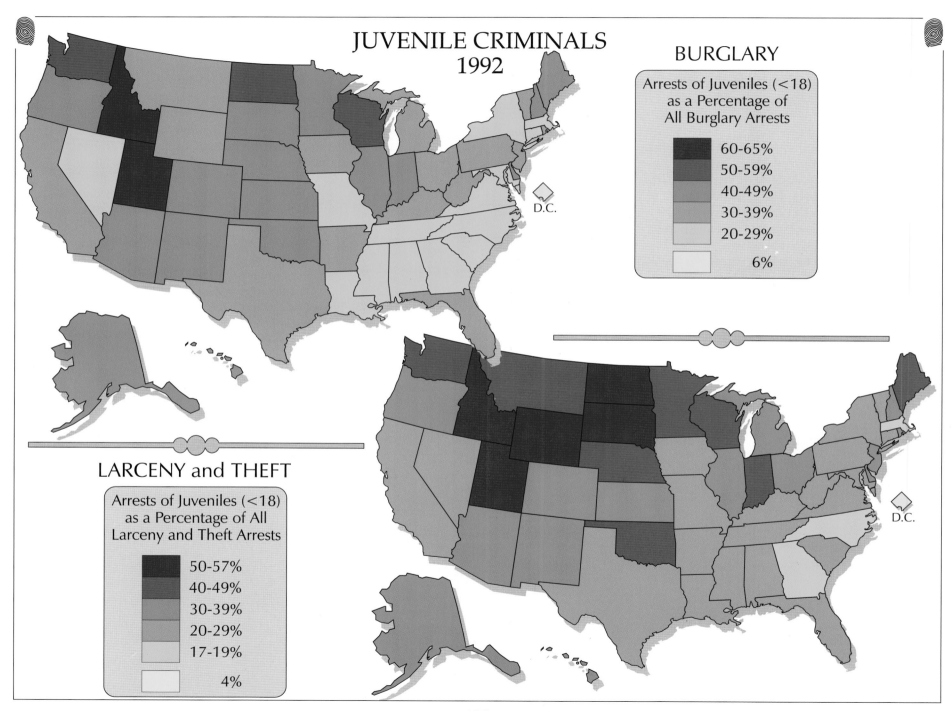

JUVENILE CRIMINALS
1992

BURGLARY

Arrests of Juveniles (<18)
as a Percentage of
All Burglary Arrests

60-65%
50-59%
40-49%
30-39%
20-29%
6%

D.C.

LARCENY and THEFT

Arrests of Juveniles (<18)
as a Percentage of All
Larceny and Theft Arrests

50-57%
40-49%
30-39%
20-29%
17-19%
4%

D.C.

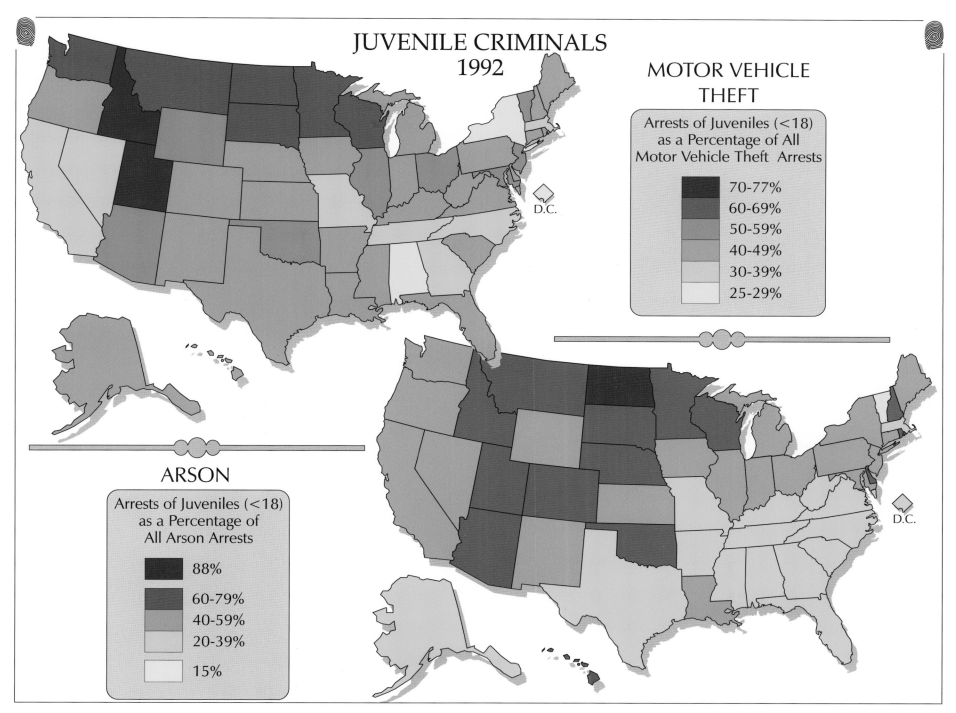

JUVENILE CRIMINALS
1992

MOTOR VEHICLE THEFT

Arrests of Juveniles (<18) as a Percentage of All Motor Vehicle Theft Arrests

- 70-77%
- 60-69%
- 50-59%
- 40-49%
- 30-39%
- 25-29%

D.C.

ARSON

Arrests of Juveniles (<18) as a Percentage of All Arson Arrests

- 88%
- 60-79%
- 40-59%
- 20-39%
- 15%

D.C.

JUSTICE SYSTEM

"We the people of the United States, in Order to form a more perfect Union, establish Justice, insure domestic Tranquillity, provide for the common defense, promote the general Welfare, and secure the Blessing of Liberty to ourselves and our Posterity, do ordain and establish this Constitution for the United States of America."

—Preamble, Constitution of the United
States of America

The drafters of the Constitution of the United States so valued living in a just society that they referred to the establishment of justice in the preamble of that great document. In order to establish this justice in the young United States, they said in Article III, Section 1 of the Constitution, "The judicial Power of the United States, shall be vested in one supreme Court, and in such inferior Courts as the Congress may from time to time ordain and establish." This judicial power was given a status equal to that of the executive and legislative branches of government.

The federal judicial branch includes the Supreme Court of the U.S.; the U.S. courts of appeals; the U.S. district courts; the Court of International Trade; the U.S. bankruptcy courts; any court created pursuant to Article I of the U.S. Constitution, including the Court of Military Appeals, the U.S. Court of Veterans Appeals, the U.S. Court of Federal Claims, and the U.S. Tax Court, but not including a court of a territory or possession of the U.S.; the Federal Judicial Center; and any other agency, office, or entity in the judicial branch.[1]

STRUCTURE AND ORGANIZATION

The government of the United States includes both the three federal branches and state government. The United States has 51 separate judicial systems, one for the federal government and one for each of the 50 states. Over the years this system of courts has developed into a four-tiered system of justice, as illustrated in the chart "Current Structure of the Federal Courts." The top two levels of courts deal mainly with cases that are being appealed and have previously been heard in a court on one of the lower levels. A case may proceed through this system, beginning in a trial court of either general or limited jurisdiction. If the judgment at the trial level is unsatisfactory, the decision can be reviewed in a court of appeal. Finally, if the decision is still not favorable to the parties involved, the case may be reviewed by either a state supreme court or, in certain circumstances, the Supreme Court of the United States. Other classifications of courts include civil and criminal courts, trial and appellate courts, and courts of general and limited jurisdiction.

Whether a case is heard in a federal or a state court depends on the nature of the case. More and more, legal battles in the United States occur in state courts. Judith S. Kaye, Chief Justice of New York State, notes that from 1985 to 1992 criminal cases increased 22 percent in the federal courts, but at nearly twice that rate in the state courts. States handle more than 97 percent of all litigation, including criminal, housing and family-related cases. These are the types of cases that tend to affect people most directly. In fact, state courts handle most criminal cases, divorces, land dealings, the probate of estates and other ordinary types of legal disputes. These state courts are subject to the limitations of state law, their own state constitutions and the Constitution of the United States.

Federal courts, however, are limited by the Constitution as to the types of cases they may hear. These cases generally include those in which the government of the United States or one of its officers is either suing or being sued; cases for which state courts are for some reason inappropriate; cases

CURRENT STRUCTURE OF THE FEDERAL COURTS

U. S. Supreme Court

13 Courts of Appeals (Circuit Courts)

94 District Courts Specialized Courts (Limited or General Jurisdiction)
{including: Tax Court, Court of Federal Claims, Court of Veteran Appeals, Court of International Trade}

involving interstate commerce; cases involving other nations' representatives or citizens; and finally cases involving the Constitution as a law, federal laws, treaties and laws relating to navigable waters.

Supreme Court of the United States

The highest court in the land is the Supreme Court of the United States, created as directed by the Constitution and the Judiciary Act of 1789. It is comprised of nine justices appointed for life by the President with the consent of the U.S. Senate.

The U.S. Supreme Court mediates disputes between the states, and also between a state and the federal government. It hears appeals from other federal courts and from the highest state courts when a federal law or constitutional issue is at stake, thus ensuring uniformity on constitutional issues. In cases involving a question of state law, the individual state's supreme court is the ultimate authority, and in these cases it is not possible to appeal to the U.S. Supreme Court.

Courts of Appeals or Circuit Courts

The courts of appeals are usually referred to as circuit courts. Early in our nation's history, judges of the courts of appeals traveled to courts in a region in a particular order or "circuit." Today, the United States is divided into 13 judicial circuits comprised of from one to fifteen districts each. The first eleven circuits cover the 50 states and U.S. territories. The twelfth circuit is comprised solely of the District of Columbia. In addition, there is a Court of Appeals for the Federal Circuit (item 13 on the map "Federal Judicial Circuits & Districts") created in 1982 by the merging of the U.S. Court of Claims and the U.S. Court of Customs and Patent Appeals. It has nationwide jurisdiction over specific types of cases, hearing appeals from various federal courts, such as the U.S. Court of Veterans Appeals, the U.S. Court of International Trade and the Patent and Trademark Office. Appeals from federal trial (district) courts in each state must be taken to the federal court of appeals for that circuit. Circuits in the more sparsely populated western half of the country tend to contain fewer districts but cover a larger geographic area than do the eastern circuits.

The map "U.S. Circuit Courts—Division of Appeals 1992" illustrates the division of cases in each of the thirteen U.S. circuit courts. The map examines the percentage of six types of appeals heard in U.S. circuit courts and categorizes them as cases that had been commenced, terminated or were pending in 1992. In the district court maps that follow, the largest percentage of cases being heard at that time were generally civil appeals, with prisoner petitions and criminal appeals placing either second or third, depending on the district. The percentages shift a bit when examining cases terminated or pending, but overall, civil cases are still prevalent. The exception to civil cases being in the majority can be found in the Court of Appeals for the Federal Circuit, where administrative appeals outnumber all other types of appeals in all three categories.

The division between felony and misdemeanor cases is presented in the map "U.S. Circuit Courts—Division of Criminal and Civil Cases, 1992." Cases at the felony level represent the majority of cases that the circuit courts hear. Felony cases outnumber misdemeanors at a rate of approximately three to one. One would expect such a pattern to exist because misdemeanor cases are rarely serious enough to justify hearings at the circuit level. However, in the fourth, ninth and eleventh circuits, misdemeanor cases represent nearly 50 percent of the total cases that are commenced or terminated.

FEDERAL JUDICIAL CIRCUITS & DISTRICTS

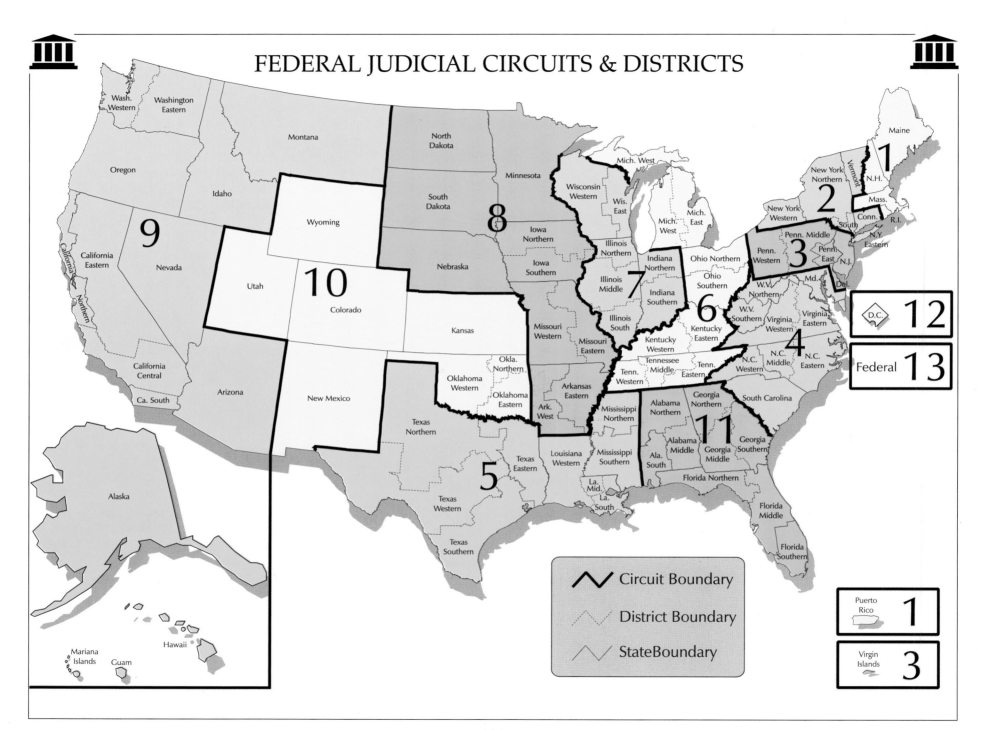

Circuit Boundary

District Boundary

StateBoundary

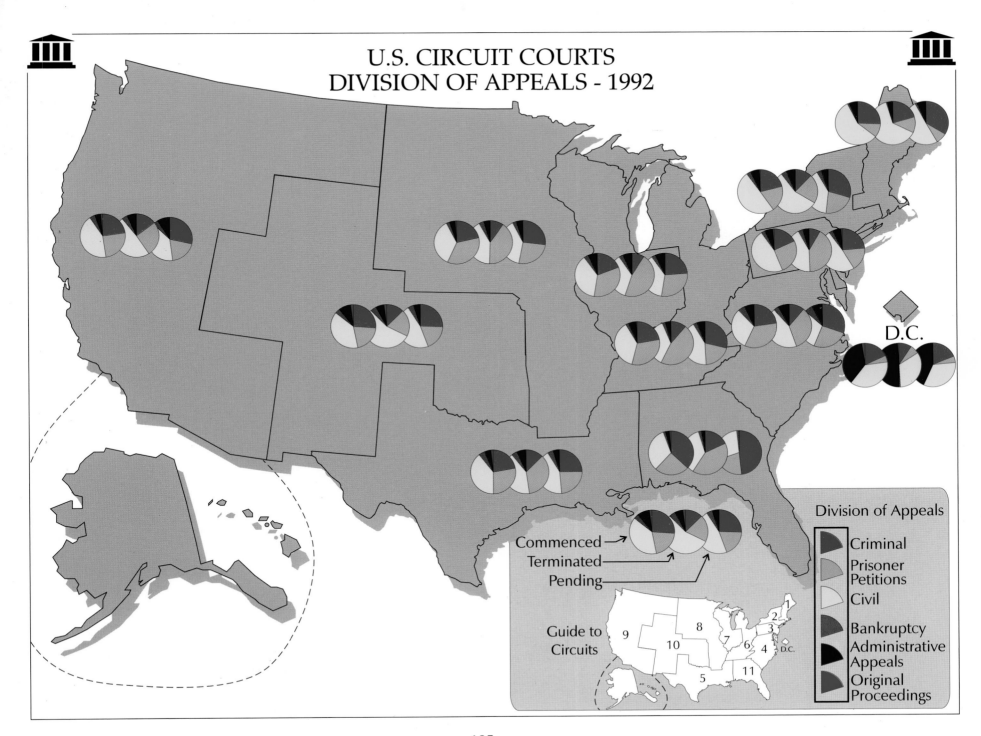

U.S. CIRCUIT COURTS
DIVISION OF APPEALS - 1992

D.C.

Commenced →
Terminated →
Pending →

Guide to Circuits

Division of Appeals

Criminal

Prisoner Petitions

Civil

Bankruptcy

Administrative Appeals

Original Proceedings

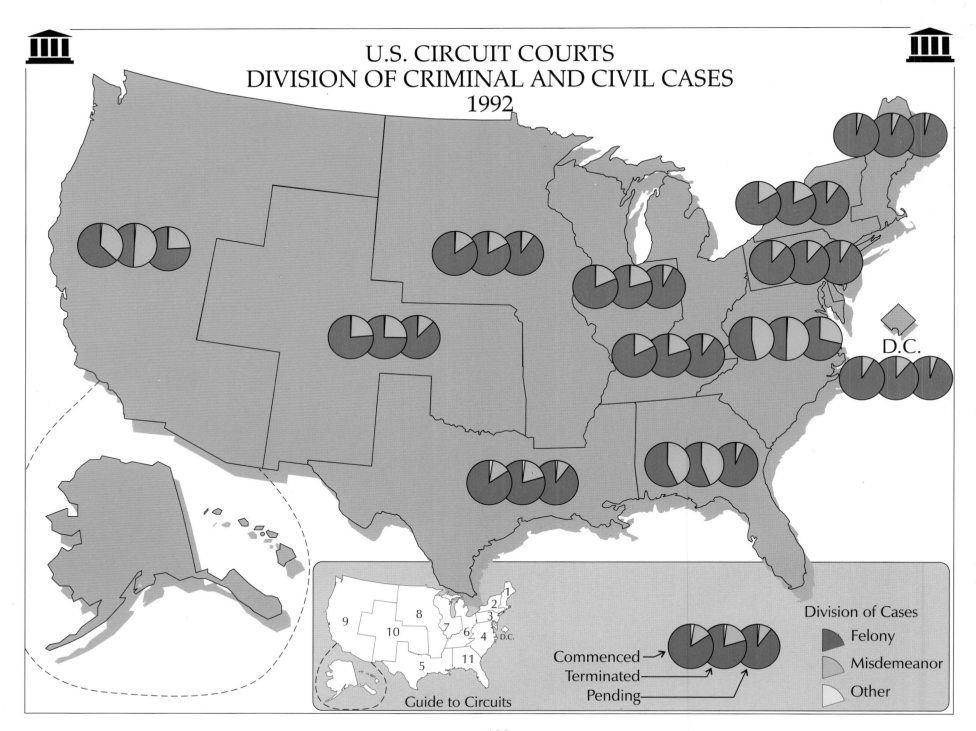

U.S. CIRCUIT COURTS
DIVISION OF CRIMINAL AND CIVIL CASES
1992

D.C.

Guide to Circuits

Commenced
Terminated
Pending

Division of Cases

Felony

Misdemeanor

Other

District Courts

—Courts Of General Jurisdiction

The district courts are the federal courts of general jurisdiction. These courts can hear almost any type of case, either civil or criminal. The map "Federal Judicial Circuits & Districts" shows how the United States and its territories are divided geographically into 94 U.S. district courts. While some of the more sparsely populated states, mostly in the West and Midwest are comprised of only a single district, more populous states have multiple districts.

—Courts of Limited Jurisdiction

The majority of court cases, either civil or criminal, in this country take place in the courts of limited jurisdiction, the lowest tier of the judicial system. Courts of limited jurisdiction specialize in one particular area of law and are the most common type of trial court. On the state level, traffic court is the most well-known of this type of court. Small claims court, family court, juvenile court, county court and the office of the Justice of the Peace are other familiar examples. Federal courts of limited jurisdiction include the Court of Claims of International Trade, the Court of Veteran Appeals, the Court of Federal Claims and Tax Court.

The majority of trials occur at the district court level, so the number and types of cases heard in these courts by state are depicted on the maps "U.S. District Courts, Total Civil Cases, 1992" and "U.S. District Courts, Total Criminal Cases 1992." When comparing the two maps, it is immediately apparent that in 1992 there were many more civil cases under way or pending than there were criminal cases. In all but a handful of districts, there were between 50 and 199 civil cases commenced or pending per district, compared with between one and 39 commenced or pending criminal cases per district. The Southern District of New York and the District of Columbia lead the nation in civil cases commenced, with 533 and 443 cases per 100,000 people, respectively. New York's Southern District takes the lead, however, in civil cases pending, at 741 per 100,000, while the District of Columbia is second with 522 cases per 100,000 people. Interestingly, the Northern District of New York, adjacent to the district with the greatest number of civil cases in the nation, has a rate of less than 50 per 100,000, about one-tenth of the rate of the Southern District. Seven other districts scattered throughout the country rank in the lowest group in both the number of civil cases commenced and in those pending.

LAWYERS

Apart from the judge, the most prominent persons in a courtroom are the lawyers. As an officer of the legal system, a lawyer is a representative of his client and functions as the client's advisor, advocate and negotiator.[2] Before advancing to his or her position as legal advocate, the lawyer has to be admitted to the bar in one of the fifty states. The admissions process is usually accomplished after completing a degree program at an accredited law school and passing a rigorous examination known as the bar exam. Upon being admitted to the bar, each lawyer takes an oath declaring his obligations to the court, state, and country as an officer of the court, registers with the court and receives a license to practice.

The law, over the past two decades, has been an increasingly popular profession. The map "Lawyers (1990)" illustrates the number of lawyers per 10,000 people, and the increase in the number of lawyers from 1980 to 1990.

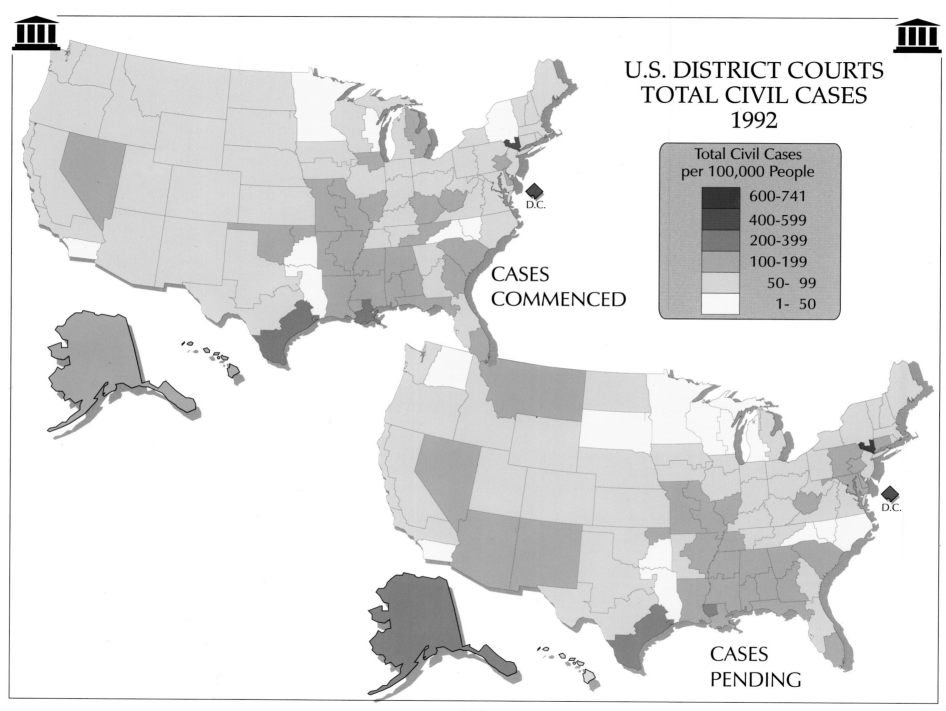

U.S. DISTRICT COURTS
TOTAL CIVIL CASES
1992

Total Civil Cases
per 100,000 People

	600-741
	400-599
	200-399
	100-199
	50- 99
	1- 50

CASES
COMMENCED

D.C.

CASES
PENDING

D.C.

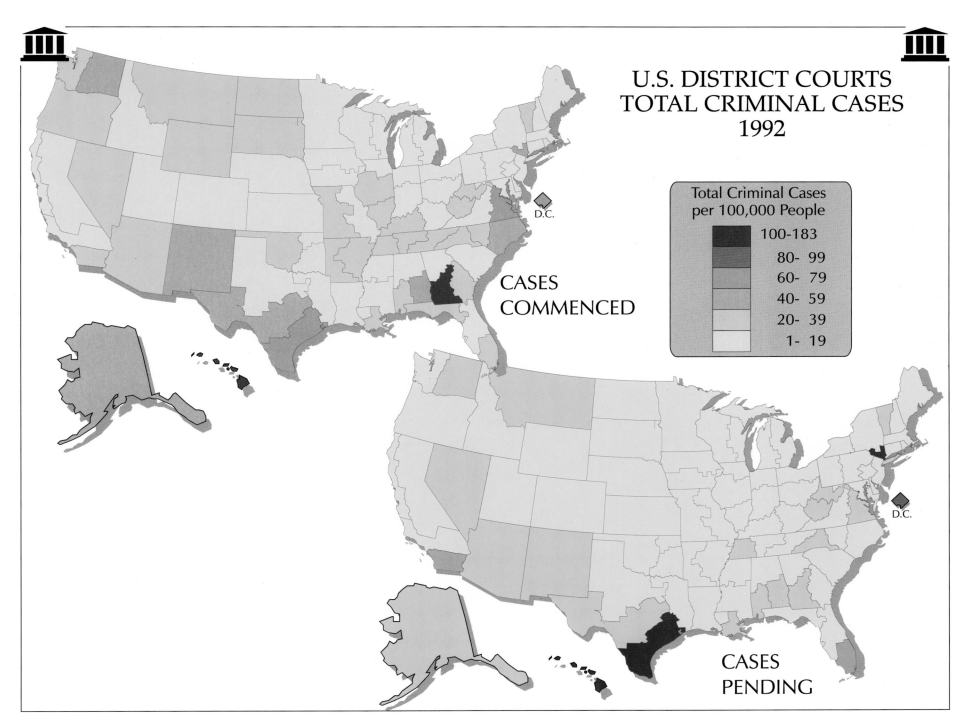

U.S. DISTRICT COURTS TOTAL CRIMINAL CASES 1992

CASES COMMENCED

CASES PENDING

Total Criminal Cases per 100,000 People

	100-183
	80- 99
	60- 79
	40- 59
	20- 39
	1- 19

D.C.

Nationwide there are an average of 29.8 lawyers per 10,000 people. At 196 lawyers per 10,000 people, the District of Columbia had by far the greatest concentration of lawyers, nearly 4 times higher than the highest states, New York and Virginia. Each of these states had 50 lawyers per 10,000 people in the state. Massachusetts and Connecticut, each with 42 and 41 lawyers per 10,000 people respectively, follow close behind. At the other end of the spectrum, North Carolina had the fewest lawyers per capita in the United States, with only 14.8 per 10,000. The South, along with the Dakotas, Indiana and West Virginia, had the lowest concentration of lawyers in the country.

Nationally, there was a 35 percent increase in the number of lawyers in the years between 1980 and 1990, with increases in all but two states and the District of Columbia. The map showing the increase in the number or lawyers from 1980 to 1990 reveals that Virginia and Maryland lead the nation in lawyers per capita, with their 138 and 125 percent increases. The District of Columbia shows a 53 percent decrease in the number of lawyers. Possible factors in this drop may be the saturation of lawyers in the market or a reflection of the current trend toward smaller government. Many of the states at the low end represent predominantly rural populations, where a market for the high salaries is not present.

Corresponding to the national increase in the number of lawyers is an increase in the number of minorities and women who have chosen the law as a profession. The maps "Racial Distribution of Lawyers" and "Women Lawyers" track the incidence of minorities and women in the legal profession. The first map shows the racial distribution of minority lawyers as simple pie charts, and also indicates the percentage of lawyers that are members of a minority with shading ranging from white to dark blue. In Hawaii, the majority of lawyers (51%) belong to a minority, Asians being overwhelmingly the largest group represented. Hawaii has by far the largest percentage of minority lawyers of any state. New Mexico places a distant second with minorities, largely Hispanic, accounting for only 17% of the total number of lawyers in the state. In the District of Columbia as well, 17% of all lawyers are members of a minority, in this case, largely African-American. In North Dakota, only about one-half of one percent of lawyers come from a minority—in this case entirely Native American, and in Maine there were no minorities at all represented in the ranks of lawyers in the state. In exactly half of the states, 4% or less of the lawyers are members of a minority. In general, minority lawyers are predominantly African-American in the Eastern half of the country and predominantly Hispanic in the Western half, with the notable exceptions of Washington and Oregon, where Asians take the lead. As expected, the distribution of minority lawyers in a state seems to coincide with the minority population of that state.

When it comes to the percentage of lawyers who are women, the map "Women Lawyers" shows that in every state, except Hawaii, women represent a greater percentage of each state's lawyers than do minorities. While minorities are better represented in the Western, Southwestern, Southern and Mid-Atlantic states, women lawyers tend be found in greater percentages in Alaska, the Southwest, New England and states around the District of Columbia. In the District of Columbia, 40% of the total number of lawyers are women. Women comprise 32% of the lawyers in Alaska and 31 and 30 percent, respectively, in Massachusetts and New Mexico. The District of Columbia and New Mexico have relatively high percentages of both women and minority lawyers, while several states, including Idaho, Montana, Wyoming, South Dakota, Iowa, West Virginia and Rhode Island, have very few members of minorities or women as members of the bar.

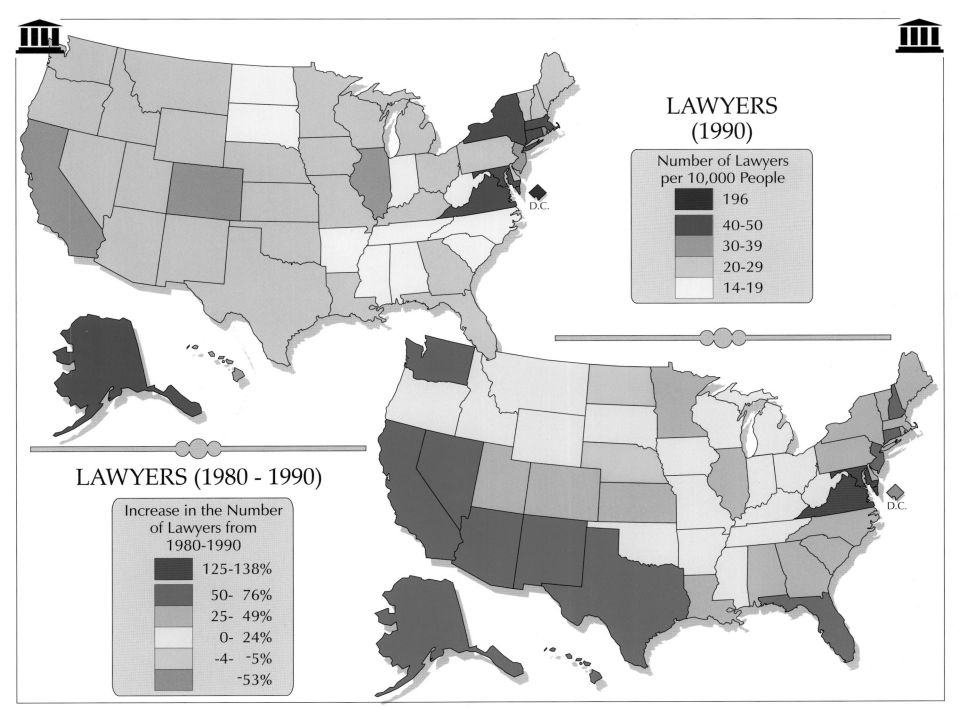

LAWYERS
(1990)

Number of Lawyers
per 10,000 People

196
40-50
30-39
20-29
14-19

LAWYERS (1980 - 1990)

Increase in the Number
of Lawyers from
1980-1990

125-138%
50- 76%
25- 49%
0- 24%
-4- -5%
-53%

D.C.

RACIAL DISTRIBUTION OF LAWYERS

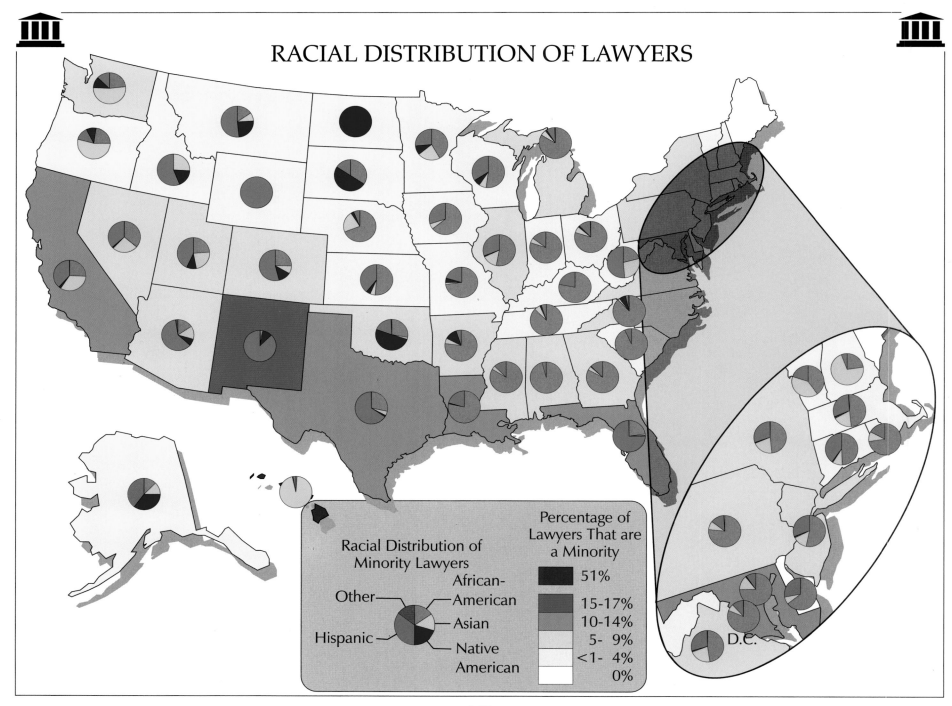

Racial Distribution of
Minority Lawyers

Other

Hispanic

African-
American

Asian

Native
American

Percentage of
Lawyers That are
a Minority

51%

15-17%

10-14%

5- 9%

<1- 4%

0%

D.C.

WOMEN LAWYERS

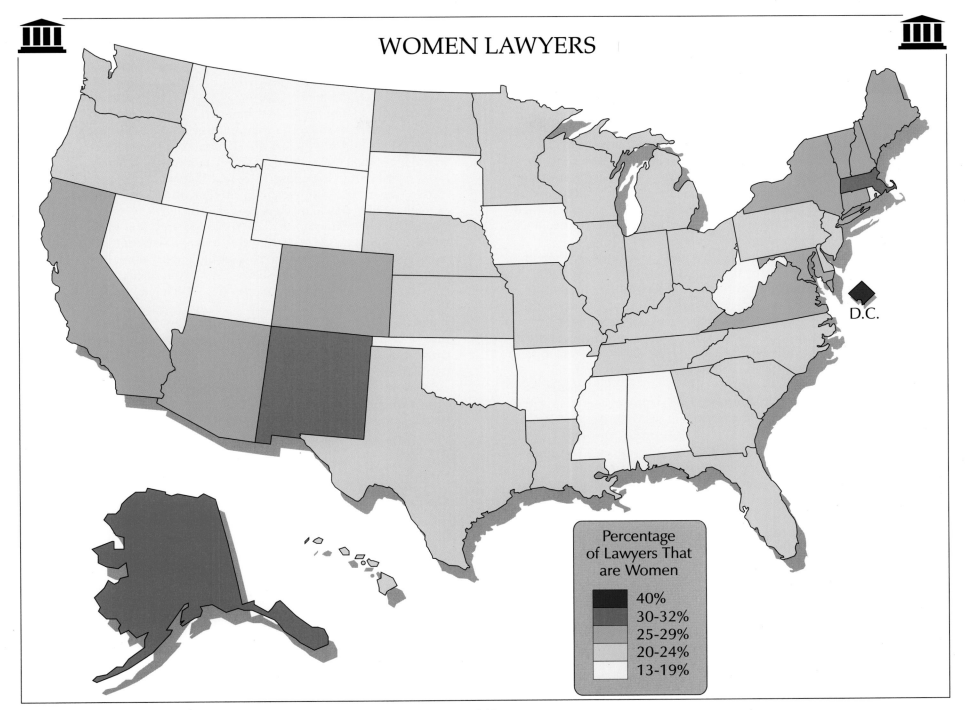

D.C.

Percentage
of Lawyers That
are Women

40%
30-32%
25-29%
20-24%
13-19%

JUDGES

In the United States, judges are public officials who have the authority to administer the law in the nation's courts. Judges apply national, state or district laws to the cases that they preside over, and when there is no jury, judges can decide the outcome of a trial. Judges at the state level need not be lawyers. Those that are not usually preside over municipal courts. State judges serve specific terms and are either appointed by state officers, or are elected.

Federal judges who preside over courts other than the four territorial courts, the U.S. Bankruptcy Courts, the U.S. Court of Military Appeals, the U.S. Court of Federal Claims and the U.S. Tax Court, are appointed to lifetime terms. Federal judges, who must be lawyers, are nominated by the president and approved by the Senate. According to the Constitution, federal judges may be removed from office against their will only through "impeachment for, and conviction of, treason, bribery, or other high crimes and misdemeanors." In addition, neither the executive nor the legislative branches of government can reduce the salary of a federal judge.

The map "Racial Distribution of Judges" tracks the percentage of judges who are members of minorities. The map shows the racial distribution of minority judges as simple pie charts and also indicates the percentage of judges who are from minorities, with shading ranging from white to dark blue. The overall pattern of the percentage of minority judges follows that of minority lawyers, but the racial breakdowns are different. As with minority lawyers, Hawaii has by far the largest percentage of minority judges, all Asian. The District of Columbia and the state of New Mexico have the second and third highest percentage of minority lawyers. In the District of Columbia, the minority judges are exclusively African-American, while in New Mexico they are largely Hispanic.

Minority judges in the eastern half of the nation tend to be African-American, with the exception of New Hampshire, where all the minority judges are Hispanic, and New Jersey, where more than 60% are Hispanic. The minority judges in the western half of the country are more often Hispanic and Native American than other minorities, with the exception of Idaho, which has more Asian judges.

Interestingly, while South Dakota ranked very low in the nation in the percentage of minority lawyers, with only 4% being members of a minority, 27% of the judges come from a minority, in this case exclusively Native American.

There are some surprises in the map "Women Judges." Women represent more that 40% of the judges in three states—Alaska and New Mexico with 49% and South Dakota with 40%. While Alaska and New Mexico have a correlating high percentage of women lawyers, South Dakota has relatively few women practicing law in the state.

Delaware, Hawaii and Montana have the smallest percentages of women judges, with fewer than 9%. These states also have a correspondingly low percentage of women lawyers.

SUPREME COURT JUSTICES

The Supreme Court has two basic functions: to interpret and expound all congressional enactments brought before it, and to examine federal and state statutes and executive actions to see if they conform to the United States Constitution. Its decisions are intended to guide legislation, execute authority and mold the development of the law.

The Supreme Court of the United States began in 1789 per Constitutional mandate. This first court began with six members, and in 1807 increased to seven. In 1837, the court

RACIAL DISTRIBUTION OF JUDGES

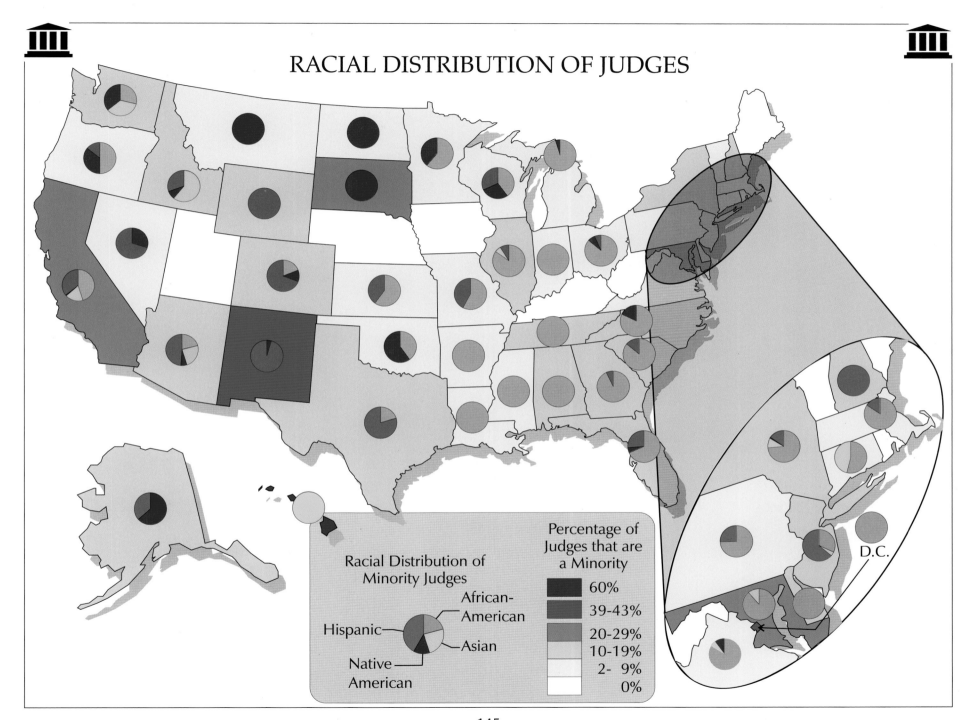

Racial Distribution of Minority Judges

African-American

Asian

Hispanic

Native American

Percentage of Judges that are a Minority

60%

39-43%

20-29%

10-19%

2- 9%

0%

D.C.

WOMEN JUDGES

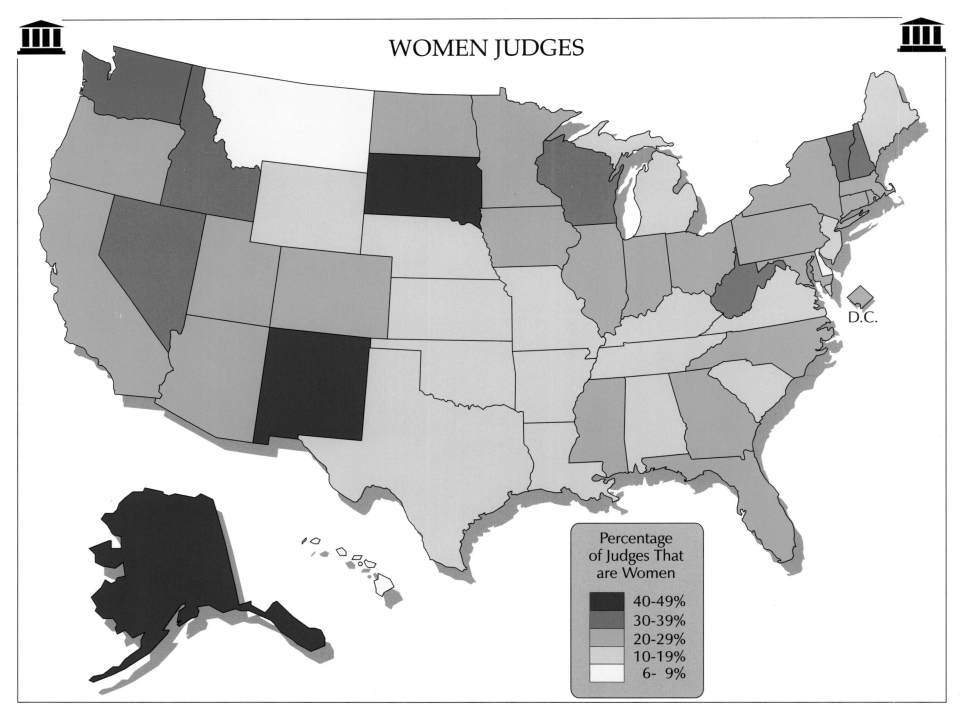

Percentage
of Judges That
are Women

40-49%
30-39%
20-29%
10-19%
6- 9%

D.C.

was increased again to nine members, and to ten in 1863. In 1866, the court was reduced to eight members in order to prevent President Andrew Johnson from filling any vacancies. Since 1869 there have been nine members.

The pattern of states from which Supreme Court justices have been appointed roughly follows the pattern of settlement in the United States. As illustrated in the map "Supreme Court Justices (State Appointed from)" the majority of justices have been from the Eastern states, along with clusters in California and Arizona. There have been no Supreme Court justices from the Pacific Northwest or the Northern High Plains states.

Traveling back in time, we find that, before 1861, there were no Supreme Court justices from west of the Mississippi. During the next half-century there were seven from five predominantly Western states, Wyoming, California, Kansas, Louisiana, and Iowa. Utah, Iowa and Minnesota contributed three justices during the next 30 years.

From 1947 to 1972, there were five justices from west of the Mississippi, and today there are four. Wisconsin, Florida, Delaware, Vermont, and West Virginia are the only states east of the Mississippi not to contribute a Supreme Court justice. Eleven states west of the Mississippi, plus Alaska and Hawaii, have not yet seen a Supreme Court justice appointed from them. Among the justices who are presently serving, there is one from California and two from Arizona, one each from Minnesota, Illinois and New Hampshire, two from Virginia and one from the District of Columbia.

LAWSUIT AWARDS

To close this section, we present a graph that shows the median dollar amount awarded for various types of trial cases. Although there has been recent press over the trend of ever-increasing awards, they generally fall into a few types of trial cases—libel, medical malpractice and product liability. Of added interest is the percentage of the outcome verdicts in each of the categories. Note that a higher median award does not necessarily favor either the plaintiff or the defendant. Malpractice and liability cases favor the defendant, while the more difficult cases of libel, fraud and personal injury favor the plaintiff.

SUPREME COURT JUSTICES
(State Appointed From)

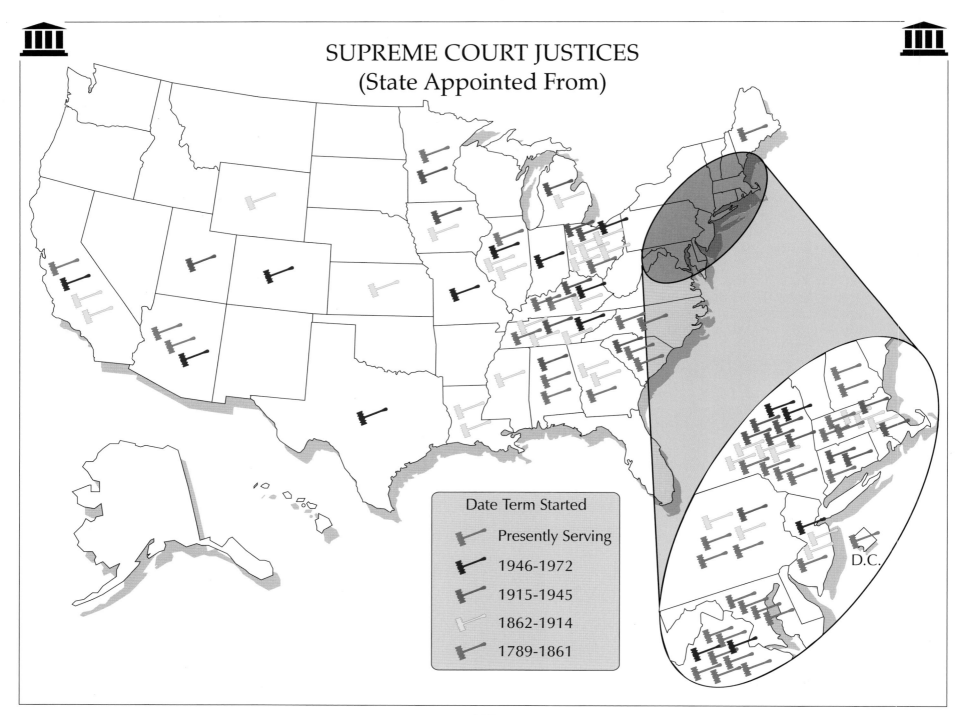

Date Term Started

Presently Serving

1946-1972

1915-1945

1862-1914

1789-1861

D.C.

LAWSUIT AWARDS
1992

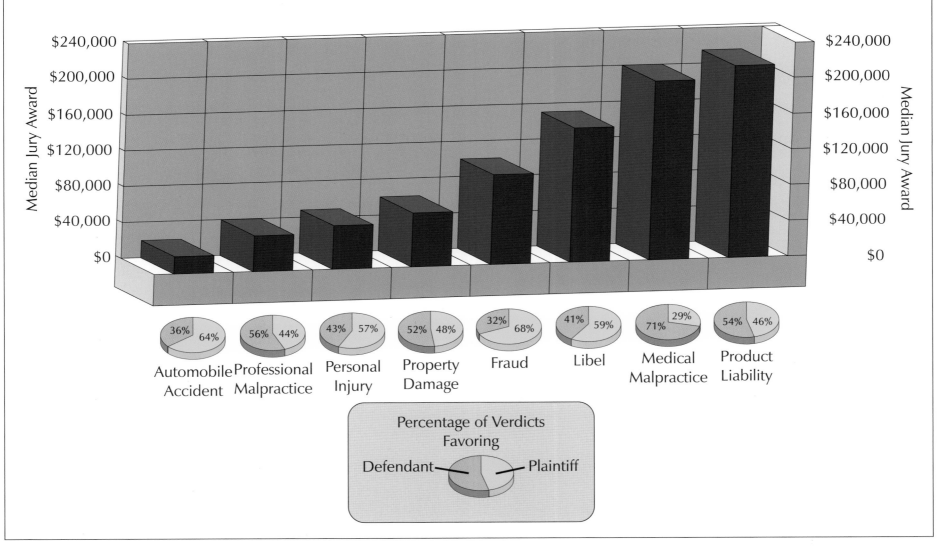

Median Jury Award

$240,000	
$200,000	
$160,000	
$120,000	
$80,000	
$40,000	
$0	

Median Jury Award

$240,000
$200,000
$160,000
$120,000
$80,000
$40,000
$0

36% / 64% — Automobile Accident

56% / 44% — Professional Malpractice

43% / 57% — Personal Injury

52% / 48% — Property Damage

32% / 68% — Fraud

41% / 59% — Libel

71% / 29% — Medical Malpractice

54% / 46% — Product Liability

Percentage of Verdicts Favoring

Defendant —— Plaintiff

 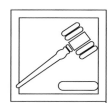

CORRECTIONS

Crime in the United States has ramifications far beyond its effect on victims. The maps in this section examine the results of crime in the United States, the law enforcement personnel necessary to control crime and the prison system that holds the criminals. They also consider just who the criminals are in terms of gender, race and age.

What happens to the prisoners within the prison system is perhaps one of the most important determinants in terms of recidivism. While some states have programs in place to educate their prison inmates, other states do little to improve the minds of their inmate population.

Parole is a method of reducing the prison population and allowing prisoners to return to society before they have served their full terms. The various states have different requirements for parole and different regulations as to what constitutes breaking parole and warrants a return to prison.

LAW ENFORCEMENT PERSONNEL

Since demographic and jurisdictional situations change from one location to another, it is difficult to assess the needs of any community for law enforcement personnel or to understand the impact of such personnel on the community. For example, if a community has a variable seasonal population, its law enforcement needs will be quite different from those of another, more stable community.

Where a community is located geographically also contributes to its law enforcement needs. A small town, located between two large cities, will need a larger police force than one located away from any sizable urban area, even if both towns have comparable populations.

Throughout the United States, the duties of law enforcement personnel vary from one location to the next. In some places sheriffs are responsible only for civic functions and administering the county jail facilities. In the same way, the responsibilities of state police and highway patrol agencies vary in different locales. Therefore, any one particular number of law enforcement personnel does not tell us anything about the total impact of law enforcement.

Nevertheless, the ratio of police officers as a percentage of the population, as shown on the map "Police Officers, 1991," serves as one indication of strict law enforcement, since the number of police is almost always proportional to the

POLICE OFFICERS
1991

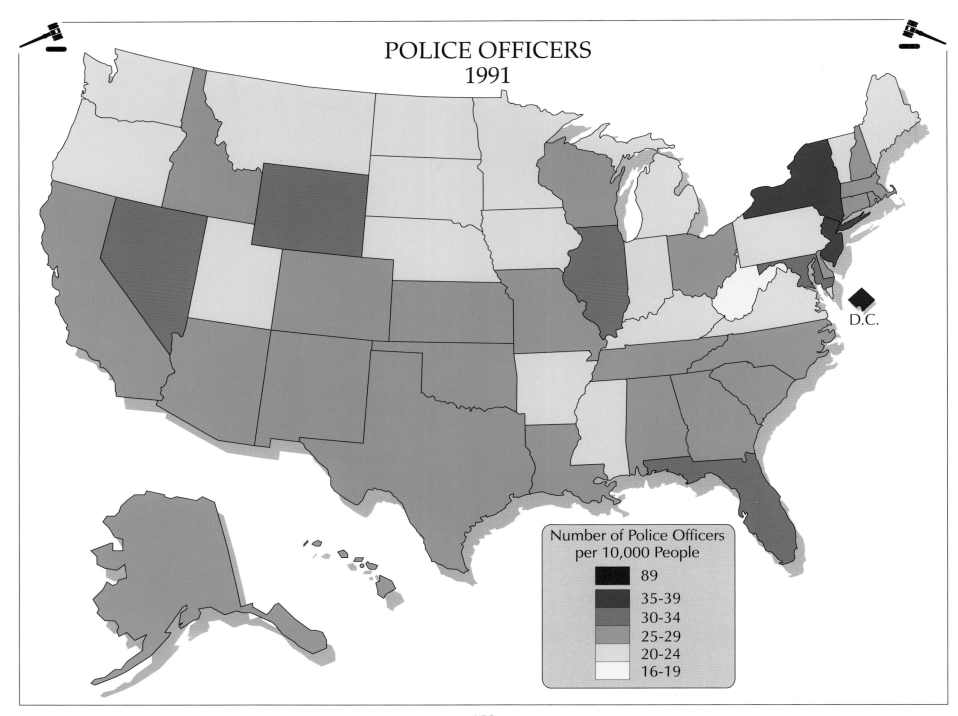

D.C.

**Number of Police Officers
per 10,000 People**

89
35-39
30-34
25-29
20-24
16-19

number of law enforcement personnel in any state.

The highest ratio of police officers to population in the country is to be found not in a state, but in the District of Columbia, where there are 89 officers for every 10,000 people. At first, the District of Columbia would seem to be the crime capital of the United States; however, it should be noted that the District of Columbia is composed entirely of an urban population. Violent crime rates are typically lower in rural than in urban areas. Therefore, when considering the overall crime rate of an entire state, the rate is lowered due to the influence of rural areas. Since the District of Columbia is entirely urban, the crime rate is correspondingly higher. Therefore, the rate in the District of Columbia cannot really be compared to the rate of any state.

The state with the highest number of police officers is New Jersey, with 39.4 officers for every 10,000 people. New York is a close second, with 37.1. In general, the South, along with southern New England, exhibits overall higher numbers of police officers per capita than Northern and Western states.

PAYING FOR ENFORCEMENT

In our current political climate, there is demand for crime control. Usually this demand has been interpreted as being "tough" on criminals, and promotes spending on law enforcement by increasing the police force and building more jails.

West Virginia spends the least on law enforcement—$90 per resident. However, the map "Law Enforcement Expenditures" shows that the amount spent on law enforcement does not always correspond to the rate of crimes committed in a state.

Later maps on the rates of murder, robbery and assault, however, show that those states that spend the least on enforcement are often the states lowest in these crimes. West Virginia spends the least and also has the lowest rates of murder, robbery and assault. Alaska spends the most and has one of the lowest robbery rates, but one of the highest rates of aggravated assault.

Like West Virginia, North Dakota also spends little on law enforcement and has a very low rate of crime. In states like New York and California, where there are high expenditures for law enforcement, there are also high crime rates. A countervailing argument could be that a lot is spent in these states just because there is so much crime, or that little is spent in other states because there is little crime there. Keep in mind that both California and New York have very large metropolitan areas that are not present in predominantly rural North Dakota and West Virginia.

Alaska is by far the heaviest spender, as the map "Law Enforcement Expenditures" shows. Alaska also pays the highest salaries to judges, probably because of the higher cost of living in Alaska.

HOW STATES PUNISH

It is generally thought that the way to reduce crime is to put criminals in jail. Yet a comparison of the two maps, "Punitiveness of States" and "Inmates in Local Jails, 1988" shows that there is not always a correlation between a state's punitiveness and the number of incarcerations. The ranking of punitiveness is achieved by dividing the imprisonment rate by the arrest rate. The percentages resulting from this method range from a low ranking of 1.3 to 2.4 percent, in states such as Minnesota, North Dakota and Washington, to a high of 5.3 to 10 percent in states such as Alaska, Louisiana and Alabama.

Among the most punitive are states in the Southeast, while

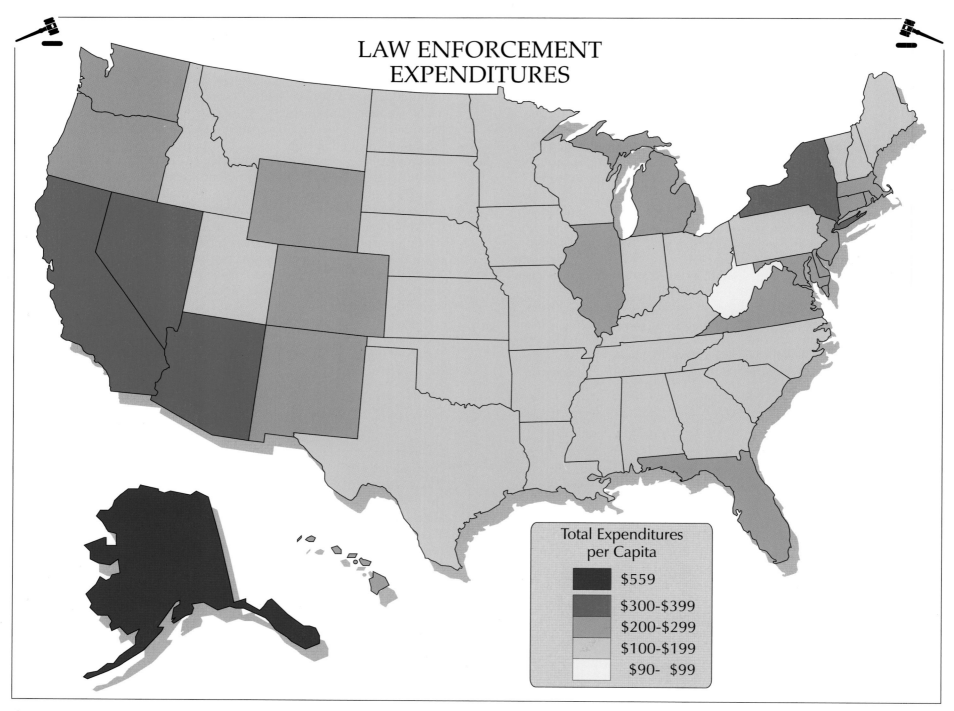

LAW ENFORCEMENT EXPENDITURES

Total Expenditures per Capita

- $559
- $300-$399
- $200-$299
- $100-$199
- $90- $99

PUNITIVENESS OF STATES

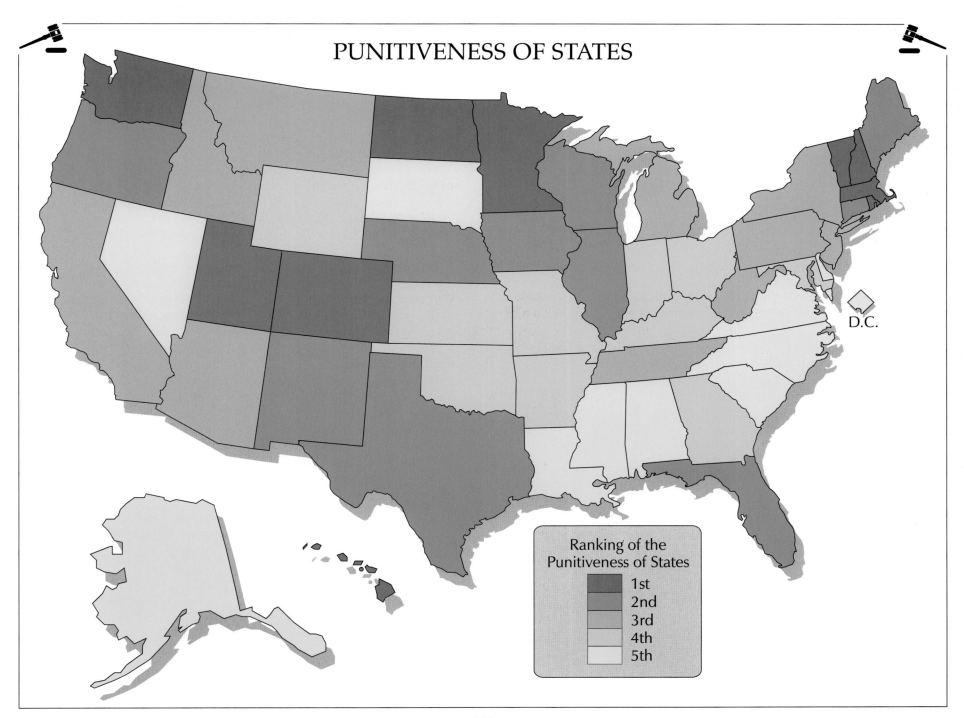

D.C.

Ranking of the
Punitiveness of States

- 1st
- 2nd
- 3rd
- 4th
- 5th

the least punitive tend to be in the North and Northeast. One explanation for the increased rate in the Southeast is offered by Alida V. Merlo and Joycelyn M. Pollack, in their book *Women, Law and Social Control*. It is often claimed, according to the authors, that "there may exist a conservative 'Southern Mentality' that breeds an ideology more favorable to punishment and harsh criminal sanctions."[1]

JAILS

For the United States as a whole, jails (where people are kept before trial and for short sentences, as opposed to prisons, which are used for longer term incarcerations) held about 400,000 inmates in 1988. An additional 2.5 million were on probation, with another 400,000 on parole. The map "Inmates in Local Jails, 1988" gives some idea of the problem. In early 1994, the prison population for the United States topped one million for the first time.

In general, the states in the South had the greatest jail inmate population, as did the West and East coasts. The states with the lowest number of inmates in local jails are North Dakota, with 43 per 100,000, and Iowa, with 37.

WHAT IT COSTS

With the current public demand to lock up criminals to get them off the streets, it would be well to pause and consider what individual states spend to do just that. The maps "Local Jail Expenditures, 1988" give an idea.

The first of the two maps, "Expenditures Per Capita," represents the amount each state spends per inhabitant (in the form of taxes) to house its local jail inmates. Not surprisingly, the overall pattern is similar to the distribution of the local jail inmate population. The second map, "Expenditures per Inmate," presents expenditures as a rate per inmate. In an ideal situation, there would be a match between the per capita expenditure and inmate expenditure. However, this is not always the case.

The two states with the highest per capita expenditure, New York and Wyoming, also spend the most on each inmate. Texas, which has a heavy per capita expenditure, is one of the states that spends the least on its prisoners. The same is true for Georgia, Tennessee and the District of Columbia.

Outside of New York and Wyoming, the four states that spend most heavily on each prisoner are Iowa, North Dakota, Maine and Oregon. It is important, however, to note that per capita spending depends on the population of the state. Wyoming, with a population below a million, spends almost as much per prisoner as New York, with a population well over 15 million.

When comparing the map "Prisons, 1994" to "Inmates in Local Jails, 1988," it is well to bear in mind that Wyoming has only two state prisons, while New York has 51. This differential tends to even up differences in expenditure. In 1988, it cost each citizen in New York State $48.61 to maintain the prison population that year. In Wyoming, it cost each resident $41.05. New York State spent $33,643 dollars on each prisoner, while Wyoming spent $41,768.

Nevada, while being among the highest in per capita expenditures, did not rank among the highest states for expenditure per individual inmate—$15,811. Likewise, the District of Columbia had a per capita expenditure of $22.37, but spent only $8,336 per prisoner. Mississippi spent the least per prisoner, $6,041, and was also among those states that had the lowest per capita expenditure, $8.19. West Virginia had the smallest per capita expenditure, $6.67, and one of the lowest expenditures per inmate, $8,766.

INMATES IN LOCAL JAILS
1988

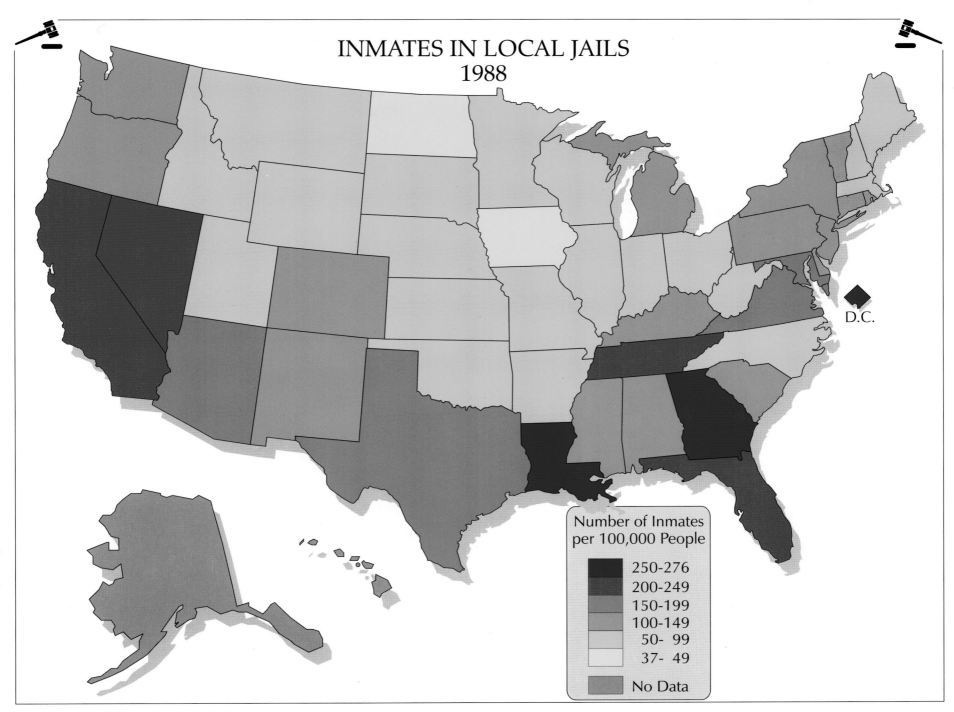

D.C.

Number of Inmates
per 100,000 People

250-276
200-249
150-199
100-149
50- 99
37- 49

No Data

LOCAL JAIL EXPENDITURES
1988

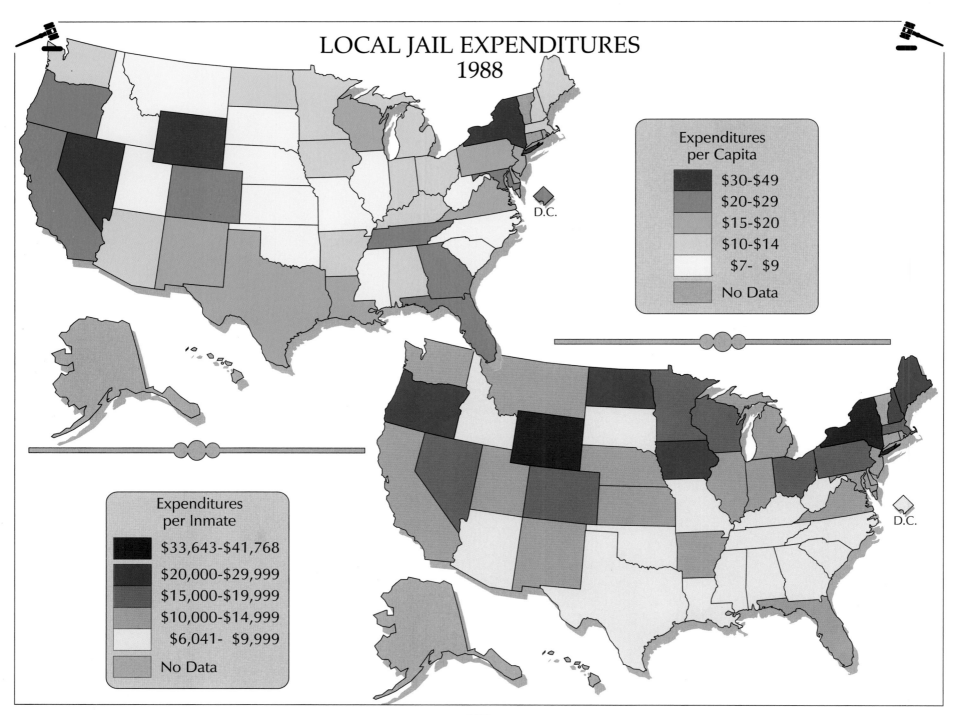

Expenditures per Capita

- $30-$49
- $20-$29
- $15-$20
- $10-$14
- $7- $9
- No Data

Expenditures per Inmate

- $33,643-$41,768
- $20,000-$29,999
- $15,000-$19,999
- $10,000-$14,999
- $6,041- $9,999
- No Data

D.C.

PRISONS

There is a weak correlation between the number of prisons in any state and the number of crimes committed in that state. This correlation holds even if the crime rate of a state is assumed to be a combination of the rates of aggravated assault, robbery and murder (see maps entitled "Aggravated Assault," "Robbery" and "Murder Rate").

Comparing the crime rates with the number of prisons shows that North Carolina, with almost twice as many prisons as any other state, has only a moderate crime rate. This finding would indicate that a large portion of North Carolinian prisoners are brought in from out of state. New York, with half the number of prisons of North Carolina, has one of the highest crime rates. A breakdown of the number of prisons for adult offenders and correctional facilities for juveniles is shown in the map "Prisons, 1994."

North Carolina, with 94 prisons for adults leads the nation. Michigan with 51 and Florida with 41 come next. Wyoming, Montana and North Dakota have the least number of prisons, two each. South Dakota, Mississippi and New Hampshire have three prisons and West Virginia has four. The crime rates for these states, except for aggravated assault, correlate with the number of prisons. In general, while the number of prisons seems highest in the North Central, Northeast and Mid-Atlantic states, crime rates are highest in the Southwest and Deep South.

Juvenile correctional facilities follow a similar pattern, with states in North Central and Mid-Atlantic states having a greater number of facilities. None of the four states with the greatest number of juvenile correctional facilities (Michigan, New York, Massachusetts and Ohio) has a high arrest rate for juveniles. The highest rates are in the Northern High Plains states, Idaho, Utah, Oregon, North Dakota, Minnesota and Wisconsin. The lowest juvenile arrest rates cluster in the Deep South, where juvenile correctional facilities are fewer.

PRISONERS

There has been a dramatic increase in the number of prisoners in the United States from 1980 to 1994, as the chart "Prison Population through Time" shows. In the span of only 14 years, the prison population has quintupled. By 1994, the number of people incarcerated topped one million, the largest for any industrialized nation. This exponential growth, along with the current atmosphere of "getting tough on crime," seems to guarantee that the increase will continue.

The map "Increase in Prison Population, 1980–1990" gives us a breakdown of this fivefold increase in prison population. Surprisingly, New Hampshire, a state with rates for aggravated assault, robbery and murder that are among the lowest in the country, has the highest percentage increase in prison population at 312 percent.

California follows with 296 percent growth, a more logical increase, since its crime rates are among the highest in the nation. The Northeast shows a sharp increase of over 100 percent, as do the West and some of the Rocky Mountain States. The three states with the smallest increases, less than 50 percent, are North Carolina, Tennessee and West Virginia. While 15 states had increases of less than 100 percent, the majority of the states more than doubled their prison populations.

The increases in prison population do not match the number of prisons. New Hampshire, for example, had the highest percentage increase in prison population, yet was one of the states with the least number of prisons. North Carolina, with its small increase of prisoners, had the most prisons, 94.

The map "Prisoners, 1994" gives an idea of the distribution of prisoners who were sentenced to more than one year. For the United States as a whole, there is an average of 373 prisoners for every 100,000 people. The District of Columbia has the greatest number of prisoners—1,578 for every 100,000 people, nearly triple the rate for the second highest state, Texas, with a rate of 545 prisoners per 100,000 people.

North Dakota has the smallest rate, 75 for every 100,000 inhabitants, while Texas, Oklahoma, Louisiana, and South Carolina have the greatest number of prisoners—all have over 500 prisoners for every 100,000 people. Generally, the Southern states have more people incarcerated than the Northern states, with the exception of Michigan.

A MATTER OF RACE

A look at the racial breakdown of the prison population provides some interesting facts. The map "Prison Population, Racial Breakdown, 1993" shows that in four of the major regions of the United States, the North Central, the Deep South, the Mid-Atlantic and the Northeast, the proportion of African Americans in prison is very high. Only three states within these four regions, Kentucky, West Virginia and Indiana, indicate more whites in prison than African Americans.

This proportion might cause one to link crime with African-Americans. The perceived link was the reason that the Willie Horton incident, used by George Bush's campaign in 1988, was so successful against the Democratic candidate, Michael Dukakis. Horton was serving a sentence for murder in a Massachusetts prison. On a weekend furlough in 1986, he escaped, raped a white woman and stabbed her fiancee. Using the prison furlough system in Massachusetts as an issue, the Willie Horton story, according to the *New York*

Times in 1988 "was highly effective in damaging Mr. Dukakis's image."[2]

The Horton story shows, not only how important crime is as a political issue, but also how easily racial stereotypes are linked to crime. If Horton had been white, the campaign would not have been half as effective, if at all.

The map may show a biased criminal justice system where African-American men, once convicted, face a one-in-five chance of serving a sentence in an adult state prison, according to the United States Bureau of Justice statistics in 1985. Statistics on race in the United States are further distorted by the "one drop" rule. It holds that even the smallest amount of African-American blood defines a person as African American.

The classification "other" in the map is defined as people who do not consider themselves to be in any of the other racial categories listed. Natives of India are an example. They are not listed as Asian, but fall into the category "other."

WOMEN IN PRISON

Prisons in the 1800s were terrible places for both men and women, but worse for women. Originally, prisons were built for men without any facilities for women. In addition to the abysmal physical conditions, women prisoners were frequently abused sexually by both guards and male prisoners.

It was only after 1873 that separate facilities for women, staffed by women, were built. The prisons were built, in part, because of the action of women involved in the temperance and abolition movements. There was some improvement in the condition of imprisoned women, but unequal treatment still remained. Even today sexual inequality persists among prisoners. Most states find it too

PRISONS
1994

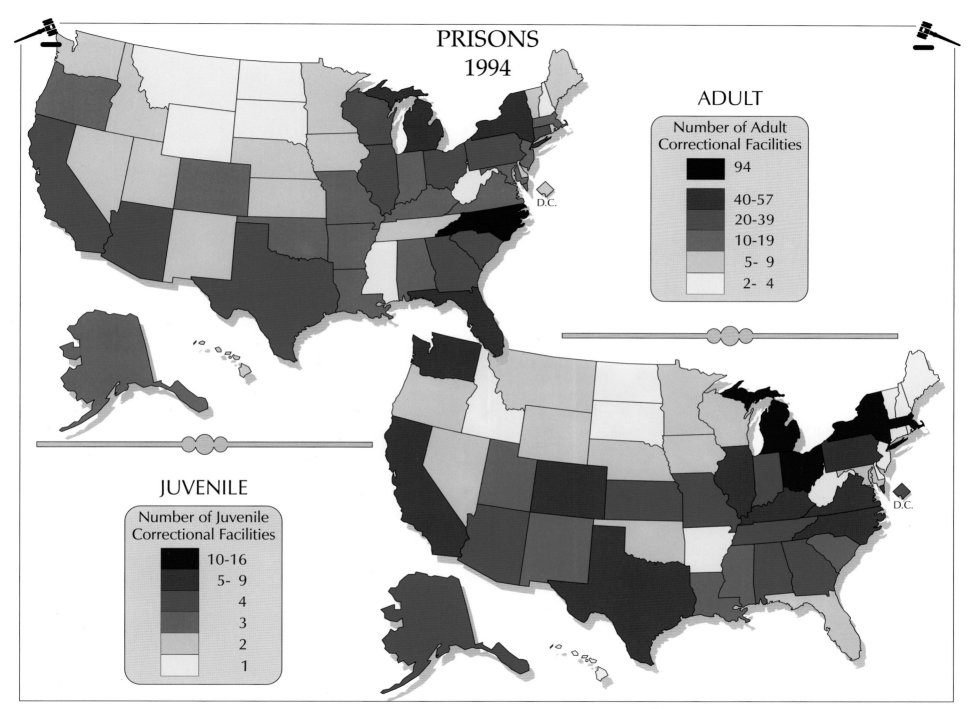

ADULT

Number of Adult Correctional Facilities

- 94
- 40-57
- 20-39
- 10-19
- 5- 9
- 2- 4

D.C.

JUVENILE

Number of Juvenile Correctional Facilities

- 10-16
- 5- 9
- 4
- 3
- 2
- 1

D.C.

PRISON POPULATION THROUGH TIME

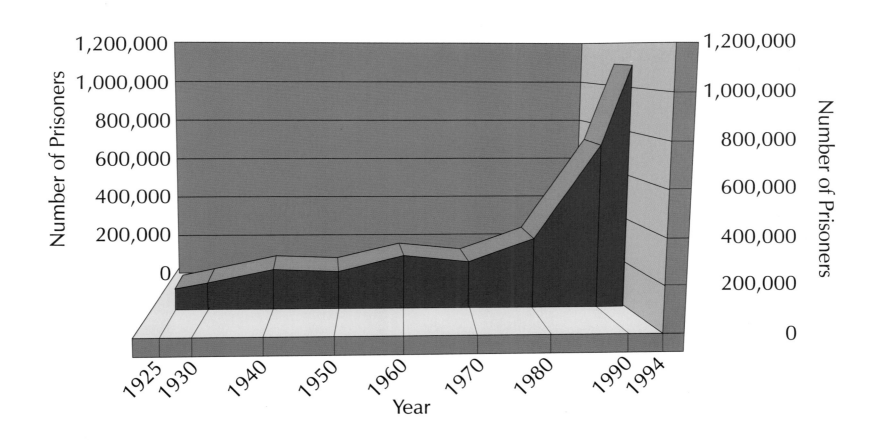

Number of Prisoners

1,200,000
1,000,000
800,000
600,000
400,000
200,000
0

1,200,000
1,000,000
800,000
600,000
400,000
200,000
0

Number of Prisoners

1925 1930 1940 1950 1960 1970 1980 1990 1994

Year

INCREASE IN PRISON POPULATION
1980-1990

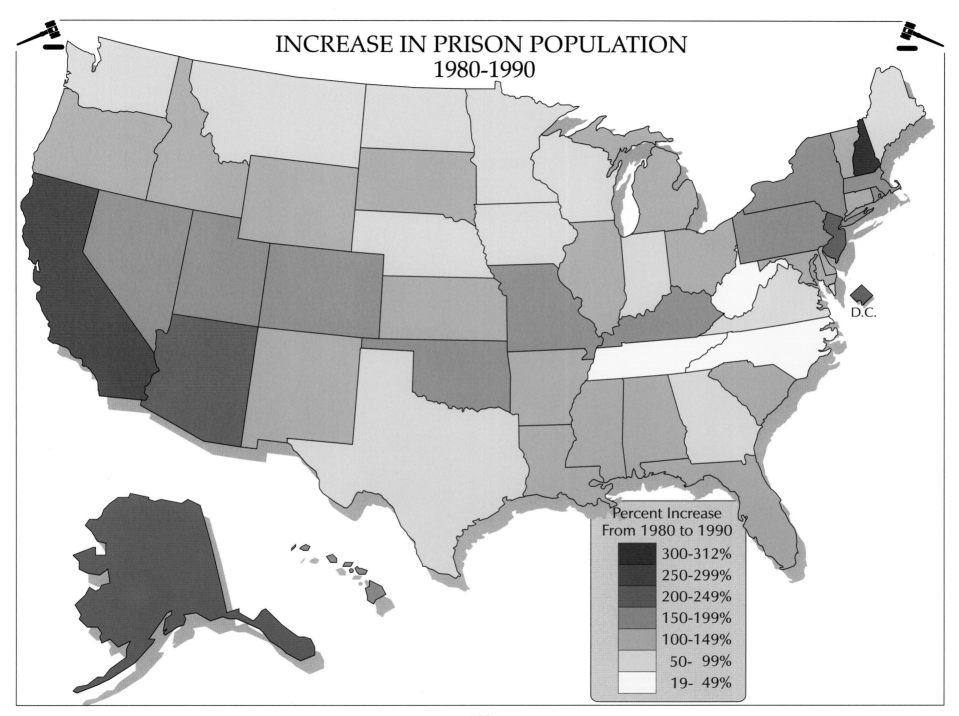

D.C.

Percent Increase
From 1980 to 1990

	300-312%
	250-299%
	200-249%
	150-199%
	100-149%
	50- 99%
	19- 49%

PRISONERS
1994

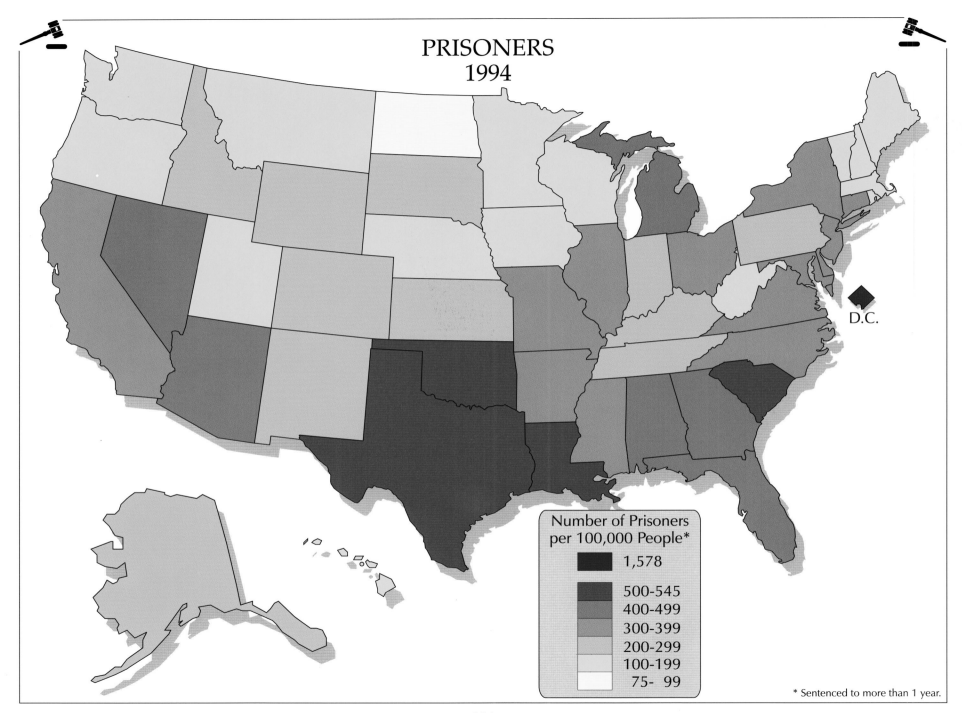

D.C.

Number of Prisoners
per 100,000 People*

	1,578
	500-545
	400-499
	300-399
	200-299
	100-199
	75- 99

* Sentenced to more than 1 year.

PRISON POPULATION
RACIAL BREAKDOWN
1993

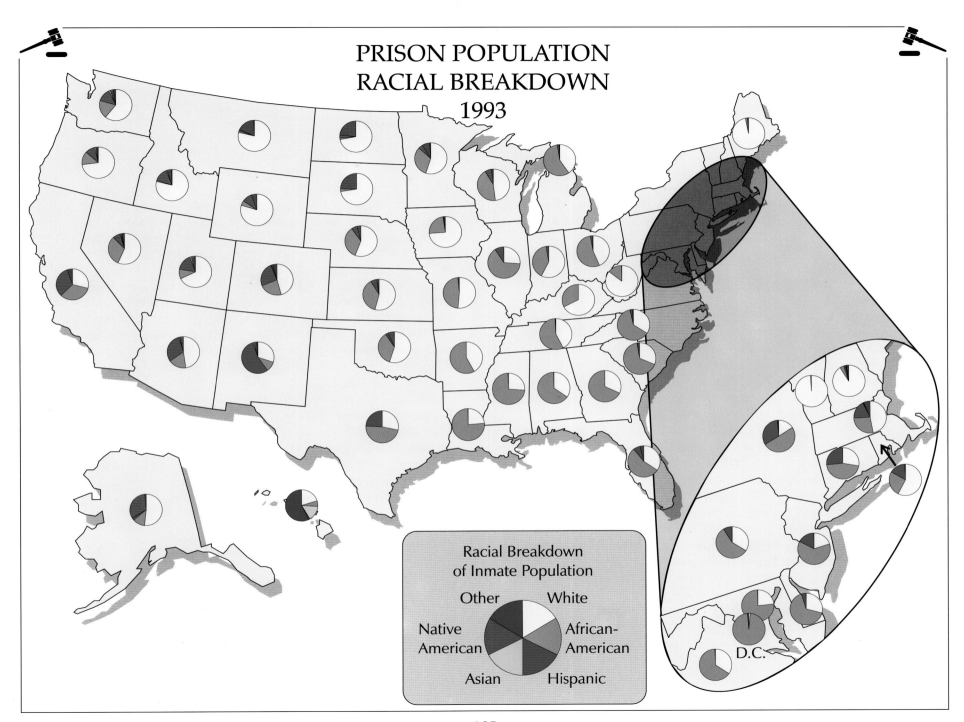

Racial Breakdown
of Inmate Population

Other   White

Native   African-
American   American

Asian   Hispanic

D.C.

expensive to allow women the same education and job training that men have.

The map "Female Prisoners, 1993" shows that the total percentage of prisoners who are women is narrow, on the order of only 5.7 percent. With the exception of California, Ohio and the District of Columbia, the highest percentages of women in prison are in predominantly rural states. A comparison with the map "Prisoners, 1994" shows no clear relation between the number of prisoners as a whole and the number of women in prison.

JUVENILES IN CUSTODY

Since the Juvenile Justice reforms of the 1970s, large numbers of children are no longer held in adult jails. Children who range in age from 10 to 15 years are considered juveniles. Detention centers, which are essentially jails for juveniles who have been arrested and are awaiting trial, are intended to hold those thought to be most dangerous or most likely to take off before court hearings.

The map "Juvenile Custody Rate" exhibits some apparent contradictions when compared to the juvenile section of the map "Prisons, 1994." While Nevada, Wyoming and South Dakota have the highest juvenile custody rates, they have the lowest number of juvenile custody facilities, a function of their low population. Massachusetts, with one of the lowest juvenile custody rates, 88 per 100,000 youths, ranks among the highest in numbers of juvenile correctional facilities. It is important to note that the map Juvenile Custody Rate" presents data from 1990, four years prior to the data in the "Prisons, 1994" map.

California, the most heavily populated state, also has a large number of juvenile correctional facilities and a high juvenile custody rate. The same is true of New York, Ohio and Michigan. In general, the Northern states exhibit a higher juvenile custody rate than does the South.

SENTENCED TO LIFE

The map "Sentenced to Life" shows the percentage of prisoners sentenced to life imprisonment. Nevada has the most prisoners who are serving life sentences. Aside from Nevada, New York, Delaware, California and Michigan, the greatest number of prisoners serving life sentences are in the Southern states.

The map "Without Parole" shows the percentage of life prisoners who have no possibility of parole. While Nevada has the greatest number of "Lifers," only 25 percent of them are serving sentences with no possibility of parole. However, a life sentence does not necessarily mean parole is not possible. Seventeen states, along with the District of Columbia, have no provisions for life sentences without parole. Of those states that do have provisions for prisoners serving life sentence without parole, four states, Utah, Oregon, Minnesota and Vermont, have no prisoners serving life without the possibility of parole. At the other end of the spectrum, in five states, South Dakota, Iowa, Louisiana, Pennsylvania and New Hampshire, all criminals who are sentenced to life have no possibility of parole.

THE DEATH PENALTY

"There will never be another execution in this country." This was the optimistic and completely erroneous statement of Supreme Court Chief Justice Burger in 1972.

Before 1790, the death penalty was mandated for certain crimes, but in 1794 Pennsylvania adopted "degrees" of

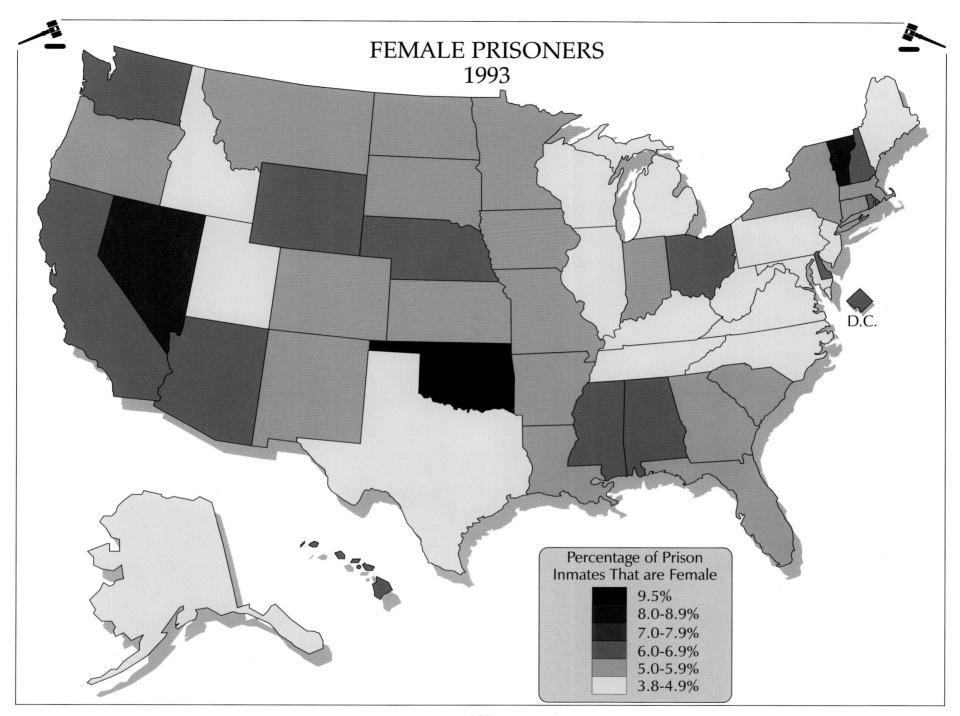

FEMALE PRISONERS
1993

D.C.

Percentage of Prison
Inmates That are Female

9.5%
8.0-8.9%
7.0-7.9%
6.0-6.9%
5.0-5.9%
3.8-4.9%

JUVENILE CUSTODY RATE

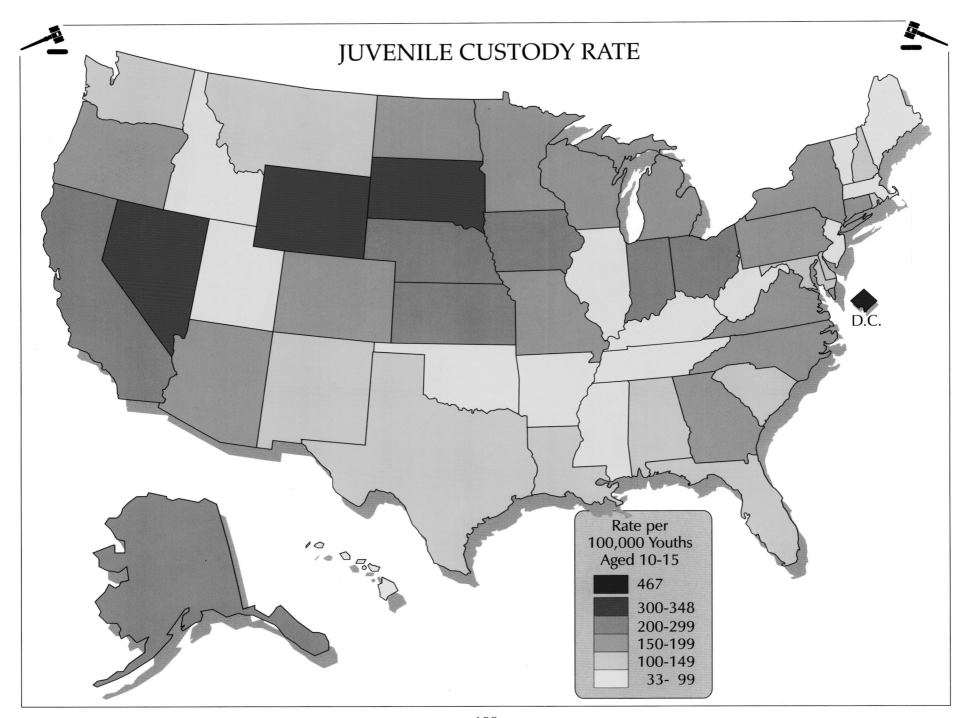

D.C.

Rate per
100,000 Youths
Aged 10-15

467
300-348
200-299
150-199
100-149
33- 99

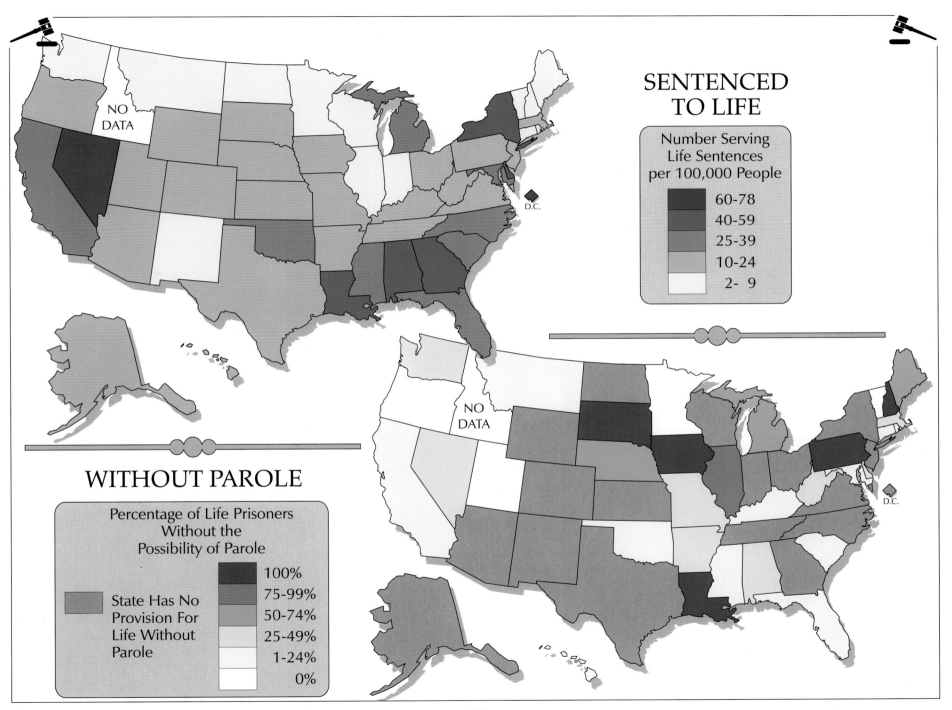

SENTENCED TO LIFE

Number Serving Life Sentences per 100,000 People

- 60-78
- 40-59
- 25-39
- 10-24
- 2- 9

NO DATA

D.C.

WITHOUT PAROLE

Percentage of Life Prisoners Without the Possibility of Parole

- 100%
- 75-99%
- 50-74%
- State Has No Provision For Life Without Parole
- 25-49%
- 1-24%
- 0%

NO DATA

D.C.

murder. First degree, or premeditated murder, could be punished by death, while non-premeditated murder did not carry the death sentence.

In the late 1960s, the Supreme Court, which at first had refused to hear death sentence cases, began to consider them. In 1972, a number of cases were argued, and on a tentative note, five Supreme Court judges, citing the Eighth Amendment to the Constitution which "prohibits the infliction of uncivilized and inhuman punishment," found the death penalty to be unconstitutional.

The five justices who agreed that capital punishment was unconstitutional believed they represented the "will of the American People." They were apparently wrong, for, according to the elected legislature, the American people wanted the death penalty. Eventually, the Supreme Court left the imposition of the death penalty to the discretion of judge and jury. The Supreme Court, however, did not give the states a free hand in deciding which acts would receive the death penalty. It was not to be inflicted for crimes other than murder.

When the issue of responsibility in a murder is not clear—for example, if two people rob a store and one stays in the car while the other kills the store owner—the one in the car is an accomplice to committing a felony murder. He can be convicted of murder, but cannot be given the death penalty. Youth, mental retardation and insanity are all considered mitigating factors in assigning the death penalty, but these factors are still being debated.

As the map "Capital Punishment—Minimum Age, 1992" shows, of the 37 states that have instituted the death penalty, only nine do not specify the minimum age at which a person can be executed. In Utah and Arkansas, the death penalty can be imposed on children as young as 14. In 11 states, the usual age of majority, 18, is also the minimum age for execution.

For nearly every prisoner who is condemned to death, the sentence is not carried out in an expedient manner. Numerous appeals can stretch over many years. Because of this, every state with the death penalty has a "death row" in its prison system. The map "Prisoners on Death Row, 1992" shows the greatest number of "death row" inmates are in Texas, California and Florida.

New Mexico was the only state with just one prisoner on death row in that year. Colorado, Montana, Washington, New Jersey and Connecticut had less than 10 awaiting execution. These figures are current for 1992 and do not reflect the pace at which death penalties are now being imposed in various states. Nationally, 51 percent of all prisoners on death row are white, while only 39 percent are African-American. In eight Eastern states, the majority of prisoners on death row are African-Americans.

There are, at present, five accepted methods of execution in the United States shown on the map "Methods of Execution, 1995." Thirteen predominately Eastern states use the classic electric chair. The majority employ the use of lethal injection, and three states, New Hampshire, Montana and Washington, use hanging as well as lethal injection. Lethal gas or lethal injection is used in California, Arizona, Missouri, Mississippi and Maryland, while one state, Utah, also uses a firing squad.

The maps "Executions" and "Change in the Murder Rate, 1973–1993" show that, while in some states high rates of executions are accompanied by a decrease murder rates, it is clear that execution is not always a deterrent to murder. three states—Louisiana, Arkansas and Missouri—that record a high number of executions, the murder rate has increased. Executions are more prevalent in the South, from Texas with 101 executions to Florida with 35, Virginia with 28 and Louisiana and Georgia with 21 and 20, respectively. In states that have no death penalty, the change in the murder rate is split nearly 50/50 between states that have exhibited increases and those that have had decreases.

Perhaps the Supreme Court itself has created a situation about the death penalty that no one finds acceptable. Opponents of the penalty are upset because it remains on the books; proponents are upset because it is only occasionally carried out. An accepted legal definition for administering the death penalty still remains to be worked out by the Supreme Court.

As the court removes obstacles to capital punishment, we can expect an increase in death sentences. In 1991, there were 2,500 people under sentence of death. Each year there are more people sentenced to death than are executed. However, if the public demand for the death sentence continues, the courts may increase the rate of executions.

EDUCATING PRISONERS

Many sociologists believe that there is a negative correlation between education and crime. If this is so, then educating prisoners may be one way to reduce recidivism. It is also a way of giving some purpose to the long days and years of a criminal's sentence.

The map "Academic Education Programs in Prisons" points out that there are education programs in most prisons in the United States. In Indiana and Maryland, prisoners can earn doctoral degrees. In Utah, Texas and New York, prisoners can earn master's degrees. In 20 other states they can obtain a bachelor's degree.

Eighty-five percent of the prisoners in Kansas and Hawaii participate in prison education programs, the highest percentage in the United States. Connecticut, with 78 percent, is next, followed by Alaska, with 75 percent. Ten

states have over half the eligible inmates participating in an educational program.

In general, it seems that the greatest educational participation is in the North Central states, although Texas and Louisiana have half or more of their prisoners working toward degrees.

PAROLE

Not everyone who goes to prison for a definite sentence serves that sentence. There is an "escape clause" called parole. Parole comes before the entire sentence is served. It should not be confused with probation which is granted at the time of sentencing. Probation is given instead of a jail or prison term.

The concept of parole arose in the late nineteenth century when Massachusetts authorized magistrates to release prisoners arrested for vagrancy as soon as they had reformed and were willing to return to an orderly course of life. Parole laws, passed in the 1890s, gradually spread through the United States. In some states, special boards of pardon were installed, along with grading systems, to facilitate parole of prisoners who could be returned to society "reformed."

In our present society there are two basic reasons for parole and probation. One is to help rehabilitate the criminal by reintegrating him into society; the other is a result of the pressure of prison overcrowding which has forced early release of inmates. The latter has come under fire recently in light of the current anti-crime wave in the United States.

Good behavior is a third justification for parole. Release for good behavior becomes an incentive for inmates to behave and makes the running of a prison easier. It is also an incentive for the paroled prisoner to behave on the outside because of the risk that parole may be revoked.

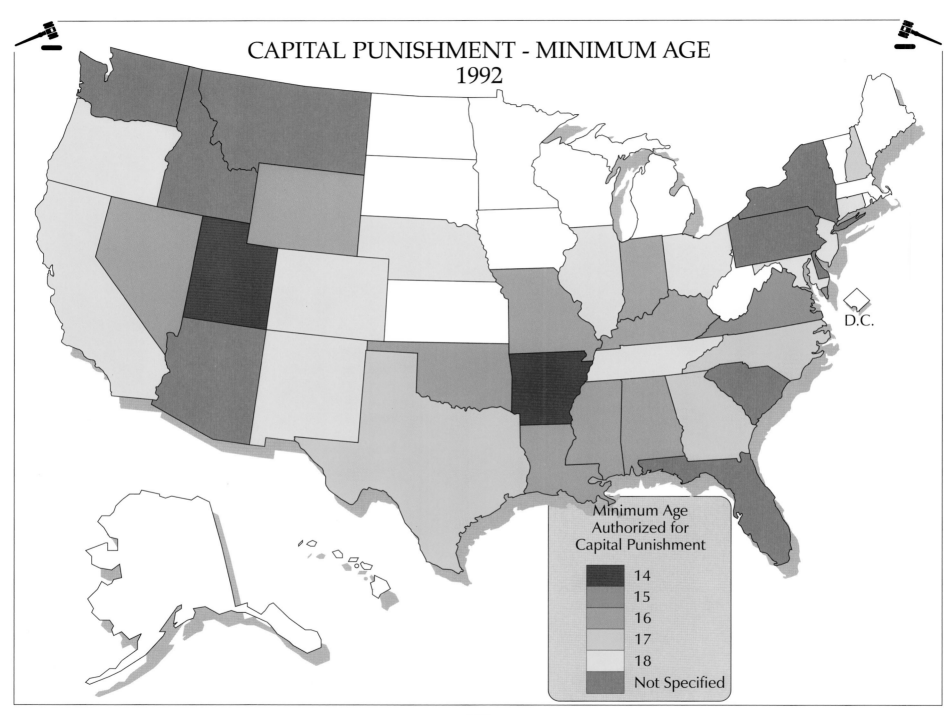

CAPITAL PUNISHMENT - MINIMUM AGE
1992

D.C.

Minimum Age
Authorized for
Capital Punishment

14
15
16
17
18
Not Specified

PRISONERS ON DEATH ROW
1992

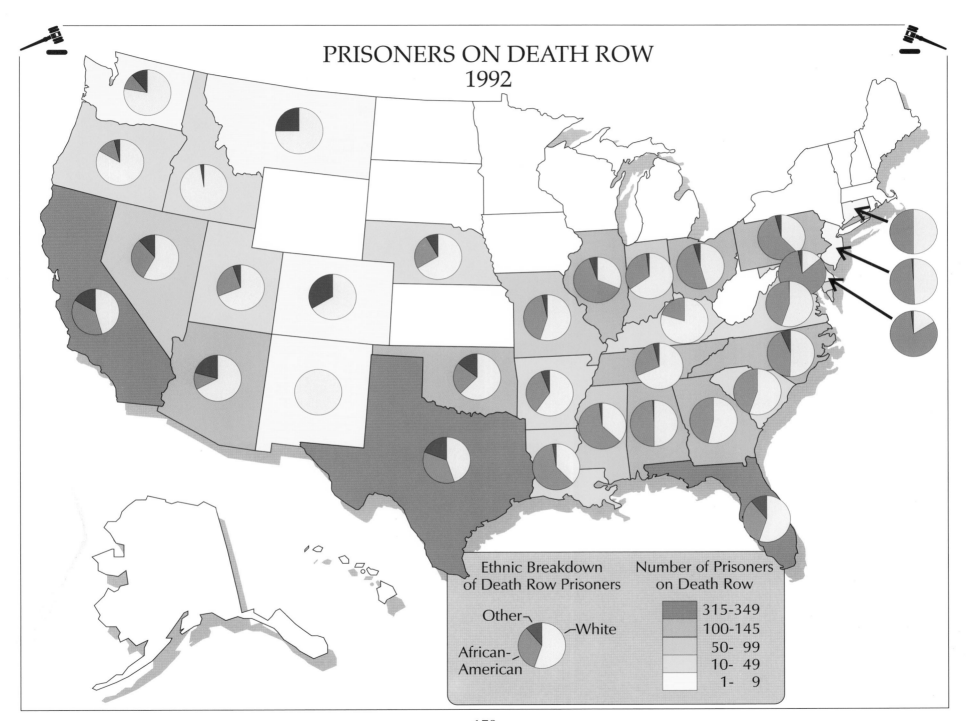

Ethnic Breakdown of Death Row Prisoners

Other
White
African-American

Number of Prisoners on Death Row

- 315-349
- 100-145
- 50- 99
- 10- 49
- 1- 9

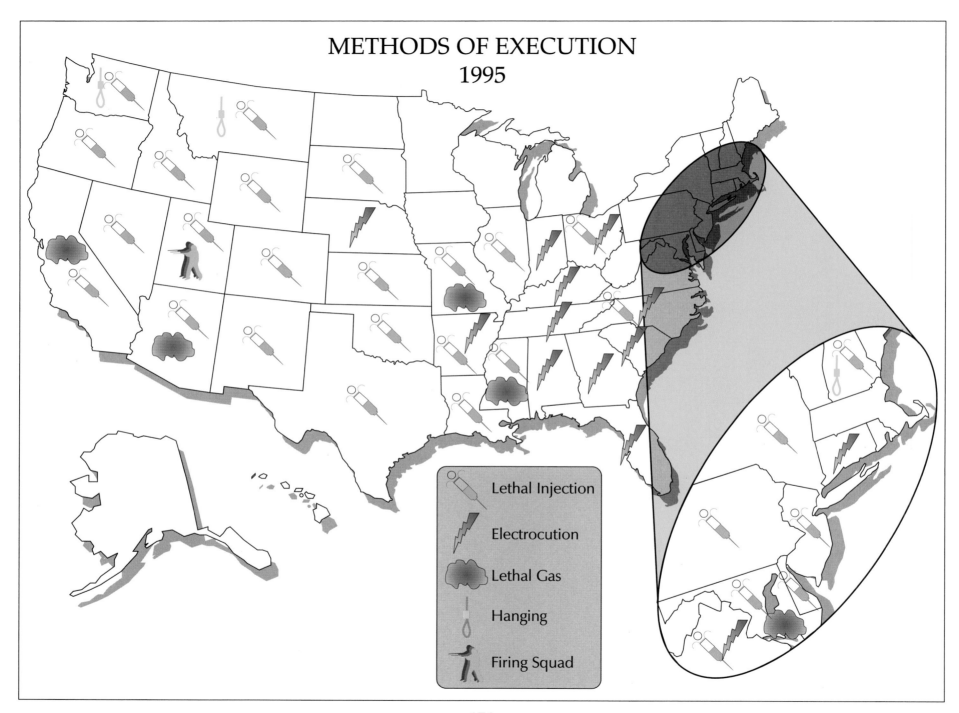

METHODS OF EXECUTION
1995

Lethal Injection

Electrocution

Lethal Gas

Hanging

Firing Squad

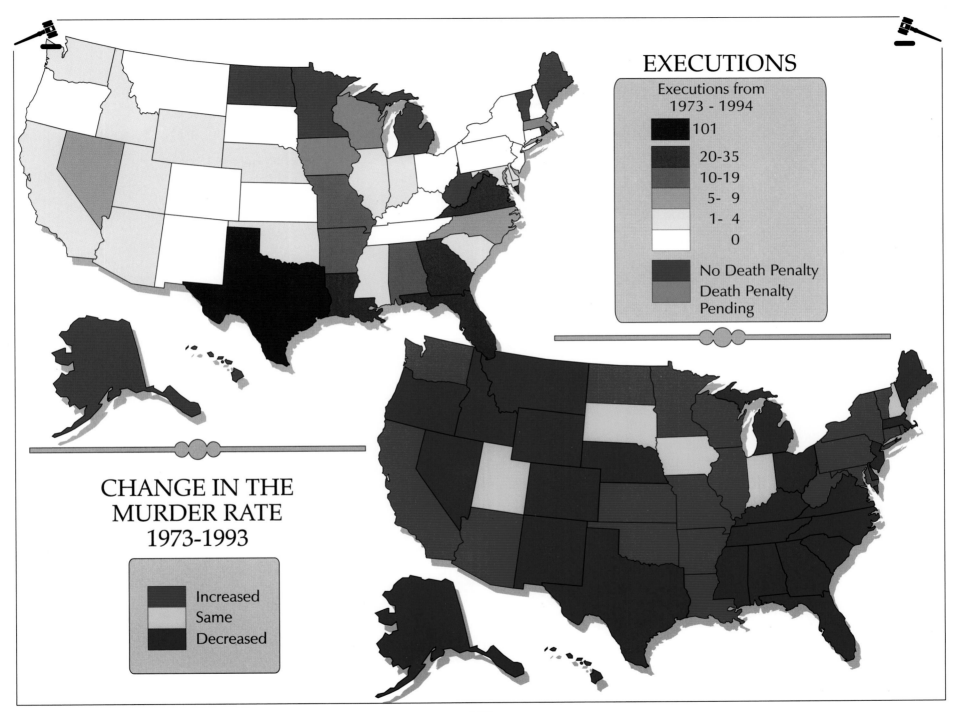

EXECUTIONS

Executions from
1973 - 1994

101

20-35

10-19

5- 9

1- 4

0

No Death Penalty

Death Penalty
Pending

CHANGE IN THE
MURDER RATE
1973-1993

Increased
Same
Decreased

ACADEMIC EDUCATION PROGRAMS IN PRISONS

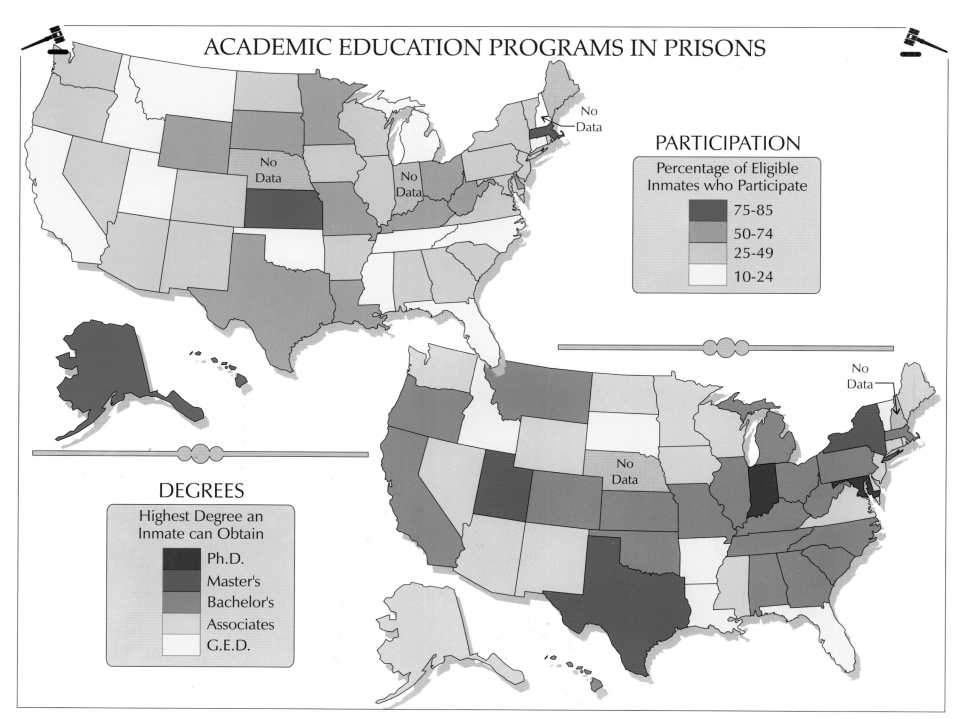

PARTICIPATION

Percentage of Eligible Inmates who Participate

- 75-85
- 50-74
- 25-49
- 10-24

DEGREES

Highest Degree an Inmate can Obtain

- Ph.D.
- Master's
- Bachelor's
- Associates
- G.E.D.

No Data

The two maps "Criteria for Release Via Parole" show that Maine, Connecticut, Mississippi and Oregon are the only states that deal directly with rehabilitation. Maine favors parole when it appears that the prisoner has reformed, and Oregon upholds an interest in "personality change." As a condition for release of sex offenders, Mississippi requires certification by a psychiatrist that the prisoner is "normal." In Connecticut, if a prisoner is denied parole, the parole board must offer suggestions to facilitate rehabilitation.

All but five states allow a prisoner to be paroled after the minimum sentence has been served. In California, Idaho, North Dakota, Minnesota, Iowa, Arkansas and Indiana, a prisoner can be released at any time, at the discretion of the parole board.

North Dakota allows parole on the basis of good behavior alone. Nine states require a minimum sentence to be served before parole based on good behavior can be granted. Montana, Kansas, Iowa and Vermont add the stipulation that the prisoner's release on parole must not be detrimental to himself or to society. Three states, Arizona, Montana and Delaware, have definite plans and guidelines for parole.

Altogether, there are more than 500,000 parolees from state prisons. The map "State Parolees" shows that the greatest number of adults under parole supervision are in the District of Columbia, with 88 parolees per 10,000 inhabitants. The rate for the District of Columbia is more than four times the national average of 20 parolees per 10,000 people. Texas and Pennsylvania follow with rates of 65 and 48, respectively. Of the remaining states, eleven rise above the national average and 37 fall below. Maine has no adults under parole supervision. The lowest rate of parolees tends to cluster in the Mountain states, the northern Midwest, the North Central states and New England.

VIOLATING PAROLE

A parole is no guarantee that a prisoner will stay out of jail. There are certain rules s/he must live up to. The eight maps "Conditions for Violation of Parole" point out these rules and the various states where they are in effect.

In every state except Oklahoma and West Virginia a violation of the law can return the parolee to prison. Washington, Idaho, Iowa, Missouri, Mississippi, Alabama, Massachusetts and Maine are the only states where possessing a weapon does not revoke parole. It is curious that in 21 states and the District of Columbia associating with other criminals does not break a parole, while in all but 16 states using drugs or alcohol can send a criminal back to jail.

In every state except Alaska, South Dakota, Minnesota, Delaware and Massachusetts, parole can be canceled for failure to make a periodic report to the parole counselor. Washington, Wyoming, Wisconsin, Illinois, Michigan, Pennsylvania and Vermont are the only seven states where failure to notify the authorities of a change of address does not land a prisoner back in prison. A more lenient attitude is taken about a failure to notify the authorities of a marriage or divorce. Only 27 states revoke parole because of it. Failure to hold a job or support a family are grounds for revoking parole in all but 13 Northern states.

PRISONER ESCAPES

It is one thing to put a criminal in prison. It is quite another to keep him there. Literature is filled with stories of prisoners, usually innocent, who escaped. *The Count of Monte Cristo*, and currently, *The Shawshank Redemption*, are two popular examples. In fact, in 1991 alone, there have been thousands of prisoners who have escaped from jails in the United States, or

CRITERIA FOR RELEASE VIA PAROLE

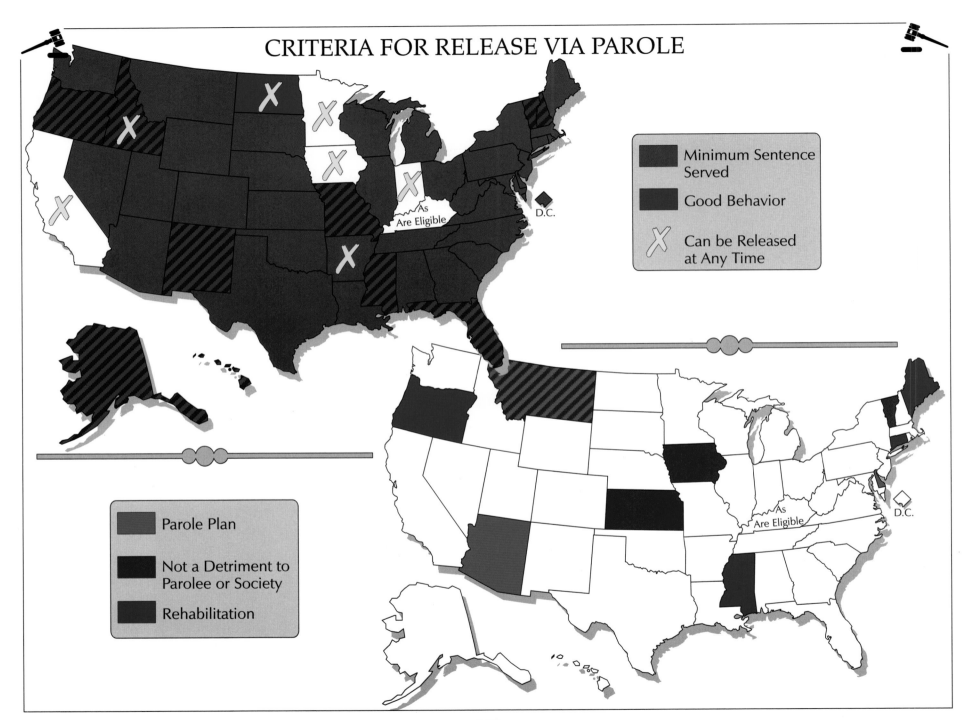

Minimum Sentence Served

Good Behavior

Can be Released at Any Time

As Are Eligible

D.C.

Parole Plan

Not a Detriment to Parolee or Society

Rehabilitation

STATE PAROLEES

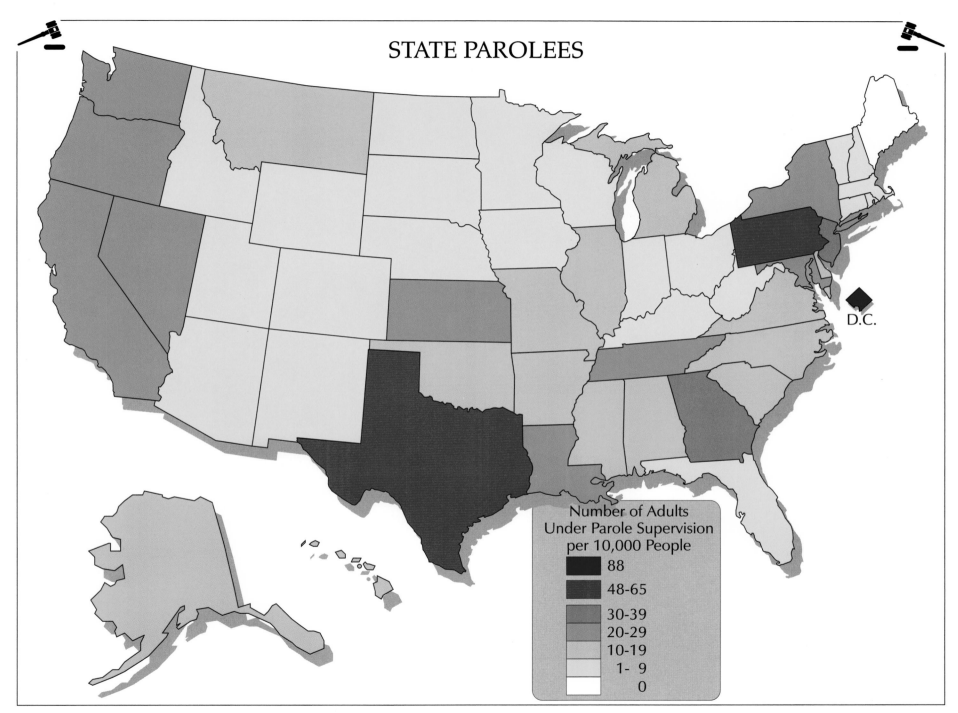

D.C.

Number of Adults
Under Parole Supervision
per 10,000 People

- 88
- 48-65
- 30-39
- 20-29
- 10-19
- 1- 9
- 0

CONDITIONS FOR VIOLATION OF PAROLE

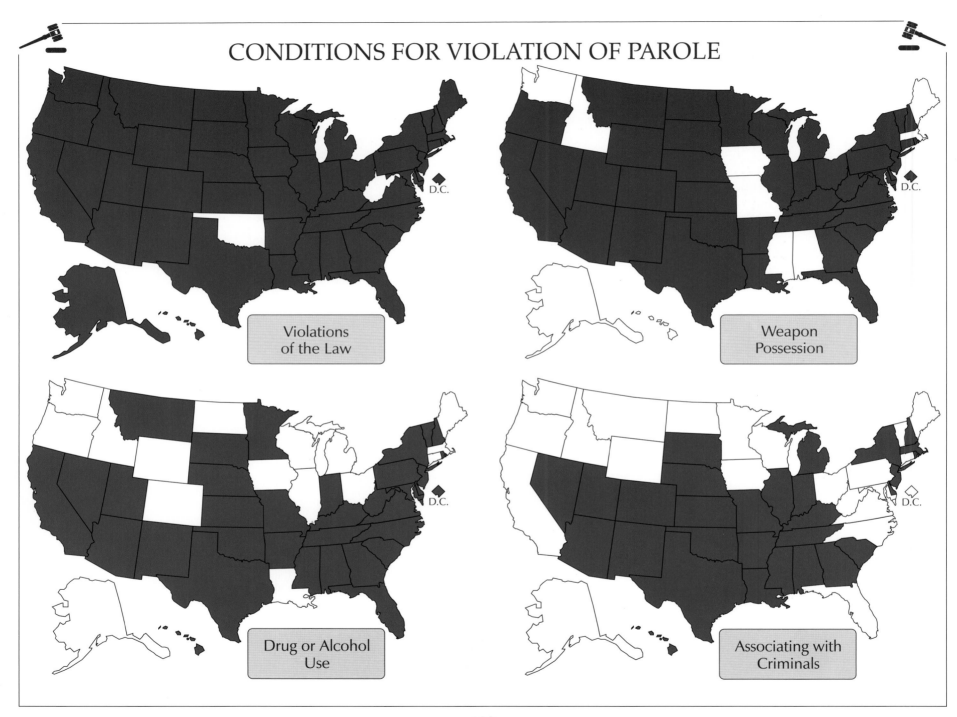

Violations of the Law

Weapon Possession

Drug or Alcohol Use

Associating with Criminals

CONDITIONS FOR VIOLATION OF PAROLE

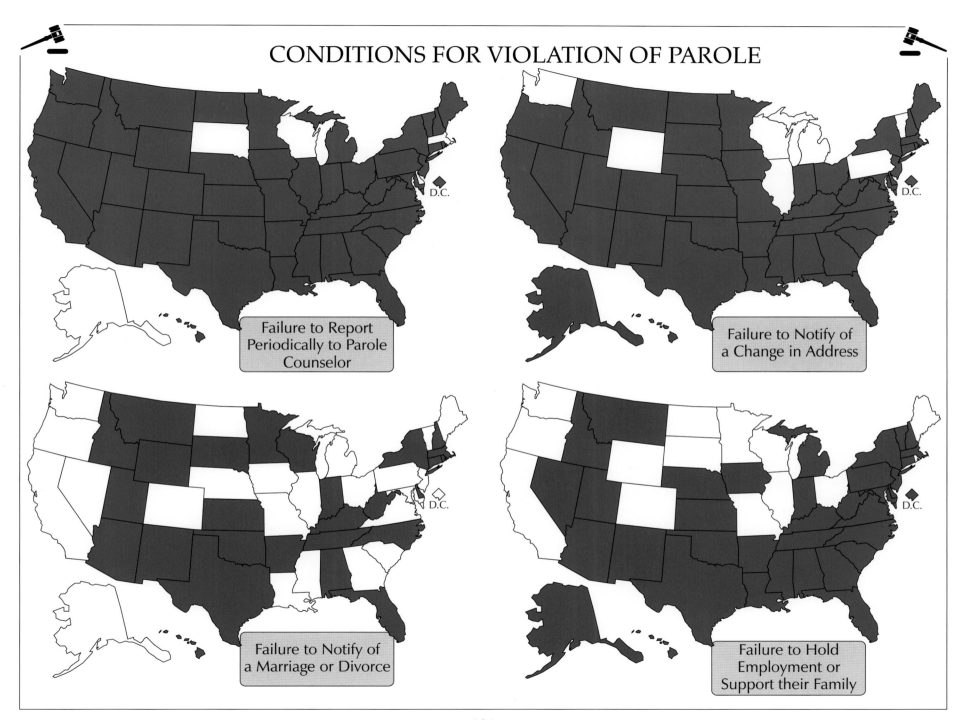

Failure to Report Periodically to Parole Counselor

Failure to Notify of a Change in Address

Failure to Notify of a Marriage or Divorce

Failure to Hold Employment or Support their Family

D.C.

even more common, gone AWOL from parole.

The map "Prisoner Escapes, 1991" shows that New York has the largest number of escapes and AWOLs. The 1,952 escapes represent about three percent of New York's prisoner population. The District of Columbia comes a close second with 1,788 escapees. The only other state with over 1,000 escapes is Michigan with 1,161, approximately four percent of its prisoner population.

Sixteen states have between 100 and 1,000 escapees and in six states the escapees number between 50 and 95. The states with the lowest number of escapees are Hawaii and Virginia, each with three.

A look at the map "Prisoners, 1994" shows some correlation between the number of prisoners and the number of escapees, although there are some notable exceptions. Ohio, which has a high incarceration rate, is very low in escapes—about 0.9 percent of the total prison population. Washington, with a low incarceration rate, has a high number of escapes—about 10 percent of its prison population.

BENEFITS FOR CRIME VICTIMS

Until recently, victims of crime have not been able to participate in the criminal justice system. In recent years, however, there has been growing awareness of the need for victims' rights in criminal cases, and this need is reflected in state laws.

In the late 1980s, victims' rights commissions were formed, and there was a call for changes in the laws and in court procedures. Because of this pressure, victims have gained a voice in criminal cases. Every state now has a crime victims' compensation board that pays part or all of victims' medical bills and lost wages. There are also a number of national victims' rights organizations, such as the National Association for Victims' Assistance and the National Victims Center.

We have considered various criminal laws throughout this book, and now, at the end, we focus briefly on some benefits available to the victims of crime. Far too often the victims are forgotten or given short shrift, and even when there is compensation available, it rarely relieves either the physical or psychological trauma of being a victim. Nevertheless, there have been efforts made to reimburse the victims of crime and help them get over their pain and suffering.

The set of three maps "Crime Victims—Eligibility for Reimbursement Programs" shows three aspects of the reimbursement program. Intervenors—people who intervene against the perpetrator of a crime and are harmed by their intervention—can collect some reimbursement in all but 20 states. Third parties refers to programs that will reimburse people who provide services or pay bills for victims. These programs exist in all but 12 states and the District of Columbia.

The "Residents Only" map lists 34 states and the District of Columbia that do not restrict damages to residents. Connecticut, Delaware, Kentucky, South Carolina and Virginia have programs that, while restricting recovery to residents, still allow nonresidents to recover if the state in which they live has reciprocity with the state where the crime took place. Federal funding is available for programs which compensate nonresidents.

The map "Crime Victims—Eligibility for Recovery Programs" considers both the physical and mental problems that crime victims may incur and what programs are available to help them. "Counseling" shows that all states except for North Dakota, Nebraska and New York have programs available for counseling. Federal funds are also available for counseling programs.

All but 18 states have programs to help crime victims who

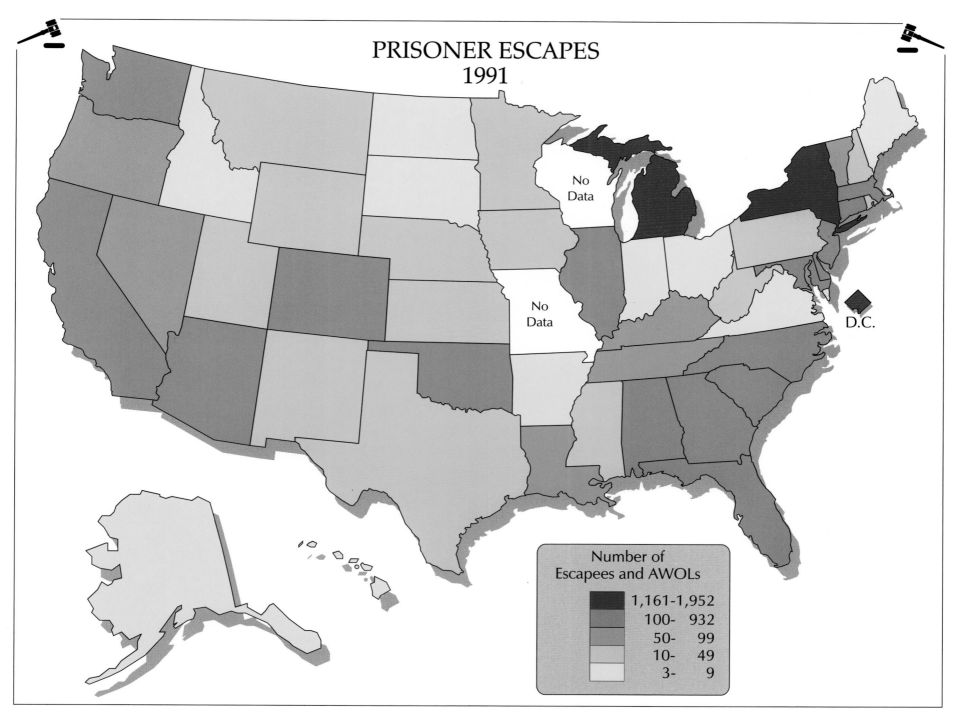

PRISONER ESCAPES
1991

No Data

No Data

D.C.

Number of
Escapees and AWOLs

■	1,161–1,952
	100– 932
	50– 99
	10– 49
	3– 9

have some disability. As for rehabilitation, only Hawaii, Louisiana, Massachusetts, Montana, New Jersey, Rhode Island, Texas and Virginia have no programs for rehabilitation. Only four states, Hawaii, Delaware, Rhode Island and Tennessee have no programs that address pain and suffering.

The final map in this section is "Crime Victims—Benefits." In 39 states and the District of Columbia, victims of violent crime who have suffered personal injury can be compensated for loss of earnings, support or out-of-pocket losses.

The top map shows the maximum benefits available to victims. Maryland allows the largest available benefit, at $45,000, followed by Alaska with $40,000. In general, the Northern states allow higher benefits, and the Southern states, except for Texas, lower benefits. Tennessee stands out as the lowest, with a maximum of only $5,000.

In 13 states and the District of Columbia, the maximum benefit may be denied by the amount of any payment to the victim from the person who committed the crime, from insurance money, public funds or any emergency awards from compensation programs. In 24 states awards may be denied and reduced by these contributions. In Montana, they can only be reduced, not denied.

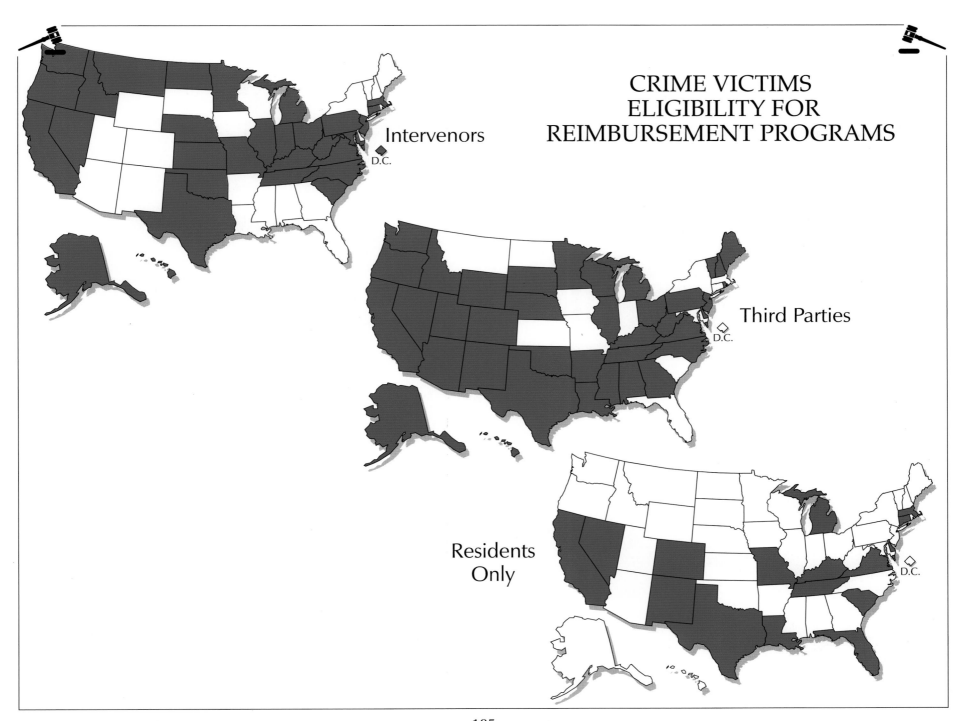

CRIME VICTIMS
ELIGIBILITY FOR
REIMBURSEMENT PROGRAMS

Intervenors

D.C.

Third Parties

D.C.

Residents
Only

D.C.

CRIME VICTIMS - ELIGIBILITY FOR RECOVERY PROGRAMS

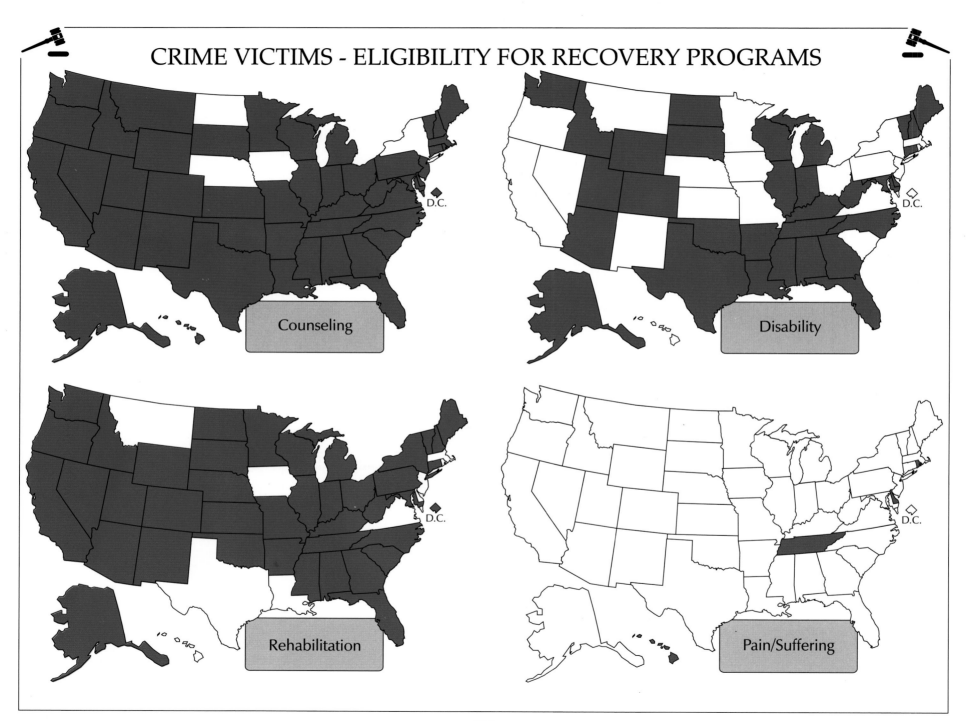

Counseling

Disability

Rehabilitation

Pain/Suffering

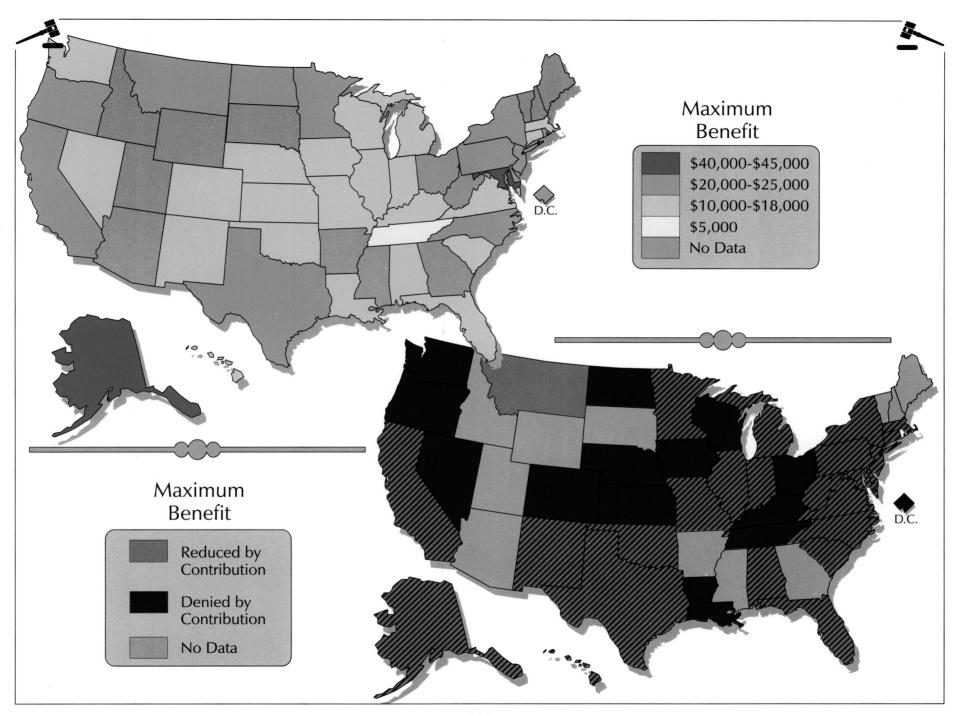

Maximum
Benefit

$40,000-$45,000

$20,000-$25,000

$10,000-$18,000

$5,000

No Data

D.C.

Maximum
Benefit

Reduced by
Contribution

Denied by
Contribution

No Data

D.C.

NOTES

PERSONAL LAW

[1] Schroder, J., *Identifying Medical Malpractice*, (Charlottesville VA: The Michie Company, 1990).

[2] 'Lectric Law Library. From the Internet: http://www.lect-Law.com.

[3] "Paramilitary Groups are Presenting Delicate Legal Choices for the States," *New York Times*. May 10, 1995. P. D21, Col. 4.

VIOLENT CRIME

[1] Belli, Mevin M., *Everybody's Guide to the Law*, (San Diego: Harcourt Brace Jovanovich, 1986).

[2] Department of Health and Human Services, *Child Abuse and Neglect: A Shared Community Concern*, (Washington, D.C. 1989).

JUSTICE SYSTEM

[1] 'Lectric Law Library. From the Internet: http://www.lect-Law.com.

[2] Rules of Professional Conduct Governing Lawyers. From the Internet http://www.law.cornell.edu/lawyers/ruletable.html.

CORRECTIONS

[1] Merlo, A. V. and Pollack, J. M., *Women, Law and Social Control*, (Boston: Allyn and Bacon, 1995).

[2] "New TV Spots Assail Dukakis on Furloughs." *New York Times*. Oct 21, 1988. P. A17, Col. 5.

BIBLIOGRAPHY FOR MAPS

INTRODUCTION

"Population"
U. S. Department of Commerce, Bureau of the Census. *1990 Census of Population General Population Characteristics United States.* CP-1-1.
"Population of Major Cities"
U. S. Department of Commerce, Bureau of the Census. *1990 Census of Population General Population Characteristics Urbanized Areas.* CP-1-1C, Table 14.

FAMILY LAW

"Laws Regulating Consenting Adults, 1993"
Personal Correspondence. Lambda Legal Defense and Education Fund, Inc. New York, 1993.
"Marriage Rate"
The 1992 Information Please Almanac. Boston: Houghton Mifflin Co., 1992. P. 806.
"Marriage Laws: Age of Consent 1991"
Famighetti, R., ed. *The World Almanac and Book of Facts.* Mahwah, NJ: Funk & Wagnalls, 1994. P. 724.
"Marriage Laws: Blood Tests & Licenses, 1993"
Ibid.

"Common Law Marriage and Cohabitation"
Duff, J. *The Spousal Equivalent Handbook.* New York: Plume, 1992. Appendix A.
"Divorce Rate"
The 1992 Information Please Almanac. Boston: Houghton Mifflin Co., 1992. P. 806.
"Selected Grounds for Divorce, 1993"
Famighetti, R., ed. *The World Almanac and Book of Facts.* Mahwah, NJ: Funk & Wagnalls, 1994. P. 725. "Family Law in the Fifty States," *Family Law Quarterly* 25 (Winter 1992), Table I.
"Durational Residency Requirements"
"Family Law in the Fifty States," *Family Law Quarterly* 25 (Winter 1992), Table II.
"No Fault Divorce"
Ibid., Table I.
"Division of Property in Divorce, 1992"
Ibid., Tables IV & VI.
"Spousal Support"
Ibid., Table VII.
"Factors Affecting Property Distribution in Divorce, 1992"
Ibid., Table V.
"Joint Custody"
National Divorce & Bankruptcy Center. From the Internet http://www.cyberstation.net/~paralegal/statelaw.html.

"Paternity Legislation, 1982"
National Conference of State Legislatures. *State Legislation on Child Support and Paternity.* Denver, 1982. Exhibit VIII-1.
"Age & Residency Requirements for Adoption"
Sack, S. M. *The Complete Legal Guide to Marriage, Divorce, Custody and Living Together.* New York: McGraw-Hill Book Co., 1987. Table 4-1.
"Adoptees' Rights"
Legal Problem Solver. Pleasantville: Reader's Digest Associates, 1994. P.18.
"Adoption Rate & Type 1986"
Adamec, C. A. & W. L. Pierce. *The Encyclopedia of Adoption.* New York: Facts On File, Inc., 1991. Pp. 316-17, Appendix Table 1.
"Statutes Concerning Involuntary Termination of Parental Rights: Legal Procedures & Issues, 1989"
Ibid.
"Statutes Concerning Involuntary Termination of Parental Rights: Issues Concerning Return to Home, 1989"
Ibid.
"Statutes Concerning Involuntary Termination of Parental Rights: Alternative Placement, 1989"
Ibid.

PERSONAL LAW

"Laws Regulating Abortions, 1992"
The Naral Foundation. *Who Decides? A State-by-State Review of Abortion Rights.* Washington D. C., 1992.
"Abortion Rate, 1988"
U. S. Department of Commerce, Bureau of the Census. *Statistical Abstract of the United States, 1993: The National Data Book.* Washington, D. C., 1993. Table 104.

"Restrictions on Smoking in Public Places, 1993"
Garbage & Other Pollution. Wylie, TX: Information Plus, 1993. Table 2.2.
"Medical Malpractice Legislation"
Schroder, J. *Identifying Medical Malpractice.* Charlottesville, VA: Mitchie Co., 1990. Table 13.1.
"Driving Age"
Hoffman, M. S., ed. *The World Almanac and Book of Facts.* New York: Pharos Books, 1992. P. 678.
"Minimum Blood Alcohol Level for DWI Offense"
The Lawyer's Almanac. New York: Prentice Hall Law and Business, 1992. Pp. 1207-30.
"Driver License Suspension Terms for Drunk Driving, 1993"
Leiter, R. A. *National Survey of State Laws.* Detroit: Gale Research, Inc., 1993. Table 8.
"Driving While under the Influence of Alcohol, 1991"
Federal Bureau of Investigation. *Uniform Crime Reports for the United States, 1991.* Washington, D. C.: 1992. Table 68.
"Legal Age for Sale of Alcoholic Beverages to Minors"
Guggenheim, M. & A. Susman. *The Rights of Young People.* New York: Bantam Books, 1985. Appendix C.
"School Prayer in Public Schools, 1993"
Leiter, R. A. *National Survey of State Laws.* Detroit: Gale Research, Inc., 1993. Table 13.
"Corporal Punishment in Public Schools, 1993"
Ibid., Table 12.
"Parental Liability"
Legal Problem Solver. Pleasantville: Reader's Digest Associates, 1994. P. 392.
"Prostitution, 1991"
Federal Bureau of Investigation. *Uniform Crime Reports for the United States, 1991.* Washington, D. C.: 1992. Table 68.
"Sex Offenses, 1991"

Ibid., Table 68.

"Gambling, 1991"
Ibid.

"Gun Control, 1992—Purchasing"
"Compendium of State Laws Governing Handguns, 1992".
The Lawyers Almanac. 1993. Pp. 1232-33.

"Gun Control, 1992—Carrying"
Ibid.

"Weapons Possession, 1991"
Federal Bureau of Investigation. *Uniform Crime Reports for the United States 1991*, Washington, D. C.: 1992. Table 68.

"Drug Possession, 1991"
Ibid., Table 68.

"State Laws Banning or Restricting the Activities of Paramilitary, Groups 1995"
"Paramilitary Groups are Presenting Delicate Legal Choices for the States," *New York Times* , May 10, 1995. P. D21, Col. 4.

"Hate Crime Laws, 1993"
Crime: A Serious American Problem. Wylie, TX: Information Plus, 1993. Table 3.37.

VIOLENT CRIME

"Murder Rate"
U. S. Department of Commerce, Bureau of the Census. *Statistical Abstract of the United States, 1993.* Washington, D. C., 1993. Table 289.

"Murder in Major Cities"
Ibid., Table 290.

"Murder Rate through Time"
U. S. Department of Commerce, Bureau of the Census. *Statistical Abstract of the United States 1993.*

Washington, D. C., 1993. Table 289 & 304.
U. S. Department of Justice, Bureau of Justice Statistics. *Sourcebook of Criminal Justice Statistics, 1991.* Washington, D. C., Table 3.127.

"Violent Crimes against Which Deadly Force is Justified"
Kramer, A. *Crime Victims.* Belmont, CA.: Wadsworth Publishing Co., 1989. Table 7.3.

"Percentage of Murders by Relationship to Victim, 1991"
U. S. Department of Justice. *Crime in the United States, 1991.* Uniform Crime Reports, Washington, D. C., 1992. Table 2.11.

"Types of Weapons Used in Murders, 1991"
U. S. Department of Justice, Bureau of Justice Statistics. *Sourcebook of Criminal Justice Statistics, 1991.* Washington, D. C. Table 3.112.

"Aggravated Assault"
U. S. Department of Commerce, Bureau of the Census. *Statistical Abstract of the United States 1993.* Washington, D. C., 1993. Table 289.

"Aggravated Assault in Major Cities"
Ibid., Table 290.

"Assault Rate through Time"
U. S. Department of Commerce, Bureau of the Census. *Statistical Abstract of the United States 1993.* Washington, D. C., 1993. Table 289 & 304.
U. S. Department of Justice, Bureau of Justice Statistics. *Sourcebook of Criminal Justice Statistics, 1991.* Washington, D. C. Table 3.127.

"Rape Rate"
U. S. Department of Commerce, Bureau of the Census. *Statistical Abstract of the United States 1993.* Washington, D. C., 1993. Table 289.

"Rape in Major Cities"
Ibid., Table 290.

"Rape Rate through Time"

U. S. Department of Commerce, Bureau of the Census. *Statistical Abstract of the United States 1993*. Washington, D. C., 1993. Tables 289 & 304.

U. S. Department of Justice, Bureau of Justice Statistics. *Sourcebook of Criminal Justice Statistics, 1991*. Washington, D. C., Table 3.127.

"Marital Rape Laws, 1987"
NOW/Legal Defense and Election Fund. *The State-by-State Guide to Women's Rights*. New York: McGraw Hill Book Co., 1987.

"Definitions of Child Abuse"
American Humane Association. *Child Abuse Reporting Legislation in the 1980s*, Denver, 1987.

"Child Abuse—General Provisions"
Ibid.

"Child Abuse"
The National Committee for Prevention of Child Abuse. *Current Trends in Child Abuse Reporting and Fatalities: The Results of the 1991 Annual Fifty State Survey*. Chicago, 1992.

"Offenses against Family and Children, 1991"
Federal Bureau of Investigation. *Uniform Crime Reports for the United States, 1991*. Washington, D. C.: 1992. Table 68.

"Robbery"
U. S. Department of Commerce, Bureau of the Census. *Statistical Abstract of the United States, 1993*. Washington, D. C., 1993. Table 289.

"Robbery in Major Cities"
Ibid., Table 290.

"Robbery Rate through Time"
U. S. Department of Commerce, Bureau of the Census. *Statistical Abstract of the United States 1993*. Washington, D. C., 1993. Tables 289 & 304.

U. S. Department of Justice, Bureau of Justice Statistics. *Sourcebook of Criminal Justice Statistics, 1991*.

Washington, D. C. Table 3.127.

"Extortion, 1992"
U. S. Department of Justice, Bureau of Justice Statistics. *Sourcebook of Criminal Justice Statistics, 1992*. Washington, D. C. Table 3.150.

"Juvenile Criminals—All Arrests, 1992"
Morgan, K. O., S. Morgan, & N. Quitno, eds. *State Rankings 1993: A Statistical View of the 50 States*. Lawrence, KS: Morgan Quitno Corp., 1993. P. 36.

"Juvenile Criminals 1992 Murder/Rape"
Ibid., pp. 40 & 42.

"Juvenile Criminals 1992 Robbery/Aggravated Assault"
Ibid., p. 44.

U. S. Department of Justice, Bureau of Justice Statistics. *Sourcebook of Criminal Justice Statistics, 1991*. Washington, D. C.. Table 4.4.

PROPERTY CRIME

"Burglary"
U. S. Department of Commerce, Bureau of the Census. *Statistical Abstract of the United States, 1993*. Washington, D. C., 1993. Table 289.

"Burglary in Major Cities"
Ibid., Table 290.

"Burglary Rate through Time"
U. S. Department of Commerce, Bureau of the Census. *Statistical Abstract of the United States 1993*. Washington, D. C., 1993. Tables 289 & 304.

U. S. Department of Justice, Bureau of Justice Statistics. *Sourcebook of Criminal Justice Statistics, 1991*. Washington, D. C. Table 3.127.

"Larceny/Theft"
U. S. Department of Commerce, Bureau of the Census.

Statistical Abstract of the United States, 1993. Washington, D. C., 1993. Ibid., Table 289.

"Larceny/Theft in Major Cities"
Ibid., Table 290.

"Larceny Rate through Time"
U. S. Department of Commerce, Bureau of the Census. *Statistical Abstract of the United States, 1993.* Washington, D. C., 1993. Tables 289 & 304.
U. S. Department of Justice, Bureau of Justice Statistics. *Sourcebook of Criminal Justice Statistics, 1991.* Washington, D. C. Table 3.127.

"Trends in Larceny & Theft"
Federal Bureau of Investigation. *Uniform Crime Reports for the United States, 1991.* Washington, D. C., 1992. Chart 2.24.

"Motor Vehicle Theft"
U. S. Department of Commerce, Bureau of the Census. *Statistical Abstract of the United States, 1993.* Washington, D. C., 1993. Table 289.

"Motor Vehicle Theft in Major Cities"
Ibid., Table 290.

"Motor Vehicle Theft Rate through Time"
U. S. Department of Commerce, Bureau of the Census. *Statistical Abstract of the United States, 1993.* Washington, D. C., 1993. Tables 289 & 304.
U. S. Department of Justice, Bureau of Justice Statistics. *Sourcebook of Criminal Justice Statistics, 1991.* Washington, D. C. Table 3.127.

"Arson"
Federal Bureau of Investigation. *Uniform Crime Reports for the United States, 1991.* Washington, D. C., 1992. Table 68.

"Arson in Major Cities"
Carpenter, A. & C. Provorse. *Facts About the Cities.* New York: H. W. Wilson Co., 1992.

"Fraud, 1991"

Federal Bureau of Investigation. *Uniform Crime Reports for the United States, 1991.* Washington, D. C.,1992. Table 68.

"Embezzlement, 1991"
Ibid., Table 68.

"Forgery, 1991"
Ibid., Table 68.

"Justifiable Use of Deadly Force when Life Is Not Threatened"
Kramer, A., *Crime Victims.* Belmont, CA.: Wadsworth Publishing Co., 1989. Table 7.3.

"Property Crimes Against Which Deadly Force Is Justified"
Ibid.

"Juvenile Criminals, 1992: Burglary/Larceny and Theft"
Morgan, K. O., S. Morgan, & N. Quitno, eds. *State Rankings 1993: A Statistical View of the 50 States.* Lawrence, KS: Morgan Quitno Corp., 1993. Pp. 50 & 52.

"Juvenile Criminals, 1992: Motor Vehicle Theft/Arson"
Ibid., Pp. 54 & 56.

THE JUSTICE SYSTEM

"Current Structure of the Federal Courts"
From the Internet. http://www.lectlaw.com/tjud.html

"Federal Judicial Circuits & Districts"
Administrative Office of the United States. *The United States Courts: Their Jurisdiction, 1989.*

"U. S. Circuit Courts, Division of Appeals—1992"
The Lawyers Almanac. New York: Prentice Hall Law and Business, 1993. Pp. 1005-09.

"U. S. Circuit Courts, Division of Criminal and Civil Cases, 1992"
Ibid., pp. 1010-19.

"U. S. Circuit Courts, Total Civil Cases, 1992"
Ibid., pp. 1010-13.

"U. S. Circuit Courts, Total Criminal Cases, 1992"
    Ibid., Pp. 1014-19.
"Lawyers—Lawyers (1980–1990)"
    U. S. Department of Commerce, Bureau of the Census.
    Statistical Abstract of the United States, 1993. Washington, D. C., 1993. Tables 314 & 315.
"Racial Distribution of Lawyers"
    U. S. Department of Commerce, Bureau of the Census.
    1990 Census of Population and Housing Summary, EEO CD-ROM.
"Women Lawyers"
    Ibid.
"Racial Distribution of Judges"
    Ibid.
"Women Judges"
    Ibid.
"Supreme Court Justices (state appointed from)"
    Hoffman, M. S., ed. *The World Almanac and Book of Facts*. New York: Pharos Books, 1992. P. 84.
"Lawsuit Awards"
    "A Brief Course in Self-Defense". *Des Moines Register*, March 19, 1995., USA Weekend Section, P. 14, Col. 1.

CORRECTIONS

"Police Officers, 1991"
    U. S. Department of Commerce, Bureau of the Census.
    Statistical Abstract of the United States, 1993. Washington, D. C., 1993. Table 325.
"Law Enforcement Expenditures"
    Ibid.
"Punitiveness of States"
    Selke, W. L. *Prisons in Crisis*. Bloomington: Indiana University Press, 1993. Table 1.1.

"Inmates in Local Jails, 1988"
    Van Son, V. *CQ's State Fact Finder*. Washington, D. C.: Congressional Quarterly, Inc., 1993. P. 62.
"Local Jail Expenditures, 1988"
    Ibid., Pp. 63-64.
"Prisons, 1994"
    American Correctional Association. *Directory of Juvenile and Adult Correctional Departments, Institutions, Agencies and Paroling Authorities, 1993*. College Park, MD.,1994.
"Prison Population through Time"
    U. S. Department of Commerce, Bureau of the Census. Personal communication.
    U. S. Department of Justice. *Crime in the United States, 1991*. Uniform Crime Reports, Washington, D. C., 1992. Fig. 1.1.
"Increase in Prison Population, 1980–1990"
    U. S. Department of Commerce, Bureau of the Census.
    Statistical Abstract of the United States, 1993. Washington, D. C., 1993. Table 331.
"Prisoners, 1994"
    "State by State Behind Bars." *New York Times*. Oct. 28, 1994. P. A25, Col. 1.
"Prison Population: Racial Breakdown, 1993"
    Crime: A Serious American Problem. Wylie, TX: Information Plus, 1993. Table 6.14
"Female Prisoners, 1993"
    Ibid., Table 6.14
"Juvenile Custody Rate"
    Van Son, V. *CQ's State Fact Finder*. Washington, D. C.: Congressional Quarterly, Inc., 1993. P. 66.
"Sentenced to Life/Without Parole"
    U. S. Department of Justice, Bureau of Justice Statistics.
    Sourcebook of Criminal Justice Statistics, 1991. Washington, D. C. Table 6.91.

"Capital Punishment—Minimum Age 1992"
Crime: A Serious American Problem. Wylie, TX: Information Plus, 1993. Table 4.2.

"Prisoners on Death Row, 1992"
U. S. Department of Justice, Bureau of Justice Statistics. Sourcebook of Criminal Justice Statistics, 1991. Washington, D. C. Table 6.140.

"Methods of Execution 1995"
American Correctional Association. Directory of Juvenile and Adult Correctional Departments, Institutions, Agencies and Paroling Authorities, 1993. College Park, MD., 1994.

Crime: A Serious American Problem. Wylie, TX: Information Plus, 1993. Table 4.3.

"Most States Kill with Needle". Des Moines Register. February 19, 1995. P. 1B, Col. 2.

"Executions/Change in Murder Rate, 1973–1993"
American Correctional Association. Directory of Juvenile and Adult Correctional Departments, Institutions, Agencies and Paroling Authorities, 1993. College Park, MD., 1994.

"Murder and the Death Penalty: A State-by-State Review". New York Times. Dec. 4, 1994. P. E3, Col. 1.

"Academic Programs in Prisons"
U. S. Department of Justice, Bureau of Justice Statistics. Sourcebook of Criminal Justice Statistics, 1991. Washington, D. C. Table 6.99.

"Criteria for Release via Parole"
Cavender, G. Parole, A Critical Analysis. Port Washington, NY: Kennikat Press, 1982. Pp. 47, 47a, 47b; Table 3.

"State Parolees"
Morgan, K. O., S. Morgan, & N. Quitno, eds. State Rankings 1993: A Statistical View of the 50 States. Lawrence, KS: Morgan Quitno Corp., 1993. P. 67.

"Conditions for Violation of Parole"
Cavender, G. Parole, A Critical Analysis. Port Washington, NY: Kennikat Press, 1982. Pp. 51-53, Table 4.

"Prisoner Escapes"
U. S. Department of Justice, Bureau of Justice Statistics. Correctional Populations in the United States. Washington, D. C., 1990. Table 5.10b.

"Crime Victims—Eligibility for Reimbursement Programs"
Stark, J. H. & H. W. Goldstein. The Rights of Crime Victims. New York: Bantam Books, 1985. Pp. 402-03.

"Crime Victims—Eligibility for Recovery Programs"
Ibid.

"Crime Victims—Benefits"
Ibid.

INDEX

Page numbers listed in italics refer to either a map or a graph.